MISSISSIPPI GARDENER'S GUIDE

To Ethel
Happy Gardening!
Noreen Winter

*The What, Where, When, How & Why
of Gardening in Mississippi*

MISSISSIPPI GARDENER'S GUIDE

Norman Winter

COOL
SPRINGS
PRESS

Library of Congress Cataloging-in-Publication Data

Winter, Norman
    Mississippi gardener's guide / Norman Winter.
        p. cm.
    Includes bibliographical references (p.   ).
    ISBN 1-888608-44-7
    1. Landscape plants -- Mississippi 2. Landscape gardening -- Mississippi I. Title

    SB407 .W578 1999
    635.9'09762--dc21

Cool Springs Press, Inc.
112 Second Avenue North
Franklin, Tennessee 37064

First printing 1999
Printed in the United States of America
10 9 8 7 6 5 4 3 2 1

Horticultural Nomenclature Editor: Joe Walker White, PhD., Extension Horticulturist,
    LSU Agricultural Center

On the cover (clockwise from top left): Tiger Swallowtail Butterfly, Purple Coneflower,
    Black-Eyed Susan, Shasta Daisy

Visit the Cool Springs Press website at: www.coolspringspress.com

DEDICATION

This book is dedicated to Mississippi Gardeners, who see the Creator every day in the plants they grow

and

to my wife Jan, who takes care of the plants I bring home like lost puppies, and to my daughter Kimberly and son James who already have a tremendous gift for plant identification.

SPECIAL THANKS

I gratefully recognize my wife Jan who assisted me by spending hours typing on the computer to make this book a reality.

I wish to thank Jan Keeling, my editor, who dedicated her time, day and night, to making this book shine. She was never too busy and it was never too early or too late for an encouraging word.

I also want to acknowledge the members of the Mississippi Nurserymen Association who generously donated new plants for me to try both at home and at various Mississippi Agricultural and Forestry Experiment Stations.

> *"What a gardener hears he might believe, what he reads he may believe, but what he tries with his own hands he does believe." —Seaman A. Knapp (paraphrase)*

CONTENTS

Mississippi Gardener's Guide

INTRODUCTION

Many other states are proud of their gardens, but not one is more beautiful than the gardens found in Mississippi. Our houses and gardens are featured in books that fill shelves and adorn coffee tables in homes everywhere. This book is designed to help you get the most out of your plant purchases. Each page is dedicated to a plant, describing what it takes to successfully grow and use that plant in the landscape.

Plant Characteristics at a Glance

Each plant entry in this guide offers pertinent information about the plant such as its height, bloom time, flower color, and cold-hardiness zones (zones in which the plant is winter hardy). Each plant's light requirements (the amount of sunlight suitable for the plant's needs) are indicated by the following symbols:

☀ ◑ ☀
Full Sun   Partial Shade   Shade

Full sun means a minimum of eight hours of sun per day. Partial sun is about six hours, and partial shade is four hours of direct sunlight. Shade is approximately two hours of sun.

Each plant that is native to Mississippi is marked by this symbol next to its common name: [N]

Some additional beneficial characteristics of many of the plants are indicated by the following symbols:

Added Benefits

 Attracts Butterflies

 Attracts Hummingbirds

 Produces Edible Fruit, Flowers, or Leaves

 Has Fragrance

 Produces Food for Wildlife

 Good for Cut Flowers

 Long Bloom Period

 Attracts Honeybees

Did You Know?

A "Did You Know?" box offers information about the plant's uses, nomenclature, history, or information that is little known or just plain interesting.

USDA Cold-Hardiness Zone Map

The USDA cold-hardiness zone map on page 10 shows the minimum temperatures that can be expected in your area or zone. Mississippi is said to have only two cold-hardiness zones, broken down into four subzones: 7a, 7b, 8a, and 8b. Many believe that zone 9 areas exist south of Interstate 10; for that reason I have designated some plants in this book as hardy to zone 9. You will notice that I have indicated some plants as hardy in zone 10, which is south of Mississippi. Such plants, most of them tropicals, can be grown in our state if treated as annuals or given winter protection.

If there are parentheses around an indicated zone, such as (7), the plant's hardiness in that zone is considered marginal. If you live in zone 7, a plant hardy for zones 8 and 9 but marginally hardy for zone 7 should be planted in the most protected area of the landscape to have a chance of surviving winter temperatures—or you may grow it in a container to be brought indoors for winter. (If there are parentheses around a zone that is *south* of the other zones indicated for a plant, that means the plant's *heat* hardiness is marginal.)

Soil Preparation: the Key to the "Green Thumb"

Have you wondered why some people are excellent container gardeners but seem to fizzle once they get into the landscape? When growing plants in a container, the gardener is providing the very best in soil conditions.

It seems everyone wants a "green thumb." In most cases it is obtained by getting it brown first by practicing good soil preparation. That container growing gorgeous flowers is undoubtedly filled with a rich organic potting mix. Organic matter has good moisture-holding capacity and allows for good drainage, providing maximum oxygen to the roots. A container gardener probably waters with a diluted fertilizer or applies a timed-release mixture that releases nutrients every time the plant is watered. In a purchased potting mix, weeds are nonexistent.

USDA COLD-HARDINESS MAP

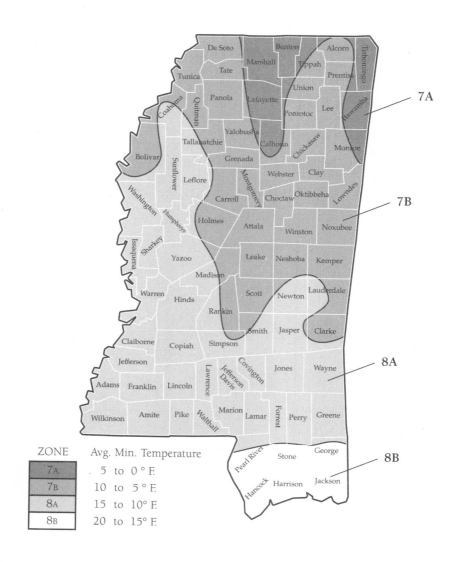

7A

7B

8A

8B

ZONE	Avg. Min. Temperature
7A	5 to 0° F.
7B	10 to 5° F.
8A	15 to 10° F.
8B	20 to 15° F.

Mississippi

How do we duplicate the success of the container garden in the herb garden, flower bed, or shrub planting? The soil in the landscape bed should be well drained to moist, loose, and nutrient- and humus-rich, with a layer of mulch added to prevent loss of moisture, deter weeds, and moderate summer temperatures. Keep in mind that the soil you prepare will be the plants' home for the life of their roots. Metal edging, landscape timbers, brick, and masonry work well to separate turf from beds, and they allow you to improve the bed with soil mixes. Soil mixes can be purchased by the bag, cubic yard, or truckful. When you look at the price per cubic yard, you'll wonder why you have been torturing your plants with heavy clay. Remember that soil improvement is an ongoing process that you work on from year to year.

Clay particles are the smallest of all soil particles, which means they become compacted easily, keeping out not only water, but air as well. By incorporating organic matter like humus, compost, or peat into your native soil, good things will happen: organic matter helps loosen the soil for better water penetration and aeration, leading to proper root development.

If you have sandy soil, organic matter is equally important. Sand is made of large particles, resulting in quick drainage and the more rapid leaching of nutrients. By adding organic matter to your soil, the water-holding capacity improves and the nutrients needed by the plant will be retained.

Train Your Plants with Proper Watering

Mother Nature usually provides supplemental water to make up for our watering forgetfulness, but watering may be entirely up to us for weeks at a time. Getting newly planted trees, shrubs, and bedding plants established is crucial, and proper watering is essential.

The first year a tree or shrub spends in your landscape is the most critical for establishment. Trees and shrubs must be nursed through intense summer heat and drought. I have occasionally been challenged by a gardener who says: "I thought you told me that plant was tough. Well, it is wilting already!" That means that a plant has not yet become established. Even drought-tolerant trees or shrubs have to first grow enough so that new roots are spreading from the ball into surrounding soil.

I have seen gardeners using a spray mist nozzle at the end of a hose, lightly sprinkling new shrubs every day. While this may be fun and relaxing, it ends up training the roots of that plant to stay near the soil's surface. These plants can die when the owner goes away for a week's vacation or a long weekend. Get in the habit of watering infrequently, but very deeply. As the top layer of soil begins to dry, roots will reach deeper and deeper for more moisture. Add a layer of mulch to prevent loss of moisture through evaporation.

Don't Be Afraid of Fertilizers

Fertilizer is a substance used to make the soil or growing medium more productive by increasing the supply of nutrients available to the plant. Fertilizing lawns, gardens, and landscape plantings is one of the least understood gardening practices. Every year countless home gardeners apply fertilizer without getting a soil test and just cross their fingers for good luck.

When I was managing a tourist site that had several gardens, I noticed huge differences in the plants' performances. These gardens had been given some special treatment by volunteers. A soil test revealed that some of the gardens with struggling plants had excessive levels of phosphorus. The volunteers believed high phosphorus encourages bloom, and they had been adding it to the soil every year without fail. They did not know that granular phosphorus lingers in the soil and that a soil test would have told them it was time to stop adding phosphorus.

There are sixteen chemical elements known to be essential for optimum plant growth. The three large numbers on bags of fertilizer refer to nitrogen (N), phosphorus (P), and potassium or potash, as it is often called (K). Nitrogen produces vegetative growth and gives a dark-green color to plants. It increases the yield of foliage, fruit, and seed. Phosphorus stimulates early root formation and gives a rapid and vigorous start to plants. It stimulates bud-set and blooming. Potassium, the last of the big three, is important for increasing vigor and producing strong, stiff stalks. It helps impart winter hardiness.

The secondary nutrients and micronutrients are also important. Calcium is part of a compound in the cell wall. Magnesium is present in chlorophyll, the green pigment in the plants. Sulfur affects cell division and formation. Manganese, iron, copper, zinc, and cobalt influence plant growth by serving as activators or catalysts. Boron is associated with calcium use and molybdenum is essential in nitrogen use.

Many gardeners do not have an understanding of how much fertilizer is in each bag. If the label on a 50-pound bag of fertilizer shows a formula of 10-20-10, that means it has 5 pounds (10 percent) available nitrogen, 10 pounds (20 percent) available phosphorus, and 5 pounds (10 percent) potassium. If the bag has trace elements or micronutrients, they will be listed as well, and the percentages will be much smaller. The other 30 pounds in such a 50-pound bag will be made up of filler or carrier for the nutrients.

Look for slow-release fertilizers. They have a long residual effect, low burn potential, and require fewer applications per unit of time.

Contact your local county extension agent to get a soil test to see what you really need for the particular crop you want to grow. If you haven't practiced regular fertilization and a soil test will have to wait until next year, talk to your certified nursery professional for recommendations. Here are some hints about fertilizing a few specific kinds of plants:

- Azaleas and camellias need fertilizing right after bloom.
- Many vegetables are heavy feeders.
- Pecan trees need a lot of nitrogen.
- Horticulturists often feed crape myrtles with a high-nitrogen lawn-type fertilizer to stimulate vegetative growth, followed by one higher in phosphorus four to six weeks later for bloom.
- Roses need fertilizer about every six weeks from spring until late summer. Fertilize azaleas and camellias after bloom and again in six weeks. Summer flowers need fertilizing every four to six weeks.

Reduce Your Utility Bill with Landscape Choices

Our landscapes can provide us with energy savings while offering an aesthetically pleasing setting for our homes. Trees and shrubs help settle, trap, and hold particulate pollutants that can damage humans. They release oxygen for us to breathe. A well-landscaped property is also more desirable than one with no landscape.

In some months your temperatures and utility bills may be moderate, but we all know what lies ahead. We can take action today which will pay great dividends in subsequent years. Trees and other plants reduce the greenhouse effect by shading our homes and office buildings. This reduces our air-conditioning needs by up to thirty percent, cutting down on the amount of electricity required to cool our homes.

We can also reduce heating bills in the winter. To install an energy-saving landscape, one must understand the position of the sun during the seasons, as well as the plants' characteristics.

In mid-December the sun rises in the southeast and stays relatively low before setting in the southwest. In June the sun rises in the northeast and stays high during the day before setting in the northwest. These angles influence the amount of sun that strikes the house.

To plan for shade from the hot summer sun, consider that trees on the east and northeast sides of the landscape provide morning shade in the summer. Trees placed on the west and northwest exposures of the house provide shade during summer afternoons.

We can also reduce heat absorption by having shrubs or vines cover east or west walls. Vines may be allowed to grow on masonry, brick, or concrete. Vines growing on a trellis are ideal for a wood-exterior home.

We can allow the warm sun to hit our home during the winter by placing deciduous trees on the south side of the house. A deciduous tree loses its leaves, allowing the sun to warm the house. Oaks, hickories, pecans, and sweetgums are among the best choices for this.

Evergreens like the magnolia, holly, eastern red cedar, and Leyland cypress also play a vital role in the winter landscape. When placed on the north or northwest side of a house, these evergreens not only look pretty but block the prevailing winds of the cold blue norther; they will block the wind to twice their height.

Prevailing summer winds come from the Gulf of Mexico, and we should take advantage of these cooling breezes. Do not plant thick screens on the southwest or south side of the property. By pruning off the lower limbs of tall deciduous trees to a height equal to the roof dripline, we can direct those breezes into the house.

Planting now may not influence this year's utility bills, but it certainly can affect them to your benefit in the future, and will add dollars to the value of your home.

Remember that newly planted landscape trees and shrubs will grow and mature to much larger heights and widths. Be sure to place them according to expected mature size.

Native Plants Define Beauty in Landscapes

An important virtue of native species is their survivability. If they grow well in the wild without our help, then they should do well in our landscapes. When you think about our weather extremes, from hot to cold and wet to dry, it makes sense to use adapted plants.

During the winter, many natives really strut their stuff. The Eastern red cedar (*Juniperus virginiana*) is Mother Nature's Christmas tree choice for the South. We may see disease and insects taking out many imported conifers, but the Eastern red cedar keeps on trucking.

When driving through Mississippi neighborhoods, I often see the statuesque river birch (*Betula nigra*) with its gorgeous peeling bark.

The bright-red berries of native hollies give some of our best winter color. The American holly (*Ilex opaca*), yaupon (*Ilex vomitoria*), possum haw (*Ilex decidua*), and the swamp or winterberry holly (*Ilex verticillata*) all deserve a place in the yard.

I feel passionate about the southern wax myrtle *Myrica cerifera*. People in my neighborhood in Brandon used this evergreen effectively as specimen plantings and also in clusters of three. The bluish berries, overlooked by most, are welcome food for the birds. Cold temperatures in northern Mississippi may singe the leaves a little, but I have seen enough of these trees thrive to believe they can be grown statewide.

It's not hard to determine when spring is here—Eastern redbud (*Cercis canadensis*) and dogwood (*Cornus florida*) announce its arrival. These two trees put on a show as understory plants in the forests and can do the same in the home landscape.

When you mention springtime in Mississippi, azaleas quickly come to mind, particularly the imports from Japan. We have native azaleas, however, that rival the beauty of those imports. The Florida azalea (*Rhododendron austrinum*) is a boldly colored plant with fragrant flowers in orange, red, and yellow. Another is the honeysuckle azalea (*Rhododendron canescens*), which has fragrant white to pink and rose flowers.

In late spring we are welcomed by the oak-leaf, one of the most beautiful hydrangeas anywhere. The 12-inch white blossoms and fall red leaf color give this plant superstar status.

This is just a tiny sampling of the hundreds of native plants we can and should use in our landscapes, not only because they are adaptable, but also because they are so beautiful.

Use a Color Wheel When Selecting Companion Plants

It is fairly obvious that you should use plants that have similar cultural requirements, such as light and water, when making selections to be planted close together (companion plants). Consider color compatibility as well: you can use a color wheel for garden harmony when selecting flowers (see page 144).

1. The most basic color scheme is called *monochromatic*, meaning that all the flowers are the same color, or lighter or darker shades of the same color. Monochromatic color creates a feeling of spaciousness because it is not broken or interrupted by another color.

2. When you use colors next to each other on the color wheel, you are using an *analogous* color scheme. This scheme works exceptionally well because all the plants have similar tones that visually tie them together.

3. Use colors directly opposite each other on the color wheel, and you are using a *complementary* color scheme. This attractive scheme makes use of colors from the hot side and cool side of the wheel. Opposites attract!

4. Use three or four colors that are equal distances apart on the color wheel, and you have created a scheme or harmony called *triadic* or *quadratic* (depending on the number of colors used). Such a scheme not only gives you more color, but offers the opportunity to use a greater variety of plants.

Unless your house is a neutral color, you may wish to consider its color or trim color as well when you are making flower color decisions.

Gardens Can Yield Butterflies

A famous line from a movie: *Build it and they will come.* This can apply to butterflies as well as baseball.

Building a butterfly garden is not difficult, and many of these plants are the kind you don't have to babysit throughout the summer. Whether you have a large house with flower gardens at every corner, or a small apartment garden with little or no yard, you can attract and enjoy butterflies.

My children like to spend hours watching and identifying swallowtails, viceroys, monarchs, and many others, so we choose plants annually that are known to provide food for butterflies. Plants like the Mississippi Medallion winner 'New Gold' lantana, 'Biloxi Blue' verbena, and melampodium are among the best butterfly plants. Other favorites are salvias, pentas, rudbeckias, coneflowers, butterfly bush, butterfly weed, ruellia, and zinnias.

The design possibilities are limitless. You are the artistic director of the production, so experiment and have fun. First learn about which butterfly species occur in your particular region and which plant species they use for nectar and larval food. Make the most of your natural setting. Butterflies like edges. Planting low flowers at the edge of a lawn and high flowers at the edges of treelines or along a fence is a way to enhance edge habitat.

Locate a large part of the garden in a sunny, protected area. Butterflies are cold blooded and need sun to warm their body temperature enough to fly on cool mornings. They also use the sun for orientation. Place flat stones in several locations in the garden to make butterfly basking spots.

Butterflies hate high winds and appreciate windbreaks. Evergreen shrubs, rock walls, large boulders—even the potting shed—can temper the buffeting wind, and you may notice butterflies congregating in those places on windy days.

Most butterflies are drifters looking for a meal, stopping off temporarily at your garden to partake of food, water, and shelter. If food sources disappear, butterflies will go elsewhere.

Design gardens with large drifts of color. Butterflies are first attracted to flowers by color, and a large mass is easier to spot. Some experts believe butterflies' favorite color is purple, followed by blue, yellow, white, pink, and orange.

If you really love butterflies, learn to provide for their larvae, too. Caterpillars will devour plants, but something wonderful happens inside you the first time you see that monarch or swallowtail caterpillars have fed on the plants you grew for them. Being able to watch the graceful flight of butterflies is well worth the sacrifice.

Some of the best nectar sources are coreopsis, zinnia, goldenrods, and sunflowers. I have seen one joe-pye weed with twenty swallowtails feeding from its flowers. Other key plants are buddleia (butterfly bush), lantana, ruellia, honeysuckle, lobelia, salvia, clematis, and hibiscus. Some of the better larval food sources are dill, parsley, legumes, mustards, clovers, sunflower, and ruellia. The leaves of my roses seem to be a delicacy. Some trees, like cottonwood, red bay, sweet bay, green ash, sycamore, hackberry, black willow, and cedar elm, also serve as larval food sources.

Make Your Backyard Welcome to "Everybirdy"

From the simplest backyards to the most complex gardens, any landscape can be made more beautiful with the presence of birds. Birdbaths and feeders are readily available at all garden centers and can put you on the road to identifying birds you were not even aware of until now. Attracting an assortment of colorful birds to your lawn is an easy project the whole family can enjoy.

Birdfeeders are great educational projects for children. Give children the responsibility of choosing a location and maintaining a feeder. Armed with a bird guide or encyclopedia, your child will be identifying the birds that feast in your yard in no time. Birds that feed during spring and summer will come to rely on feeders during the fall and winter, too.

Birds need more than just food. Birdbaths supply water for drinking and bathing. Not only are they functional, they can also become an attractive focal point in the landscape. Be sure to locate your birdbath away from trees or shrubs where cats could spring a surprise attack.

Birdhouses have become all the rage, from very simple single-story bungalows to decorative gourds to those that look like churches, schools, and even antebellum homes. I have seen some birdhouses that almost make me wish I could live there. I have seen some that cost more than some cars I have owned. Remember: *If you build it, they will come.*

Birdfeeders, birdhouses, and birdbaths are fun for the family, and I also encourage you to use plants with berries or fruit that birds consider a delicacy. Good-looking trees and shrubs can serve as food and shelter for birds:

- The southern wax myrtle is native in much of the South and can be used effectively as a small tree or large shrub. You may not have even noticed its waxy blue berries, but forty species of birds, including bobwhite quail and turkey, feast on them.
- Hollies—like the yaupon, possumhaw, and American—produce the red berries we associate with Christmas, and are also food for a number of birds.
- Gorgeous spring dogwoods provide fruit that turns bright red in the fall and is quickly devoured by twenty-eight species of birds, as well as by deer and squirrels.
- The blue-gray fruit of the eastern red cedar, Tupelo tree, sweetgum, and blackhaw viburnum, and the bright-purple fruits of American beautyberry are considered food for birds.
- Staghorn sumac may be the king of bird trees. Ninety-four bird species like its fruits, including the mourning dove, bobwhite quail, pheasant, and grouse.

When it's time to choose new trees or shrubs, make smart decisions. We can select those that are native to the South and produce an abundance of fruit or berries for urban wildlife. Add birdhouses, feeders, and baths, and you will have created your own wildlife sanctuary.

ANNUALS

nnuals work well when planted in bold drifts of single colors, and they also play an important role in mixed borders, in which they can be combined with perennials and woody evergreen foundation plants. Most annuals are planted in spring and die with either the onslaught of late summer heat or the first fall frost.

Many tough annuals such as zinnias, moss rose, and gomphrena can be sown or transplanted in midsummer with great success. Fall is the second season for annual planting. Millions of pansies, violas, and flowering kale and cabbage can be planted each fall and survive through the winter, giving color at what many consider the dreariest time of the year.

Annuals get their name from the fact that they complete their life cycle in one growing season. They are known to go from seed to plant to flower to seed and then die, all in a relatively short period of a few months. Despite this "bloom-once" reputation, there are several annuals that reseed with ease, offering a perennial-like performance in the landscape. Plants like cosmos, melampodium, gomphrena, and cleome return every year with an abundance of seedlings that can be thinned and even transplanted throughout the flower border.

Many annuals are compact; others are trailing. They are great for the front of the flower border and also excel in baskets, containers, and windowboxes. Large annuals work well when placed toward the middle or back of the border. Some annuals are vines and can climb a trellis or pergola, covering it in a single season. Look for these in the Vines chapter.

Gardeners may find that they have great success growing flowers in containers yet continue to struggle to grow flowers in the landscape. The problem can usually be attributed to poor soil preparation. Roots of annuals have to penetrate soils quickly to get established and to anchor the plants. They must

> No group of flowering plants provides as much color as quickly and as economically as annuals.

absorb water and nutrients in one season under all kinds of weather conditions.

The first step in preparing a bed for annual plants is to remove unwanted vegetation using a nonselective herbicide or a hoe. The soil should then be turned to about the depth of the shovel. To prevent resprouting, remove grass and weed roots while turning the soil.

Add three to four inches of organic matter such as compost, humus, pine bark, or peat moss and an inch or two of sharp sand if the soil is really heavy. Many garden centers sell bulk or bagged landscape soil mixes and blends that are ideal for flower and shrub bed plantings. Such soil mixes provide excellent drainage and should allow you to plant in beds raised above the natural soil level.

It is always best to get a soil test before adding fertilizer. If you are unable to get a soil test, you can simply broadcast 2 pounds of a 12-6-6 with slow-release nitrogen fertilizer per 100 square feet of bed space, and till it in with the organic amendments.

Annual flowers can be grown from transplants or by direct-seeding, but it is always important to plant them at the proper spacing and to plant enough to create a show.

After planting, apply a good layer of mulch to conserve moisture, keep soil temperatures moderate, and discourage weeds. Keep flowers deadheaded (remove old flowers) to keep them looking their best and to increase production.

Many annuals will require a monthly application of fertilizer to keep them growing. Those in containers will need frequent watering during the summer as well as frequent fertilizing.

> Use a color wheel to help find out which colors and combinations give the best display . . .

Ageratum

Ageratum houstonianum

Other Name:
Floss Flower

Light Needs:

Added Benefits:

Bloom Time:
Spring, summer, fall

Bloom Color:
Blue, pink, white

Height: 6 to 30 in.

Spacing: 9 to 12 in.

Water Needs:
Moderate

Soil:
Moist, well drained

Uses:
Flower border, mixed containers

Did You Know?
Mississippi has a wonderful later-summer flower called the mist flower that is closely related to ageratum.

Color photo on page 129

In a world longing for blue flowers, the ageratum is most welcome. There are other colors available, but it is the blue we treasure. The dime-sized daisylike flowers are borne in clusters that persist for months.

How to Grow

Prepare beds by incorporating 3 to 4 inches of peat or compost, along with 2 pounds of slow-release 12-6-6 fertilizer per 100 square feet. Set out healthy transplants in the early spring in a site that is in full sun for best flower performance. The shorter varieties lend themselves to the front of the border, while the taller cutflower types can be planted to the middle or back. These cutflower types also make nice dried flowers.

Companion Planting

The complementary color for the blue ageratum is orange. The look is breathtakingly bold and colorful when tall orange marigolds are planted behind the ageratums. Pink flowers also look good with the ageratum, for a baby blanket look. Try pink shrub or groundcover roses behind the ageratums.

Care and Maintenance

The ageratum is easy to grow and maintenance-free in well-drained soil. Keep watered and fed with light applications of the same fertilizer as above every 4 to 6 weeks. Occasionally spider mites can be a problem; be watchful and treat as needed.

Recommended Varieties

'Blue Blazer' and 'Blue Danube' are among dwarf favorites, while 'Blue Mink' and 'Blue Horizon' are taller types. 'Summer Snow', a white variety, and a pink selection called 'Pinkie' are also recognized.

Angelonia

Angelonia angustifolia

The tall, wispy snapdragon-like flowers of the angelonia may be the best of recent plant introductions. They thrive in Mississippi heat and humidity, blooming from spring until frost.

How to Grow

Plant in the spring after frost in deep, well-prepared, well-drained beds that are rich in organic matter. Till in 3 to 4 inches of compost or humus, along with 2 pounds of a slow-release 12-6-6 fertilizer per 100 square feet of bed space. For best flower production, plant in full sun. Angelonia reaches a height of 18 to 30 inches, so plant to the middle or back of the border.

Companion Planting

'Hilo Princess', the most popular variety, is on the blue side of purple and works great with plants like the 'New Gold' lantana or 'Pink Wave' petunia. Though not as tall as larkspurs, angelonia gives much the same look, thereby lending itself to the cottage garden.

Care and Maintenance

Angelonias perform for a long time. In central and south Mississippi it is not uncommon for them to return in the spring. Once established they are drought tolerant but will benefit from a layer of mulch. Water during long dry periods, and fertilize monthly with light applications of the above fertilizer. Deadhead flower spikes during rest cycles to stimulate new blooms

Recommended Varieties

'Hilo Princess' has been the most widely recognized, along with 'Tiger Princess' (a blue-and-white-striped variety), 'Pandiana' (a pink form), and a white selection called 'Whitiana'. A new group called 'Angel Mist' will feature plum and a deeper purple.

Light Needs:

Added Benefits:

Bloom Time:
Spring, summer, fall

Bloom Color:
Blue, blue and white striped, purple, white, pink

Height: 18 to 30 in.

Spacing:
24 to 30 in.

Water Needs: Low

Soil:
Slightly moist, well drained

Uses:
Cottage gardens, contemporary flower borders

Did You Know?

The angelonia is related to the snapdragon.

Color photo on page 129

Begonia

Other Name:
Wax Begonia

Light Needs:

Added Benefit:

Bloom Time:
Spring, summer, fall

Bloom Color:
Pink, orange,
red, white

Height: 8 to 10 in.

Spacing:
8 to 12 in.

Water Needs:
Moderate

Soil:
Warm, moist, well
drained

Uses:
Beds, borders, baskets,
mixed containers

Did You Know?
There are 900
species of begonias, in
eight classes.

Color photo on page 129

Begonia Semperflorens-Cultorum Hybrids

It's hard to beat a plant that has striking flowers and shiny succulent-looking foliage in green, bronze, and variegation. Long-lasting saucer-shaped flowers in crimson, pink, orange, salmon, and white make the begonia appealing to almost every gardener.

How to Grow
Plant in spring after the last frost, in well-drained beds rich in organic material. Till in 3 to 4 inches of compost or peat, along with 2 pounds of slow-release 12-6-6 fertilizer per 100 square feet. Plant in full sun to partial shade, depending on variety. Bronze-leafed types can take the most sun, green-leafed types appreciate a little afternoon protection.

Companion Planting
Begonias really look great planted in front of ever-green shrubs like hollies. Plant in bold drifts adjacent to other begonias. In partially shady areas, plant with hostas or dwarf bananas.

Care and Maintenance
Keep well watered and feed monthly with light applications of the above slow-release fertilizer. Apply a good layer of mulch to conserve moisture and keep soil temperatures moderate. If plants become straggly in late summer, shear back to regenerate new growth and blooms. Plants may be dug up and potted for enjoyment indoors.

Recommended Varieties
There are a lot of good varieties, including the 'Cocktail' series with 'Brandy' (pink), 'Rum' (white with rose), 'Vodka' (scarlet), 'Gin' (rose), and 'Whisky' (white). The 'Pizzaz' hybrids and the 'Ambassador' series should also be tried. Try new angel wing types, 'Dragon Wing' and 'Torch'—they may be the best of all the begonias.

Black-Eyed Susan

Rudbeckia hirta

Bright-yellow daisylike flowers make black-eyed Susan one of the showiest wildflowers. The 1999 Mississippi Medallion–winning 'Indian Summer' produces gigantic blooms 6 to 9 inches wide.

How to Grow

Plant in early spring from nursery-grown transplants into well-prepared, well-drained beds amended with 3 to 4 inches of organic matter and 2 pounds of slow-release 12-6-6 fertilizer per 100 square feet. Rudbeckias work pretty well in any soil that is not waterlogged. They can also be direct-seeded with great success.

Companion Planting

Plant in bold drifts adjacent to salvia 'Indigo Spires' or behind 'Victoria' blue salvia. Perennial verbenas like 'Biloxi Blue', 'Homestead Purple', or 'Temari' (red) also combine nicely with the black-eyed Susan. 'Hilo Princess' angelonias make nice companion plants.

Care and Maintenance

Rudbeckias can produce for a long time. If direct-seeded, thin plants to the correct spacing. Air circulation is essential with this plant. Maintain moisture should rains be infrequent. Fertilize lightly every 4 to 6 weeks with the above fertilizer. Deadhead flowers for increased production and to prevent too many seedlings from appearing next year.

Recommended Varieties

The 1999 Mississippi Medallion winner 'Indian Summer' produces huge flowers for weeks. 'Sonora' has petals of burgundy red surrounded by yellow. 'Toto' is one of the prettiest small varieties, only 10 inches tall. 'Goldilocks' is another dwarf form. Read more about rudbeckias in the perennials chapter.

Other Name:
Gloriosa Daisy

Light Needs:

Added Benefits:

Bloom Time:
Spring, summer

Bloom Color:
Yellow, orange, burgundy

Height: 24 to 42 in.

Spacing: 18 to 24 in.

Water Needs:
Low/moderate

Soil:
Moist, well drained

Uses:
Cottage gardens, natural settings, large mixed containers

Did You Know?

Blue gazing globes with black-eyed Susans makes a bed worthy of a photograph.

Color photo on page 129

Blue Daze

Light Needs:

Added Benefits:

Bloom Time:
Spring, summer, fall

Bloom Color:
Clear light blue

Height: 8 to 12 in.

Spacing:
12 to 24 in.

Water Needs:
Low/moderate

Soil:
Moist, well drained

Uses:
Edging for flower border, baskets, mixed containers

Did You Know?

The evolvulus is in the morning glory family, but doesn't climb.

Color photo on page 129

Evolvulus pilosus

Rare clear-blue flowers are produced from spring until frost on this 1996 Mississippi Medallion winner. 'Blue Daze' is among the toughest plants for a climate of extremes. Its low-growing compact form makes it ideal for the border front.

How to Grow
Plant in a sunny location to the front of the flower border in early spring after the last frost. This plant has the ability to perform for a very long season, so prepare the bed properly. Work in 3 to 4 inches of organic matter, along with 2 pounds of a slow-release 12-6-6 fertilizer per 100 square feet. The bed must be well drained; soggy conditions can prove fatal.

Companion Planting
Along with the blue flowers, the olive gray-green foliage is unique and combines well with ornamental blue fescue grass. Pink verbenas, like 'Temari', give a great baby blanket effect.

Care and Maintenance
Not too many plants are this maintenance-free. Watering during dry periods and light monthly applications of the above slow-release fertilizer will keep your plants performing until frost. The evolvulus also responds exceptionally well to water-soluble fertilizers. 'Blue Daze' makes a nice indoor plant in brightly lighted areas, so dig up one or two before the first frost. You will be able to take cuttings in the spring for outdoor planting.

Recommended Varieties
The 1996 Mississippi Medallion winner was 'Blue Daze', which is still the most common in the market. 'Hawaiian Blue Eyed' is good, but rarely seen in our area.

Celosia

Celosia argentea

With feathery plumes or cockscomb-type flowers in brilliant colors, celosia is drought tolerant. It is among the best for drying and for bringing indoors.

How to Grow

Plant from healthy transplants with minimal buds showing, or direct-seed in spring or summer into well-drained, well-prepared beds that have 3 to 4 inches of organic matter incorporated into them. Celosias cannot tolerate cold soils. Try planting in late to midsummer to produce intensely colored flowers for fall.

Companion Planting

Do not spot-plant the celosia. Massing the plants in large groups gives the best look. They look good in mixes, yet single colors like orange apricot and gold are bold when planted with 'Victoria' blue salvia. Red celosia and white periwinkles combine nicely.

Care and Maintenance

Keep plants vigorous and actively growing to avoid stress and premature blooming. Celosia is one of the most drought tolerant plants, so do not over-water. Feed every 6 to 8 weeks with applications of complete fertilizer, like a 12-6-6. Celosia is sensitive to overfertilization. Apply a good layer of mulch to keep soil temperatures moderate and conserve moisture.

Recommended Varieties

'Castles' that grow to 12 to 14 inches high, 'Centuries' that reach 20 inches, and the dwarf 'Kimono' at 8 inches are among the best feathery types. 'Coral Garden', which reaches 12 inches tall, and 'Jewel Box' at 6 inches are favorites in the cockscomb type. Look also for *Celosia spicata*, which gives the appearance of wheat flowers in shades of pink and purple.

Other Name:
Cockscomb

Light Needs:

Added Benefits:

Bloom Time:
Spring, summer

Bloom Color:
Pink, orange-yellow, red

Height: 1 to 2 ft.

Spacing: 8 to 12 in.

Water Needs:
Low/moderate

Soil:
Moist, well drained

Uses:
Landscape beds and mixed containers

Did You Know?

'Prestige Scarlet' is a 1997 All-America Selection that is a branching or multiflora cockscomb celosia.

Color photo on page 129

Cleome

Other Name:
Spider Flower

Light Needs:

Added Benefits:

Bloom Time:
Summer, fall

Bloom Color:
Cherry, rose, white, violet

Height: 4 to 5 ft.

Spacing: 18 to 24 in.

Water Needs:
Low/moderate

Soil:
Moist, well drained

Uses:
Flower borders, cottage gardens, large planter boxes

Did You Know?
There are 14,000 cleome seeds per ounce!

Color photo on page 129

Cleome hassleriana

Cleome's tall spiderlike flowers have a unique look, with long stamens that border on spectacular. They are excellent for cutflowers and give a perennial performance by reseeding yearly. The flowers are a favorite for hummingbirds.

How to Grow
Cleome can be planted from young transplants or direct-seeded into warm spring soil. Plant in well-drained beds in full sun. If drainage is suspect, add 2 to 3 inches of organic matter. Morning sun and afternoon shade will also work well. These are large plants, so pay attention when spacing transplants and thinning seedlings.

Companion Planting
Place plants to the rear of the border in a bold group. Violet-colored salvia planted in front of violet 'Queen' cleome, with two-toned petunias of the same colors in front, makes one of the prettiest displays. 'Royal Sonata' cosmos, purple coneflowers, and groundcover roses like 'Baby Blanket' work well with cleome. Cleomes look good in a cottage-style garden up against a white picket fence.

Care and Maintenance
Cleomes are drought tolerant; keeping them on the dry side will help keep them in bounds. Pruning back before bloom will improve branching. A light application of a 5-10-5 fertilizer in midsummer is all that is needed. Saying that cleome reseeds prolifically is an understatement. If this bothers you, remove seedpods as they form. Though drought tolerant, they do appreciate a good layer of mulch.

Recommended Varieties
The 'Queen' series has captured the lion's share of the market with violet, rose, cherry, and a white also known as 'Helen Campbell'.

Coleus

Coleus × hybridus

Bold, colorful foliage in solid colors and wild variegation is produced on shrubby plants all season
long. This plant is becoming one of the hottest
trends in the Southern garden.

How to Grow

Plant cutting-grown coleus after the soils have
warmed in the spring. They prefer loose, well-
drained beds high in organic matter. It pays to know
your varieties; some take full sun, others grow
in sun to partial shade, and some like almost all
shade. Coleus are grown for spectacular foliage.
Blooms, which may form, detract from the plant's
appearance. Cutting-grown coleus are superior to
seed-produced coleus.

Companion Planting

Be courageous: mass-plant large beds of coleus for a
season of color. Coleus looks great in front of evergreen shrubs or in gardens with a tropical flare,
planted around bananas. Coleus such as 'Lemon
Twist', a lime-green variety for shade, excels with
fuchsia impatiens. Full-sun coleus like 'Burgundy
Sun' and 'Plum Parfait' look great next to the 'Salsa'
salmon salvias.

Care and Maintenance

Most coleus produce flower buds; pinch these as
they form. Pinching also helps keep the plant bushy.
Monthly applications of a water-soluble fertilizer, or
a slow-release 12-6-6, will keep your coleus growing luxuriantly. Apply a good layer of mulch to
prevent the loss of moisture to evaporation and
keep soil temperatures moderate.

Recommended Varieties

The 'Solar' series has become the hottest group of
coleus, with 'Solar Sunrise' being a personal
favorite. Extensive testing has shown 'Burgundy
Sun' and 'Plum Parfait' to take full sun well.

Other Name:
Flame Nettle

Light Needs:

Bloom Time:
Foliage spring,
summer, fall

Bloom Color:
Grown for brightly
colored foliage

Height: 2 to 4 ft.

Spacing:
12 to 24 in.

Water Needs:
Moderate

Soil:
Moist, well drained

Uses:
Landscape borders,
baskets, containers

Did You Know?

Coleus is in the mint
family and will root in
days from cuttings.

Color photo on page 129

Cosmos

Other Name:
Mexican Aster

Light Needs:

Added Benefits:

Bloom Time:
Spring through fall

Bloom Color:
Pink and magenta blends, white, orange, red, and yellow

Height: 2 to 8 ft.

Spacing: 12 to 36 in.

Water Needs:
Moderate

Soil:
Moist, well drained

Uses:
Cottage gardens and flower beds

Did You Know?
Cosmos is a Greek word for harmony.

Color photo on page 129

Cosmos bipinnatus and *Cosmos sulphureus*

Showy daisylike flowers in pastel shades of pink, rose, lavender, and white with bright golden centers are produced on feathery fernlike foliage (*Cosmos bipinnatus*). Bright yellow or orange flowers, some semi-double, are produced all season, becoming huge by fall (*Cosmos sulphureus*).

How to Grow
Choose a site in full sun for best flower performance. Plant in early spring to summer from nursery-grown transplants, or direct-seed into well-prepared, loose, well-drained beds that are not very rich in organic matter. Space plants at the recommended distance for their variety to allow for growth.

Companion Planting
Cosmos bipinnatus excels in a cottage-style or country flower garden with summer phlox, larkspurs, and salvias. The cosmos sulphureus needs to be planted with salvias like 'Indigo Spires', 'Mexican' bush sage, or 'Victoria' blue. They also look striking when grown with black-eyed Susans and zinnias.

Care and Maintenance
The cosmos is great at reseeding, so thin young seedlings to proper spacing. Larger cosmos will probably need staking, but pinching can help in branching. A light application of a 12-6-6 slow-release fertilizer in midsummer will give your plants a pick-me-up. Keep plants deadheaded for increased flower production. Harvest cutflowers early in the morning.

Recommended Varieties
'Sea Shells' mix and 'Sensation' mix are favorites in the large group *Cosmos bipinnatus*. 'Royal Sonata' is the best dwarf. 'Ladybird' and the 'Cosmic' series are among the best of *Cosmos sulphureus*. 'Cosmic Orange' is a 2000 All-America Selections winner.

Dianthus

Dianthus chinensis

Dianthus has delicate and showy clove-scented flowers. Many varieties have fringed blossoms in shades of pink, burgundy, white, purple, and lavender. Dianthus blooms in late winter and early spring, with the biggest displays from those planted in fall.

How to Grow

Excellent drainage is mandatory if you are to be successful with dianthus. Choose a site in full sun and prepare the soil by adding 3 to 4 inches of organic matter and 2 pounds of a slow-release 12-6-6 fertilizer per 100 square feet. Take care to plant at the same depth the plants were growing in the containers or they may suffer from crown rot, often dying.

Companion Planting

Dianthus bloom at a great time of year, giving opportunities to combine with flowering kale and cabbage or single-colored pansies and snapdragons. Base your scheme on opposite or complementary colors, as well as those of similar blends.

Care and Maintenance

Dianthus is fairly maintenance-free when prepared and planted properly. They usually endure temperatures in the middle teens. Be prepared to protect during unusually cold weather. Be sure to mulch! Feed with a light application of the above fertilizer every 6 to 8 weeks. Deadhead to keep tidy and induce blooms. They may survive the winter and bloom again in fall and spring, but are best treated as annuals.

Recommended Varieties

There are many varieties. 'Telstar' is the recognized Southern landscape winner for its tolerance of our extreme climate. Others that are noteworthy are the 'Parfait' and the 'Floral Lace' series.

Other Name:
Pinks

Light Needs:

Added Benefit:

Bloom Time:
Late winter, early spring

Bloom Color:
Pink, rose, white

Height: 8 to 12 in.

Spacing: 6 to 8 in.

Water Needs:
Moderate

Soil:
Moist, well drained

Uses:
Landscape beds, and mixed containers

Did You Know?

The dianthus is in the 'Pink' family and is related to the carnation.

Color photo on page 129

Flowering Kale and Cabbage

Other Names:
Ornamental Kale
and Cabbage

Light Needs:

Bloom Time:
Grown for foliage

Bloom Color:
Pink, maroon, and
white foliage

Height: 6 to 12 in.

Spacing:
12 to 18 in.

Water Needs:
Moderate

Soil:
Moist, well drained

Uses:
Landscape beds and
fall containers

Did You Know?
You can use these leaves
as a decorative garnish.

Color photo on page 129

Brassica oleracea

Flowering kale and cabbage excel in the Southern winter landscape, producing brightly colored foliage in shades of green, purple, lavender, and white. In the northern third of the state, they should be used in late winter or spring.

How to Grow
Prepare soil by incorporating 3 to 4 inches of organic matter and 2 pounds of slow-release 12-6-6 fertilizer per 100 square feet. Plant from nursery-grown transplants in October and early November, or in March. Set the transplant slightly below the bottom set of leaves.

Companion Planting
Flowering kale and cabbage look great with brightly colored pansies and snapdragons. For a showy display, try bold drifts of pink or purple kale next to drifts of a white variety. Try planting a large bed of narcissus behind the kale or cabbage.

Care and Maintenance
Flowering kale and cabbage need good drainage yet must be kept moist and fed for vigorous growth. Add a layer of mulch and feed with light applications of the above fertilizer every 4 to 6 weeks. The colors will intensify as temperatures start to grow cold. The same cabbage loopers that attack your broccoli can plague these plants as well. Watch and treat as needed with *Bt*.

Recommended Varieties
The 'Chidori' series has captured the hearts of many gardeners recently with its fringed ruffled leaves and intense colors. The 'Peacock' and 'Sparrow' series also are recommended as two of the prettiest. If you prefer the round-leaf types, try the 'Dynasty' series.

Geranium

Pelargonium × hortorum

Showy, erect, baseball-sized blossoms make the geranium one of the most popular landscape and container plants. Zonal geraniums come in colors that are sure to suit almost everyone's taste.

How to Grow
Prepare soil by incorporating 3 to 4 inches of organic matter with 2 pounds of a slow-release 12-6-6 fertilizer, tilling under to a depth of 8 to 10 inches. Geraniums need well-drained soil and plenty of light to perform well. Plant at the recommended spacing for your variety after all danger of frost has passed.

Companion Planting
Zonal geraniums are tall and well suited to having a low-growing plant like white trailing petunia planted in front. Try growing in planter boxes where the preferred color of geraniums is towering above sufinias or supertunias that are cascading over the walls.

Care and Maintenance
Geraniums are not hard to maintain. Keep moist and add a layer of mulch to conserve moisture and to moderate summer temperatures. Feed monthly with light applications of the above slow-release fertilizer or every two weeks with a diluted water-soluble fertilizer. When deadheading, break off a flower stalk at the base where it attaches to the stem. It is easy to root stem cuttings or to overwinter indoors.

Recommended Varieties
Geraniums like 'Glamour', 'Orbit', and 'Ringo' are good, but the cutting-grown varieties of zonal geraniums like 'Starburst' are more than equal. If you haven't tried ivy geraniums (*Pelargonium peltatum*) or scented geraniums such as *Pelargonium odoratissimum*, you are missing a treat.

Other Name:
Zonal Geranium

Light Needs:

Added Benefit:

Bloom Time:
Spring, summer

Bloom Color:
Pink, lavender, red, orange scarlet, white, salmon

Height: 12 to 20 in.

Spacing:
10 to 12 in.

Water Needs:
Moderate

Soil:
Moist, well drained

Uses:
Landscape beds, boxes, containers

Did You Know?
Scented geraniums can be used to flavor jams, jellies, and potpourris.

Color photo on page 129

Gomphrena

Gomphrena globosa

Other Names:
Globe Amaranth,
Bachelor Buttons

Light Needs:

Added Benefits:

Bloom Time:
Summer, fall

Bloom Color:
Red, purple, white,
pink, rose

Height: 1 to 3 ft.

Spacing: 6 to 12 in.

Water Needs:
Moderate

Soil:
Moist, well drained

Uses:
Landscape beds,
planters, boxes

Did You Know?
Gomphrena balls make
interesting additions to
bowls of potpourri.

Color photo on page 130

Tough as nails, resistant to heat and humidity, and great for drying, the tall purple, pink, and lavender flowers of gomphrena are a must in the Southern flower border. Many reseed, offering a perennial-like performance.

How to Grow
Plant after the danger of frost is past in beds that have had 3 to 4 inches of organic matter tilled to a depth of 8 to 10 inches. While tilling, incorporate 2 pounds of a 12-6-6 slow-release fertilizer per 100 square feet. Select healthy-growing transplants and set in holes at the same depth they were growing in the container. Place plants at the recommended spacing of the variety chosen.

Companion Planting
This plant is much underused, especially by those who want color in a trouble-free environment. Plant purple varieties in bold drifts with 'New Gold' lantana. Try pink or lavender varieties behind the 'Blackie' ornamental sweet potato or 'Purple Heart'.

Care and Maintenance
Gomphrenas are a pleasure to grow. Mulch to conserve moisture and keep weeds in check. Deadhead flowers after they have become brown to induce more flowers and keep tidy. Feed twice during the summer with light applications of the above fertilizer. Harvest flowers for drying while colors are bold.

Recommended Varieties
Often sold generic in purple, white, and rose, 'Lavender Lady' and the 'Gnome' series are catching on and easy to find. *Gomphrena haageana* 'Strawberry Fields' produces showy bright-red flowers.

Impatiens

Impatiens wallerana

By fall the colorful show of impatiens blossoms rivals the azalea, making this plant number one for partially shady areas. There is sure to be a color or form that will give summer-long performance at your home.

How to Grow
These plants have the ability to show off your landscape from May until the first frost, so give them a proper home. Incorporate 3 to 4 inches of organic matter to raise the beds and give good drainage. As you till, work in 2 pounds of a slow-release 12-6-6 fertilizer per 100 square feet. Impatiens get large, so set out at the proper spacing for your variety, and plant at the same depth they were growing in the container.

Companion Planting
Impatiens combine wonderfully with caladiums, which have the same water and light requirements. Try red-veined white caladiums with red impatiens. Plant bold drifts with complementary colors or colors of the same family.

Care and Maintenance
Keep impatiens mulched and watered, and feed every 6 to 8 weeks with light applications of the above slow-release fertilizer. In late summer, should they look leggy, trim back about one-third to induce branching and growth. Taking care of them during late summer pays off with color all fall.

Recommended Varieties
There are almost as many varieties as grains of sand. 'Super Elfin', 'Dazzler', and 'Accents' are just a few. Recent introductions that are showy are the 'Mosaic' and 'Cajun' series. The double forms which look like roses, and semi-double forms, also create a show.

Other Name:
Sultana

Light Needs:

Added Benefits:

Bloom Time:
Late spring, summer, fall

Bloom Color:
Lots of colors and variegation

Height: 12 to 24 in.

Spacing: 8 to 12 in.

Water Needs:
Moderate/heavy (late summer)

Soil:
Moist, well drained

Uses: Flower borders, baskets, containers, boxes

Did You Know?
The old fashioned touch-me-not is a close relative.

Color photo on page 130

Marigold

Tagetes species

Bold colors and flowers that range from the size of a quarter to a tennis ball adorn these plants. The marigold excels for massing in spring and fall flower beds.

How to Grow

Incorporate 3 to 4 inches of organic matter and 2 pounds of a slow-release 12-6-6 fertilizer per 100 square feet of bed space. In late spring, direct-seed or set out transplants that have little or no color showing. Thin seedlings to proper spacing for the vigorous growth that is about to occur. Leggy marigold transplants can be planted to a depth just below the first set of leaves. Plant in mid-August for a trouble-free fall of great color.

Companion Planting

The list of companion plants is enormous. The prettiest shows come from selecting colors opposite the brightly colored marigold: violets, purples, and blues, depending on whether you use orange, yellow, or cream-colored marigolds.

Care and Maintenance

Mulch marigolds when seedlings are large enough, or after setting out transplants. Feed every 6 to 8 weeks with light applications of the above slow-release fertilizer. Deadhead to encourage more blooms. Spring-planted marigolds are susceptible to spider mites, so treat as needed. August-planted marigolds are not plagued by spider mites nearly as much.

Recommended Varieties

Large-flowered compact varieties like 'Antigua' and 'Discovery' excel in the landscape, as do the slightly larger 'Inca' and 'Marvel'. The not-so-large-flowered but multi-colored 'Safari' and 'Bonanza' are well worth using.

Other Names:
African, French, or American Marigold

Light Needs:

Added Benefits:

Bloom Time:
Spring, summer, fall

Bloom Color:
Yellow, cream, orange, rusty red

Height: 6 to 30 in.

Spacing: 8 to 14 in.

Water Needs:
Moderate

Soil:
Moist, well drained

Uses:
Flower borders, mixed containers, fall planters

Did You Know?
Spider mites that love marigolds don't reproduce much in cool fall temperatures.

Color photo on page 130

Melampodium

Melampodium paludosum

Small buttercuplike daisies adorn the plant from spring until frost, giving even the novice gardener green-thumb success.

How to Grow
Though this plant tolerates poorer soils and is tough, go ahead and prepare the soil by incorporating 2 to 3 inches of organic matter. Your companion plants will appreciate your efforts. Choose a site with full sun for best flower performance. Space plants a little further apart than the tag recommends. These plants love our climate.

Companion Planting
Melampodium looks great planted behind 'Purple Wave' petunias or in front of 'Black Knight' buddleia. They look completely at home planted in front of ornamental fountain grass. Verbenas like 'Homestead Purple' and 'Biloxi Blue' also make nice combinations. Try 'Dreamland' zinnias in sweeping drifts with 'Showstar' melampodium behind.

Care and Maintenance
Mulch, and water during prolonged dry spells. This plant is a vigorous grower without much fertilizer, but a light midsummer application of slow-release 12-6-6 fertilizer serves as a nice pick-me-up. Melampodium is one of those annuals that gives a perennial-like performance by reseeding. In spring, thin volunteers to the correct spacing. Despite its reseeding, the melampodium never has to be dead-headed to remove ugly flowers.

Recommended Varieties
'Showstar', growing to about 24 inches tall, is the number-one variety of melampodium, followed by 'Derby', which reaches about 12 inches. For a very tall variety, try 'Medallion'. 'Million Gold' is a newer more dwarf form that still grows with vigor.

Other Name:
Butter Daisy

Light Needs:

Added Benefits:

Bloom Time:
Spring, summer, fall

Bloom Color:
Yellow, orange

Height: 9 to 36 in.

Spacing: 8 to 16 in.

Water Needs:
Low/moderate

Soil:
Moist, well drained

Uses:
Flower borders,
mixed containers,
planter boxes

Did You Know?
Melampodium was a 1997 Mississippi Medallion winner and will always be a standout performer.

Color photo on page 130

Mexican Heather

Other Name:
Florida Heather

Light Needs:

Added Benefits:

Bloom Time:
Spring, summer, fall

Bloom Color:
Violet, pink, white

Height: 8 to 12 in.

Spacing: 8 to 12 in.

Water Needs:
Low/moderate

Soil:
Moist, well drained

Uses:
Flower border, mixed planters, tropical gardens

Did You Know?
Mexican heather is in the same family as crape myrtle.

Color photo on page 130

Cuphea hyssopifolia

Small purple-to-pink flowers cover this plant, and it has some of the prettiest leaves around. Mexican heather never stops blooming.

How to Grow
This is a tough plant, tolerating poorer soils but not wet feet. Do yourself and the plant a favor by preparing a bed that has been amended with 2 to 3 inches of organic matter. Choose a site in full sun to partial shade to enjoy months of blooms. These plants spread out in width, so space accordingly and plant at the same depth they were growing in containers. Mexican heather is perennial in zone 9 and comes back from the roots in zone 8.

Companion Planting
Plant 'Showstar' melampodium behind a group of three or five Mexican heathers. Try combining with ornamental grass like the 'Ogon' Japanese sweet flag. Mexican heather is tropical by nature and looks good in tropical gardens with bananas and upright elephant ears.

Care and Maintenance
This is one of the lowest-maintenance plants you can grow. Water if in a period of drought, and give a light application of a slow-release 12-6-6 fertilizer in midsummer. Mulch to conserve moisture and add winter protection. Mexican heather responds to pruning by becoming bushier. This is a very easy plant to root from stems.

Recommended Varieties
Mexican heather is mostly sold generic, but there are some great species to try, like *Cuphea ignea* (called the cigar plant) and *Cuphea micropetala*.

MillionBells

Calibracoa × hybrida

Hundreds of bell-shaped flowers in cherry or blue with yellow throats cover these plants. They also come in white, and yellow with hints of rust red.

How to Grow
Plant MillionBells in early spring after the last frost, in full to partial sun. Prepare soil by tilling in 3 to 4 inches of compost or humus with 2 pounds of a slow-release 12-6-6 fertilizer per 100 square feet. Some varieties are mounding, others trailing or spreading. Space plants according to tag recommendations.

Companion Planting
The trailing blue varieties look great planted in front of yellow flowers like 'New Gold' lantana, melampodium, or the yellow-gold narrow-leaf zinnias. Try planting the trailing pink forms in front of 'Victoria' blue salvia or 'Biloxi Blue' verbena. The trailing white looks good planted in front of the upright pink forms.

Care and Maintenance
Keeping the plants growing vigorously is all that is needed. Monitor water during periods of drought and feed monthly with a water-soluble fertilizer. Mulch to conserve moisture and give winter protection. The trailing varieties may live through mild winters in zone 9 and occasionally zone 8. The trailing types respond well to cutting back, which regenerates new growth and blooms.

Recommended Varieties
MillionBells is available in 'Cherry Pink', 'Trailing Pink', 'Trailing Blue', and 'Trailing White'. In the year 2000 'Terra Cotta' (gold with rust red) and 'Trailing Yellow' will debut. 'Liracashower' and 'Colorburst' are two newer series that will be making their way to our market. They have already gained recognition in other southeastern states.

Other Name:
Liracashower

Light Needs:

Added Benefits:

Bloom Time:
Spring, summer, fall

Bloom Color:
White, cherry, blue, pink, yellow

Height: 6 to 18 in.

Spacing: 12 to 18 in.

Water Needs:
Moderate

Soil:
Moist, well drained

Uses:
Landscape flower border, baskets, mixed-containers

Did You Know?
The calibracoa is related to the petunia.

Color photo on page 130

Narrow-Leaf Zinnia

Zinnia angustifolia

Quarter-sized gold-centered flowers of yellow, gold, or white cover this bushy plant, suiting it for rock gardens and borders.

How to Grow

Set out transplants after the last frost of the year. Narrow-leaf zinnias are drought tolerant and cannot take wet feet. Prepare beds by incorporating 3 to 4 inches of compost or humus and 2 pounds of a slow-release 12-6-6 per 100 square feet. Plant at the same depth they were growing in the containers. These plants spread, so plant 10 to 12 inches apart.

Companion Planting

The narrow-leaf zinnia is not only excellent in rock gardens but is very much at home in the cottage garden. Plant two or three 'Victoria' blue salvia and surround with orange narrow-leaf zinnias. Plant orange varieties adjacent to 'Biloxi Blue' verbena, or plant 'Homestead Purple' verbena with the yellow varieties. 'Crystal White' narrow-leaf zinnias look exceptional with 'Purple Wave' petunias and the other orange narrow-leaf zinnias.

Care and Maintenance

These are disease-resistant low-maintenance plants that don't require much fertilizer. Mulch to conserve moisture. A light shearing in late summer, followed by a light application of the above fertilizer, will put them in great shape for fall blooming.

Recommended Varieties

'Star Gold' (yellow), 'Star Orange', 'Star White', and the All-America Selections winner 'Crystal White' are the varieties you will find each spring. 'Crystal White' is more compact in habit than 'Star White'. There is also a mix sold by the name 'Starbright'.

Light Needs:

Added Benefits:

Bloom Time:
Spring, summer, fall

Bloom Color:
Yellow, orange, white

Height: 18 to 24 in.

Spacing: 10 to 12 in.

Water Needs:
Low/moderate

Soil:
Moist, well drained

Uses:
Borders, rock gardens, mixed containers

Did You Know?

The narrow-leaf zinnia was the first group recognized as a Mississippi Medallion winner in 1998.

Color photo on page 130

Ornamental Sweet Potato

Ipomoea batatas

"Sweet potatoes grown for the landscape," these spreading ground covers have colorful foliage of lime green, dark burgundy with green, and green variegated with white and pink.

How to Grow

Plant in plenty of sunlight with a little afternoon shade in spring after the last frost. Prepare beds with 3 to 4 inches of organic matter incorporated with 2 pounds of a slow-release 12-6-6 fertilizer per 100 square feet. Space plants as recommended. Mulch to control weeds and conserve moisture.

Companion Plantings

'Blackie' combines well with pink lantanas or verbenas like 'Port Gibson'. 'New Gold' lantana, 'Blackie's' opposite color, is also a dynamite companion, as is the tall 'Coral Nymph' salvia. The lime-green or 'Marguerite' sweet potato looks striking with 'Solar Sunrise' coleus planted behind. The 'Pink Frost' or tri-color sweet potato looks spectacular cascading out of a basket that has a mandevilla climbing the chain.

Care and Maintenance

Ornamental sweet potatoes are a "watch-them-grow" kind of plant. Don't be afraid to keep them in bounds by pruning. They form tubers that are easy to dig, dry, and plant next year. They also root easily, so take your choice of propagation.

Recommended Varieties

There are several varieties, but 'Marguerite' (lime green), 'Blackie' (dark burgundy and green), and 'Pink Frost' (green-and-white variegation with pink margins) are mostly what you will find. All are good; 'Pink Frost' is not quite as vigorous.

Other Name:
Sweet Potato Vine

Light Needs:

Bloom Time:
Colorful foliage spring summer and fall

Bloom Color:
Grown for luxuriantly colored foliage

Height: 6 to 8 in.

Spacing:
24 to 36 in.

Water Needs:
Moderate

Soil:
Moist, well drained

Uses:
Ornamental ground cover, baskets, containers

Did You Know?

The morning glory is a close cousin.

Color photo on page 130

Pansy

Viola wittrockiana

No plant comes close to the fall, winter, and spring color of the pansy. Hundreds of varieties attest to the popularity of this plant.

How to Grow

Choose a site in full sun to partial shade. Set out in October and November for the prettiest displays. Till in 3 to 4 inches of organic matter (like peat moss or humus) and 2 pounds of a slow-release 5-10-5 fertilizer per 100 square feet. Pansies must be planted at the same depth they were growing in the container; any deeper will be fatal.

Companion Planting

The pansy's dark blues and purples look great with yellow daffodils. Complementary-colored 'Crown' or 'Liberty' snapdragons combine well with pansies. Flowering kale and cabbage make great winter companions, as do bold drifts of pansies of different colors.

Care and Maintenance

Temperatures may still be very warm when planting, so keep them watered and apply a layer of protective mulch. Pansies are heavy feeders; a twice-monthly application of a complete water-soluble fertilizer will keep them growing. Deadheading helps keep the flowers coming. Extremely cold weather may give them a frightful look, but they most likely will recover.

Recommended Varieties

Pansies without blotches like 'Crown', 'Crystal Bowl', and 'Delta Pure Color' have captured the hearts of commercial landscapers. 'Bingo', 'Rally', and 'Majestic Giants' are all good. Look for 'Purple Rain', a wonderful mounding, cascading type.

Other Name:
Heartsease

Light Needs:

Added Benefits:

Bloom Time:
Fall, winter, spring

Bloom Color:
All colors, clear and with blotches

Height: 6 to 12 in.

Spacing: 6 to 10 in.

Water Needs:
Moderate

Soil:
Moist, well drained

Uses:
Landscape beds, mixed containers

Did You Know?
Pansy flowers are edible.

Color photo on page 130

Periwinkle

Catharanthus roseus

Periwinkle's blooms are never-ending in the hottest days of summer. This is one of the most colorful and beloved flowers for the summer garden, and has striking foliage.

How to Grow

Do not plant until May. Cool soil temperatures are lethal to this plant, as are wet feet. Prepare beds deeply, tilling in 3 to 4 inches of organic matter and incorporating 2 pounds of a slow-release 12-6-6 fertilizer per 100 square feet. Set out plants at the same depth they were growing in the containers or slightly higher. Mulch to prevent water from splashing stems and leaves.

Companion Planting

Periwinkles look good with other periwinkles in masses of separate colors and mixes. Their glossy foliage and bright flowers also work well in tropical-looking gardens. Try 'Pacifica Red' as an understory planting for banana trees. White periwinkles with red eyes look great planted in front of tall red salvias.

Care and Maintenance

Planting after the weather has warmed and applying a good layer of mulch take care of most maintenance issues. Water during the driest periods, using a wand or soaker hose if at all possible to prevent splashing on leaves. Feed in midsummer with a light application of the above fertilizer.

Recommended Varieties

The 'Coolers' have long been a favorite, but the 'Pacifica' series with red and orchid (and a coral to come in 2000) are getting a lot of attention. The first F1 hybrid, called 'Blue Pearl', has light-blue flowers and durability in the landscape. The 'Mediterranean' series features spreading cascading-type growth.

Other Name:
Rose Periwinkle

Light Needs:

Added Benefits:

Bloom Time:
Summer, fall

Bloom Color:
Pink, white, red, lavender, and coral, some with eyes

Height: 1 to 2 ft.

Spacing: 6 to 10 in.

Water Needs: Low

Soil:
Moist, well drained

Uses:
Flower borders, baskets, containers

Did You Know?

A substance extracted from Madagascar periwinkle is used for fighting leukemia.

Color photo on page 130

Petunia

Other Names:
Surfinias, Supertunias

Light Needs:

Added Benefits:

Bloom Time:
Spring, summer, fall

Bloom Color:
various

Height: 2 to 24 in.

Spacing: 12 to 24 in.

Water Needs:
Moderate

Soil:
Moist, well drained

Uses:
Flower borders, baskets, windowboxes, mixed planters

Did You Know?
The Mississippi Medallion winners for 2000 are the 'Waves'— purple, pink, rose, and misty lilac.

Color photo on page 130

Petunia × hybrida

There has been a petunia revival, with new heat-tolerant landscape petunias that have some of the longest bloom periods in the flower garden. 'Waves', 'Surfinias', and 'Supertunias' are just a few.

How to Grow
Prepare beds by incorporating 3 to 4 inches of organic matter and 2 pounds of slow-release 12-6-6 fertilizer, and tilling to a depth of 8 to 10 inches. Plant in early spring, in full sunlight or in an area receiving morning sun and afternoon shade. Plant at the same depth they were growing in the containers and remember to space—some will spread 4 feet.

Companion Planting
Pick your favorite-colored combinations known for long durability, such as 'Purple Wave' and 'New Gold' lantana; 'Pink Wave' and 'Victoria' blue salvia; 'Purple Sunspot' and melampodium; and Midnight Madness and yellow marigolds. The 'Wave' series looks good as a mixture.

Care and Maintenance
A good layer of mulch will help keep soil temperatures cooler and conserve moisture in warm weather. Pinching or light shearing will stimulate new growth and more blooms. Feed every 4 weeks with light applications of the above slow-release fertilizer.

Recommended Varieties
The year 2000 looks exciting with the introduction of a new class called hedgiflora. The hedgiflora petunias called 'Tidal Wave' reach 3 feet in height and width. The 'Fantasy' series continues to gain converts with its appearance of having a thousand flowers. 'Supertunias' and 'Surfinias' have proven themselves worthy of a spot in the landscape.

Portulaca

Portulaca grandiflora

Brightly colored iridescent flowers produce for months on succulent-looking plants. This is a floral display that will stop traffic.

How to Grow

Plant in full sun. Prepare beds by incorporating 3 to 4 inches of organic matter like peat or fine pine bark, along with 2 pounds of a slow-release 12-6-6 fertilizer per 100 square feet. Plant after the last frost when the soil has warmed. Set out at the same depth they were growing in the container, then water deeply. Apply a good layer of mulch.

Companion Planting

When choosing a companion plant, consider its water needs. Portulaca does not like a lot of water and looks exceptional with fountain grass or maiden grass. Use in rock gardens along with purple heart or lantana. Mixtures are usually sold, but massing a single color may give the prettiest display.

Care and Maintenance

Keep the plants moist until they are established, then resist the temptation to water, especially by overhead sprinklers. Cut back the plants if needed in midsummer to rejuvenate growth and blooms. Give them a boost with a light application of the above fertilizer.

Recommended Varieties

The 'Sundial' and 'Sundance' series are among the best, with large semi-double flowers that stay open long into the day. New on the market and earning recognition are the 'Yubi' series with large clear single-petal flowers, and the 'Duet' series that has two multi-colored selections.

Other Name:
Moss Rose

Light Needs:

Bloom Time:
Spring, summer, fall

Bloom Color:
various

Height: 6 to 9 in.

Spacing: 6 to 12 in.

Water Needs: Low

Soil:
Moist, well drained

Uses:
Flower borders, baskets, containers, mixed planters

Did You Know?

Purslane, also a portulaca, is used in several French and Mexican dishes.

Color photo on page 130

Salvia

Other Name:
Scarlet Sage

Light Needs:

Added Benefits:

Bloom Time:
Spring, summer, fall

Bloom Color:
Red, white, pink, lavender, coral, and two-tones

Height: 15 to 30 in.

Spacing: 8 to 12 in.

Water Needs:
Moderate

Soil:
Moist, well drained

Uses:
Flower borders, mixed containers

Did You Know?
The red varieties are great hummingbird plants.

Color photo on page 131

Salvia splendens

1999 was the Year of the Salvia. The spiky flowers of scarlet sage are welcome in the summer garden, as are the many other colors.

How to Grow
Plant in full sun, although partial shade is tolerated. Prepare beds by adding 3 to 4 inches of organic matter and tilling to a depth of 8 to 10 inches. Work in 2 pounds of slow-release 12-6-6 fertilizer per 100 square feet. Set out plants at the same depth they were growing in the containers and space as recommended.

Companion Planting
Many red varieties are on the orange side and work well with gold lantanas and yellow or orange marigolds. The lilac or purple varieties combine nicely with the same color of 'Queen' cleomes. The 'Salsa' series has several bicolored selections that are dynamite with 'Blackie' sweet potato or 'Purple Heart'. Plant boldly in groups for the best display.

Care and Maintenance
Salvias are heavy feeders and will need feeding every 4 to 6 weeks with the above slow-release fertilizer. Keep them well watered during periods of drought. As blooms fade, deadhead and cut back in late summer to produce a bushier plant. By doing this you will ensure great fall bloom.

Recommended Varieties
There are a lot of good varieties of red salvia. 'Red Vista' has always been a favorite, as has 'Red Hot Sally' and 'St. John's Fire'. The 'Empire' and 'Salsa' series offer some of the prettiest colors.

Scaevola

Scaevola aemula

1997 Mississippi Medallion winner 'New Wonder' has blue fan-shaped flowers from spring until frost. A spreading plant, it is one of the toughest in Mississippi heat and humidity.

How to Grow
Plant in full sun for best bloom, though scaevola also performs in partial shade. Prepare beds by tilling in 3 to 4 inches of organic matter to improve drainage and aeration. Incorporate 2 pounds of a 12-6-6 fertilizer per 100 square feet. Set out plants at the same depth they were growing in the containers. They spread, so space accordingly. Add a layer of mulch after planting.

Companion Planting
For a bed that is pretty and tough, plant 'New Wonder' scaevola in front of 'New Gold' lantana. Lantanas with orange, or orange marigolds, look nice with scaevola. This plant is among the most beautiful when cascading out of an urn or basket. Plant 'Temari Patio Pink' verbenas in a basket with 'New Wonder' scaevola—the result is beautiful.

Care and Maintenance
The scaevola is drought tolerant in the landscape but needs daily summer watering. Feed monthly in the landscape with light applications of the above fertilizer, or weekly with a water-soluble fertilizer when grown in containers. Time-released granules are also suitable for containers. Should the scaevola grow leggy, or out of its desired location, it responds well to pruning.

Recommended Varieties
'New Wonder' scaevola was the Mississippi Medallion winner, but there are others worth growing, particularly the 'Outback' series that offers different colors such as white and pink.

Other Name:
Fan Flower

Light Needs:

Added Benefit:

Bloom Time:
Spring, summer, fall

Bloom Color:
Purple, white, pink

Height: 6 to 8 in.

Water Needs:
Low/moderate

Soil:
Moist, well drained

Uses: Flower borders, baskets, containers, mixed planters

Did You Know?
Scaevola is named for a Roman hero, Mucius Scaevola, who showed bravery by burning off his left hand.

Color photo on page 131

Snapdragon

Antirrhinum majus

Other Name:
Common Snapdragon

Light Needs:

Added Benefits:

Bloom Time:
Fall, (winter), spring

Bloom Color:
Bold colors—red, pink, yellow, orange, coral, two-tones

Height: 7 to 36 in.

Spacing: 10 to 12 in.

Water Needs:
Moderate

Soil:
Moist, well drained

Uses:
Cottage gardens, cutflower gardens, flower beds

Did You Know?
Many snapdragons have wonderful fragrance.

Color photo on page 131

These intensely colored flowers are an old-fashioned favorite and need to be planted again.

How to Grow
Choose a site in full sun, although partial shade is tolerated. Incorporate 3 to 4 inches of organic matter to ensure good drainage and aeration. While tilling, apply 2 pounds of a slow-release 12-6-6 fertilizer per 100 square feet. Plant snapdragons at the same depth they were growing in the containers. Since snapdragons range from small to large, space accordingly. Set out plants in October and November in the southern two-thirds of the state, and in March in the northern area.

Companion Planting
The rich colors of snapdragons provide an opportunity to combine them with pansies, flowering kale and cabbage, and early spring petunias. Plant large groups for the best show. Try planting the dwarf forms in front of the intermediates.

Care and Maintenance
You will be asking your snapdragons to survive winter, so be sure to mulch for protection. Cold weather can dry out beds, so be prepared to water during the winter. Keep plants deadheaded to encourage more blooms, especially after a good fall blooming period. As the weather starts to warm, give them a feeding of water-soluble fertilizer to get them going.

Recommended Varieties
Favorite dwarf varieties are 'Bells', 'Tahiti', and 'Floral Showers' (7 to 10 in.); intermediate selections are 'Sonnet', 'Liberty', and 'Ribbons' (18 to 24 in.); and the tall cutflower types are 'Rocket', 'Topper', and 'Madame Butterfly' (30 to 36 in.).

Sunflower

Helianthus annuus

Dwarf plants with huge colorful flowers have made sunflowers popular with gardeners, and they are among the flowers most beloved by children.

How to Grow

They plant easily by seed, but many new dwarf forms with loads of color are available as transplants from your local garden center. They are also good for fall crops. They prefer a loose, well-drained soil. If you don't have such a soil, work the soil into raised beds and incorporate 1 to 2 inches of organic matter. Till in 2 pounds of a slow-release 5-10-5 fertilizer per 100 square feet.

Companion Planting

Sunflowers, particularly dwarf types, look good massed in single colors at the border's back. Tall companion plants like salvia 'Indigo Spires' and 'Mexican' bush sage help give a cottage-garden look to sunflowers. Plant 'Victoria' blue salvia in front of both yellow and red sunflowers. 'New Gold' lantana looks handsome in front of the crimson-red sunflower called 'Prado'.

Care and Maintenance

Stake tall types. Many of the dwarf types form multiple buds and blooms; deadhead unsightly ones unless growing for seed. Feed every 6 to 8 weeks with a light application of the above fertilizer. Water during dry periods. Mulch to conserve moisture and deter weeds.

Recommended Varieties

For dwarf sizes, look for 'Sundance Kid', 'Teddy Bear', and 'Big Smile'. Intermediate sizes (less than 5 feet) are 'Del Sol', 'Prado', and 'Sonja'. Good choices over 5 feet are 'Sunrich', the 'Sun and Moon' series, and 'Park's Velvet Tapestry'.

Other Name:
Common Sunflower

Light Needs:

Added Benefits:

Bloom Time:
Summer, fall

Bloom Color:
Yellow, orange, burgundy tones

Height: 3 to 10 ft.

Spacing: 20 to 24 in.

Water Needs:
Moderate

Soil:
Moist, well drained

Uses: Flower beds, gardens, large planters

Did You Know?
American Indians used sunflowers for food, dye, and medicine.

Color photo on page 131

Viola

Other Names:
Johnny Jump-Up,
Horned Violet

Light Needs:

Added Benefits:

Bloom Time:
Fall, winter, spring

Bloom Color:
All shades

Height: 6 to 12 in.

Spacing: 6 to 8 in.

Water Needs:
Moderate

Soil:
Moist, well drained

Uses:
Flower beds, borders,
containers, fall planters

Did You Know?
The viola is native to
the high Pyrenees.

Color photo on page 131

Viola cornuta

These boldly colored flowers are similar to their larger cousin the pansy, but there are many more on a plant, giving a spectacular show from fall to summer.

How to Grow
Choose a site in full sun to partial shade. Be prepared to set out in October and November for the prettiest displays. Prepare beds by tilling in 3 to 4 inches of organic matter like peat moss or humus, and 2 pounds of a slow-release 12-6-6 fertilizer per 100 square feet of bed space. Violas must be planted at the same depth they were growing in the container—any deeper will be fatal.

Companion Planting
Violas combine well with snapdragons and flowering kale and cabbage. When you plant your bed of violas, plant spring daffodils. By the time the foliage of the daffodils emerges the violas will have spread. Try using the smaller-flowered daffodils like tazettas or jonquils. Mass your plantings of single colors for the prettiest show.

Care and Maintenance
Temperatures may still be very warm when planting, so keep plants watered and apply a layer of protective mulch. Violas are heavy feeders and twice-monthly applications of a complete water-soluble fertilizer will keep them growing. Deadhead to keep the flowers coming.

Recommended Varieties
The 'Princess' and 'Sorbet' series have become two of the most popular, with several colors offered for each. The *Viola tricolor* or Johnny Jump-up varieties, 'Alpine Summer', 'Blue Elf', and 'Splendid' series should also be planted. A cross between the pansy and viola called Panola will debut with several colors in 2000.

Zinnia

Zinnia elegans

Zinnia is queen of cutflowers, producing for months on end flowers from giants to those the size of a quarter. It is a must in the flower garden.

How to Grow
Zinnia is one of the easiest plants to grow from seed, yet we are fortunate to have transplants of many varieties at local garden centers. Prepare soil by incorporating 3 to 4 inches of organic matter to improve drainage and aeration. Poorer soils will be tolerated, but not wet feet. As you work the soil, apply 2 pounds of a slow-release 12-6-6 fertilizer per 100 square feet. Thin seedlings.

Companion Planting
Massing single-colored zinnias with complementary colors of plants like lantanas, verbenas, and a couple of 'Japanese Silver Grass' specimens will give months of landscape performance. Plant single-colored yellow or orange zinnias as understory plants to buddleias like 'Black Knight' or 'Plum Delight'.

Care and Maintenance
Feed monthly with light applications of the above fertilizer. Watch for moisture stress during dry periods and water as needed. Irrigate from underneath with a wand or soaker hose. Mulch to conserve moisture and keep weeds in check. Keep flowers deadheaded for maximum bloom.

Recommended Varieties
The narrow-leaf zinnia (*Zinnia angustifolia*) was a 1998 Mississippi Medallion winner and reaches about 18 inches in height. 'Profusion Orange' and 'Cherry' were 1999 All-America Selections winners. The 'Dreamland' series gets about 2 feet in height, has giant dahlia-like flowers, and is slow to get disease. Good tall cutflower types are 'Oklahoma', 'Ruffles', and 'State Fair'.

Other Name:
Common Zinnia

Light Needs:

Added Benefits:

Bloom Time:
Spring, summer, fall

Bloom Color:
All colors except blue

Height: 1 to 3 ft.

Spacing: 8 to 15 in.

Water Needs:
Moderate

Soil:
Moist, well drained

Uses:
Flower beds, borders, containers, planters

Did You Know?
Zinnias can germinate in only four days.

Color photo on page 131

BULBS

Every spring in Mississippi you will notice fields and patches of narcissus. If you bother to get out of the car and really look, you will see which varieties tend to naturalize over the years. The narcissi seen most often are jonquils and 'Campernelles', which is a local favorite and a jonquil hybrid. If you picnic among these flowers, you will be amazed at their delightful fragrance. You will also want them for your yard. Another narcissus that is prevalent at many of these old sites is the tazetta. The tazetta class contains the paper-whites, including an ancient variety called 'Grand Monarque', which is fragrant and more durable than the run-of-the-mill paper-white.

Tulips are also among the most popular of the bulbous plants, but they are treated as annuals in all but the far north parts of Mississippi. Even when grown as an annual, their beauty is something to behold. There are several other beautiful flowering plants from this wonderful world of bulbs, corms, tubers, and rhizomes that provide color in the landscape and come back yearly for glorious displays in both spring and summer.

A true bulb is a miniaturized plant complete with flowers packed in a self-contained "starter kit." Bulbs need several months to attain root growth that will support the foliage and flowers.

You should plant large masses of bulbs to appreciate their beauty. Before planting, visualize what will be in leaf or bloom at the same time as the bulbs.

It is important when landscaping with bulbs to plant groups of twelve or more of the same variety. Massed flowers look better; avoid the polka-dot effect. Flowers of narcissus look better scattered in natural-looking drifts, while tulips lend a more formal pattern to the garden and should be planted like a marching band, in rows.

Since there are many months between an October planting and a March bloom, gardeners can take advantage of this time

> When you see patches of narcissus in an empty field, you can guess that a house was there long ago.

to grow other beautiful flowers, combining pansies with large daffodils, or violas with smaller-blooming types.

When buying bulbs, always select those that are firm and blemish-free. Remember, larger bulbs produce larger flowers. Plant spring-flowering bulbs when the soil temperature is 40 to 45 degrees Fahrenheit. Bulb root growth occurs within this temperature range without initiation and growth of foliage. The ideal time for planting spring-flowering bulbs is mid-October through November in north Mississippi, and late December in south Mississippi. Plant summer-flowering bulbs after the danger of spring frost has passed.

If a large number of bulbs is to be planted, prepare the beds to a depth of 9 to 12 inches. Uniform bed preparation permits a uniform planting depth that helps ensure uniform flowering. There is physical agony involved in planting a couple of hundred bulbs in tight soil. Good loose soil is not only well drained, but a pleasure in which to plant.

Don't guess—get a soil test done with your local county extension agent. Bulbs grow and flower well with a soil pH between 5.5 and 7.0. Phosphorus is important for proper root and flower development. Since phosphorus is not mobile in the soil, add it to the soil before planting.

Don't be afraid to try new varieties—experimentation is what gardening is all about.

After planting, apply a complete fertilizer (such as 5-10-10 at 3 pounds per 100 square feet) in early spring before bloomtime for spring-flowering bulbs. For summer-flowering bulbs, apply 5-10-10 at 2 pounds per 100 square feet, three times during the growing season at 6-week intervals.

If you plant bulbs with a bulb planter or trowel, apply one teaspoon of bonemeal to the bottom of the planting hole 1 to 2 inches below the bulb.

Amaryllis

Other Name:
Knight's Star Lily

Light Needs:

Added Benefits:

Zones: 8 to 9

Bloom Time:
Spring

Bloom Color:
Red, white

Height: 18 to 24 in.

Spacing: 12 to 18 in.

Water Needs:
Moderate

Soil:
Moist, well drained

Uses:
Spring beds, containers

Did You Know?
It is called "Amaryllis," but it isn't one; it is a *Hippeastrum*.

Color photo on page 131

Hippeastrum species and hybrids

Nine-inch trumpet-shaped flowers herald the arrival of spring. There is not a showier bulb.

How to Grow
The first year, grow by planting in a pot with a light, airy potting mixture. Plant so that the neck and the top of the bulb are in view. Place the pot in a sunny window and maintain moisture. It will probably bloom in the winter. Keep it growing indoors until April, then plant outside. Make sure your outside garden is well drained and rich in organic material. Plant at the same depth it was growing in the container. It should bloom in the spring.

Companion Planting
Plant in front of evergreen shrubs to show off blooms. If growing red varieties with white stripes, consider planting white crystal bowl or crown pansies in front.

Care and Maintenance
In the northern region of the state, grow as an indoor crop. When finished blooming, cut the flower stalk and maintain moisture until leaves turn yellow. Withhold water and let the plant dry out, then repot in the fall. Keep bulbs well mulched in the winter. Remove foliage when it turns yellow. Feed your planting in early spring with 3 pounds per 100 square feet of a slow-release 5-10-10, followed by a light application in midsummer.

Recommended Varieties
Hippeastrum × *Johnsonii* 'St. Joseph's Lily' is the most widely planted. *H. reginae* the 'Mexican Lily' (a red variety with a white star in the throat) and *H. vittatum* (white with red veins) are also common.

Bearded Iris

Iris × germanica

Warning: if you grow bearded iris, you will get hooked!

How to Grow

Choose a site in full sun to partial shade. Prepare soil by incorporating 3 to 4 inches of organic matter like fine pine bark and compost. While tilling, add 3 pounds of slow-release 5-10-10 fertilizer per 100 square feet. Work the soil 8 to 10 inches deep. Set out container-grown plants anytime and plant rhizomes in the fall, just below the soil surface. Water deeply and apply a layer of mulch.

Companion Planting

With a little planning you can have a garden that takes your breath away. Plant irises in the fall at the same time you plant pansies or violas. One option is to plant single-colored pansies that are the opposite color of the iris blooms. There is a pansy that will show off, or combine well with, any iris.

Care and Maintenance

Monitor your moisture. Bearded irises do not like soggy soil. Trim off spent flower stalks and any yellow foliage to keep tidy. After the plants have finished blooming, side-dress with a light application of the above fertilizer. Bearded irises need dividing every three to four years in the fall. Discard old center rhizomes and replant the young outer ones.

Recommended Varieties

It has been estimated that there are now 30,000 varieties of bearded iris, which is a testimony to their beauty. Pick your favorite colors and heights. Visit with your local Iris Society; it is my guess they will have some valuable opinions on which are the best.

Other Name:
Sword Lily

Light Needs:

Added Benefits:

Zones: 7 to 9

Bloom Time:
Spring, early summer

Bloom Color:
All shades

Height: 12 to 30 in.

Water Needs:
Low/moderate

Soil:
Slightly moist, well drained

Uses:
Perennial and cottage gardens

Did You Know?

There are some bearded iris, like 'Desiderata', that repeat bloom.

Color photo on page 131

Caladium

Other Name:
Angel Wings

Light Needs:

Added Benefit:

Zone: 10

Bloom Time:
Grown for foliage

Bloom Color:
White

Height: 2 to 3 ft.

Spacing: 8 to 12 in.

Water Needs:
Frequent

Soil:
Moist, well drained

Uses:
Tropical and shade gardens, containers

Did You Know?
You can remove the central eye in the middle of the tuber to get more leaves.

Color photo on page 131

Caladium bicolor

From the Amazon Basin in Brazil, the caladium boasts some of the most exotic and beautiful foliage in the world, providing glorious color in areas where sun-loving plants fail.

How to Grow
Caladiums need warm, moist, well-drained soil. Prepare beds by adding 3 to 4 inches of organic matter like fine pine bark or compost, along with 2 pounds of slow-release 12-6-6 fertilizer per 100 square feet. Till the bed 8 to 10 inches deep. There are two choices in planting: tubers, or more often a 6-inch container with colorful leaves already showing. Potted caladiums should be planted at the same depth they were growing in containers. Set out tubers 2 to 3 inches deep, 8 to 12 inches apart.

Companion Planting
Pair white caladiums with red veins and red impatiens. Plant bold caladium drifts adjacent to ferns.

Care and Maintenance
Apply a good layer of mulch to keep soil temperatures moderate and conserve moisture. Remove flower buds as soon as they develop. Caladium tubers can be dug up and saved in fall. After drying a week, remove old foliage, dust with fungicide, and place in a box filled with kitty litter or sawdust. Don't let the tubers touch. Store where temperatures will stay above 60 degrees Fahrenheit.

Recommended Varieties
Favorite varieties are 'Candidum', 'Frieda Hemple', and 'Pink Symphony'. 'Fire Chief', 'Red Flash', and 'White Queen' are more sun-tolerant.

Canna

Canna × generalis

The lush foliage and exotic blooms of the canna reflect its tropical nature. From the dwarf to the giant, canna is one of the easiest perennials to grow.

How to Grow

Plant in full sun for best bloom. Add 3 to 4 inches of organic matter, like fine pine bark or compost, and 3 pounds per 100 square feet of slow-release 5-10-5 fertilizer. Till to 8 to 10 inches. Plant 3 to 4 inches deep and 12 to 18 inches apart. Cannas sold growing should be planted at the same depth they were in the containers.

Companion Planting

Plant in tropical Southern gardens with bananas and upright elephant ears, or around pools and water gardens. With careful selection, sun coleus can make a great companion.

Care and Maintenance

Remove seedpods for a tidy appearance. When the shoot is finished blooming, cut either just above the foliage or at ground level—new basal sprouts will develop. Canna leaf rollers roll the leaf, cement it, and chew holes in it. Light dustings of Sevin keep them in check when they are active. If they make your stalk too ugly, cut it off at the ground and destroy. Go into the winter with extra mulch.

Recommended Varieties

Favorite bicolored varieties are 'Cleopatra' and 'Yellow King Humbert'. The 'Pfitzer Dwarfs' are available in four colors. 'Tropical Rose' is a seed-produced canna that has gained acceptance. The prettiest new canna is 'Tropicanna', with variegated foliage in shades of orange, burgundy, yellow, and green, with orange flowers.

Other Name:
Canna Lily

Light Needs:

Added Benefits:

Zones: 7 to 9

Bloom Time:
Summer, fall

Bloom Color:
Many shades and blends

Height: 3 to 6 ft.

Spacing: 12 to 18 in.

Water Needs:
Frequent

Soil:
Moist, well drained

Uses:
Tropical garden, perennial garden, pools

Did You Know?

The canna has been in cultivation since the 1500s.

Color photo on page 131

Crinum

Other Names:
Confederate Lily,
Milk-and-Wine Lily

Light Needs:

Added Benefits:

Zones: 7 to 9

Bloom Time:
Spring, summer

Bloom Color:
Magenta, pink, rose,
white, striped

Height: 2 to 4 ft.

Spacing: 2 to 3 ft.

Water Needs: Often

Soil:
Moist, well drained

Uses:
Tropical and perennial
garden, groups and
specimen

Did You Know?
Crinums have a wonderful tantalizing fragrance.

Color photo on page 131

Crinum species and hybrids

Crinums are the beautiful sequoias of the bulb world—they will probably be around for generations.

How to Grow
Well-drained soil is a must. Spread a 3- to 4-inch layer of organic matter like fine pine bark and compost over the bed, along with 3 pounds of slow-release 5-10-5 fertilizer per 100 square feet. Turn the soil to a depth of 8 to 10 inches. Crinums should be planted deep, at a minimum of 6 inches. Deeper 12-inch planting will discourage offsets and produce a larger single bulb.

Companion Planting
The foliage and texture is such that tropical settings may look best. Plant a medium-tall banana like 'Bloodleaf' or 'Super Dwarf Cavendish' with clumps of crinum 3 feet in front and at the sides. *Alocasia macrorrhiza* (or, giant upright elephant ears) also work. Crinums do not want to be disturbed—allow space between all plants.

Care and Maintenance
Go into winter with extra mulch, particularly in the northern third of the state. Feed with light applications of the above fertilizer in spring and midsummer. Trim foliage that freezes during the winter. Don't disturb your clump or it may take years to bloom again. It should be years before you are forced to divide.

Recommended Varieties
Not all crinums are hardy in Mississippi. Varieties of *C. asiaticum* (St. John's Lily), *C. bulbispermum* (Hardy Crinum), *C. moorei* (Longneck Crinum), and *C. × powellii* (Powell's Hybrid Crinum) are all hardy. There are many more great ones for zones 8 and 9.

Gladiolus

Gladiolus × hortulanus

If you have not grown gladiolus, you have missed growing one of the most beautiful flowers in the garden.

How to Grow

The ideal site has morning sun and afternoon shade. Till in 3 to 4 inches of fine pine bark and compost to a depth of 8 to 10 inches. Incorporate 3 pounds of a slow-release 5-10-5 fertilizer per 100 square feet. Starting in February, plant at 2-week intervals through April to extend bloom period. These corms should be planted 4 to 6 inches deep. Water, then mulch.

Companion Planting

Gladiolus needs support—stake, or mound its soil. Some of the prettiest displays are in mixed borders where the glads are behind dwarf evergreens and in front of tall evergreens, their brilliant color serving as a contrast. Species glads that do not have to be dug up are great in the perennial garden when planted in drifts mixed with bearded iris.

Care and Maintenance

Harvest glads for cutflowers just as the lower buds begin to open. When the foliage turns yellow in summer, the glad should be dug up. Remove the remaining foliage and dry for several weeks in a shady, well-ventilated place. Dust with a fungicide and store in a frost-free ventilated area until next winter.

Recommended Varieties

The species varieties *G. communis* var. *byzantinus* and *G. dalenii* (formerly *G. primulinus*), though not quite as showy, become naturalized in the garden and are best planted in the fall. The Garden Gladiolus, grandiflora hybrids, are the showier varieties and should be treated as annuals or dug up.

Other Name:
Sword Lily

Light Needs:

Added Benefits:

Zones: 7 to 9

Bloom Time:
Summer

Bloom Color:
Red, yellow, pink, purple, orange, white, and others

Height: 30 to 60 in.

Spacing: 4 to 6 in

Water Needs:
Moderate

Soil:
Moist, well drained

Uses:
Cutflower garden, perennial garden

Did You Know?

Gladiolus means "little sword" in Latin.

Color photo on page 131

Louisiana Iris

Other Name:
Swamp Iris

Light Needs:

Added Benefits:

Zones: 7 to 9

Bloom Time:
Spring

Bloom Color:
All shades and blends

Height × Width:
1 to 6 ft.

Water Needs:
Moderate/frequent

Soil:
Moist, well drained

Uses:
Perennial garden,
water gardens

Did You Know?
It is estimated that there are now 1,500 to 2,000 varieties of Louisiana iris.

Color photo on page 132

Iris species and hybrids

Louisiana irises have outstanding color and often the ability to grow at the edges of streams.

How to Grow
Choose a site with at least six hours of sunlight. Add 3 to 4 inches of organic matter like fine pine bark or compost and till to a depth of 8 to 10 inches. Incorporate 3 pounds of slow-release 5-10-5 fertilizer per 100 square feet. Plant rhizomes in late summer and fall just below the soil surface. Keep them moist until they get established. They are vigorous growers, so space about 2 feet apart.

Companion Planting
The best companions are other Louisiana iris hybrids. The umbrella plant *Cyperus alternifolius* makes a great companion plant. Shorter Louisiana iris can be planted in front, while taller ones can be planted adjacent. They are lush and vigorous, so space correctly and thin yearly.

Care and Maintenance
Feed with light applications of the above fertilizer in October and February, maintaining moisture during this period should Mother Nature fail to contribute. Foliage may become ugly and yellow during the summer. Trim back and a new flush will occur in fall.

Recommended Varieties
There are four species of swamp iris and their hybrids under the "Louisiana" moniker. The colors are beautiful. If purple is your favorite, try 'Marie Caillet' and 'Professor Claude'. Choice yellow varieties are 'Sun Fury' and 'Dixie Deb'. 'Cajun Country' (a deep red) and 'Acadiana Sunset' (burgundy with yellow) are also highly acclaimed.

Monbretia

Crocosmia × crocosmiiflora

These showy orange flowers on long spikes reveal their relationship to the gladiolus. This is an old Southern nostalgia plant that everyone should grow.

How to Grow

Choose a site in full sun for best bloom. In zone 9, afternoon shade will be nice. Prepare soil by adding a 3- to 4-inch layer of fine pine bark and compost, and till to a depth of 8 to 10 inches. Incorporate 3 pounds per 100 square feet of a slow-release fertilizer such as a 5-10-5. Plant out clumps of corms about 2 inches deep and one foot apart. Nursery-grown plants should be planted at the same depth they were growing in the containers. Water, and apply a layer of mulch.

Companion Planting

This gladiolus relative looks tropical and it is, hailing from South Africa. It looks great planted in and around clumps of banana trees and upright elephant ears. Effective plantings can also be done with yellow cannas.

Care and Maintenance

With spring emergence, side-dress with a light application of the above fertilizer. Plants are vigorous and the clump enlarges, creating even more flowers. When it gets too large, divide in fall or early spring. Remove yellow foliage in fall and add a protective layer of mulch.

Recommended Varieties

The most common variety for sale in Mississippi is 'Lucifer'. Other well-known varieties are 'Spitfire', 'Emberglow', and 'Bressingham Beacon'. Crocosmia is a plant much traded at plant swaps.

Other Name:
Crocosmia

Light Needs:

Added Benefits:

Zones: 7 to 9

Bloom Time:
Spring, early summer

Bloom Color:
Orange, red, yellow

Height: 2 to 3 ft.

Spacing: 1 ft.

Water Needs:
Moderate

Soil:
Moist, well drained

Uses:
Tropical garden, perennial garden

Did You Know?

Crocosmia comes from the Greek meaning "saffron smell."

Color photo on page 132

Narcissus

Other Names:
Daffodil, Jonquil, Paper-whites

Light Needs:

Added Benefits:

Zones: 7 to 9

Bloom Time: Spring

Bloom Color: Pink, yellow, white, orange

Height: 8 to 16 in.

Spacing: 6 to 8 in.

Water Needs:
Moderate

Soil:
Moist, well drained

Uses: Spring gardens, natural areas, containers

Did You Know?
Narcissus was a mythological Greek youth who fell in love with his reflection in a pool of water and was turned into a flower.

Color photo on page 132

Narcissus species

Fields of narcissus bloom each spring all across the South at old homesites, showing their naturalizing ability. They have delightful fragrance that permeates the indoors when cut for a vase.

How to Grow
Choose a site in full sun or filtered light, or in the shadow of tall deciduous trees. Prepare the area by incorporating 3 to 4 inches of organic matter, like fine pine bark and compost, and tilling 8 to 10 inches deep. While tilling, add 3 pounds of a slow-release 5-10-5 fertilizer per 100 square feet. Plant bulbs in October and November. Bulbs should be planted 3 to 6 inches deep and 6 to 8 inches apart.

Companion Planting
Narcissus should be planted in the spring garden with trees like redbuds, dogwoods, and Japanese magnolia. Daffodils highlight shrubs like azaleas, flowering quince, and spiraea. Plant single varieties boldly in drifts adjacent to other varieties.

Care and Maintenance
Foliage plays an important role in the production of food for next year's blooms. After bloom time, trim the foliage when it turns yellow. Feed bulbs immediately after flowering with a light application of a 12-6-6 fertilizer. When the clumps get crowded and blooms become sparse, divide and replant in the spring after the foliage has started to decline.

Recommended Varieties
Some of the best at naturalizing are *N. tazetta* varieties 'Ziva', 'Galilee', 'Grand Monarque', and 'Soleil d'Or'. The *N. jonquilla* varieties 'Campernelle', 'Trevithian', and 'Golden Sceptor' will become at home in your landscape. Varieties of *N. cyclamineus*, *N. triandrus*, and *N. pseudonarcissus* daffodils like 'Ice Follies', 'Fortune', and 'Carlton' should also be grown.

Siberian Iris

Iris sibirica × *I. Sanguinea* hybrids

Beautiful and easy to grow, it is hard to believe that anything with the name "Siberian" can survive in the hot, muggy weather of Mississippi—maybe it is because they are just happy to be here.

How to Grow

Choose a site in full sun, or in morning sun and afternoon shade on the coast. Prepare the bed by tilling in 3 to 4 inches of organic matter like fine pine bark and compost to a depth of 8 to 10 inches. Evenly broadcast 3 pounds of a slow-release 5-10-5 fertilizer per 100 square feet, and work into the soil. Plant rhizomes 1 to 2 inches deep and 2 feet apart. Water after planting, and mulch.

Companion Planting

Like the Louisiana iris, the Siberian iris looks good with other Siberian iris and in gardens with the umbrella plant *Cyperus alternifolius*. It looks good in large clumps in the perennial garden, and spotted around water gardens.

Care and Maintenance

With spring emergence, feed with a light application of the above fertilizer. Keep this group of irises moist throughout the summer. Siberian iris stays green all summer and dies back in the winter. Remove dead foliage at this time. Clumps do not have to be divided very often. Divide in summer or fall after clumps have developed an open area in the center.

Recommended Varieties

The blue and purple varieties are the most common: 'Blue Brilliant', 'Heavenly Blue', 'Pansy Purple', 'Swank', and 'Caesar's Brother'. 'White Swirl' is a notable white variety with a splash of yellow.

Other Name:
Siberian Hybrids

Light Needs:

Added Benefit:

Zones: 7 to 9

Bloom Time:
Spring

Bloom Color:
Purple, violet, white, yellow, pink

Height: 2 to 3 ft.

Spacing: 2 ft.

Water Needs:
Frequent

Soil:
Moist, well drained

Uses:
Perennial and water garden

Did You Know?

There are now more than 150 varieties of Siberian Iris.

Color photo on page 132

Snowflake

Other Name:
Summer Snowflake

Light Needs:

Zones: 7 to 9

Bloom Time:
Winter on coast,
spring elsewhere

Bloom Color:
White

Height: 12 to 18 in.

Spacing: 3 to 6 in.

Water Needs:
Moderate

Soil:
Moist, well drained

Uses:
Perennial and
spring garden

Did You Know?

Leucojum comes from
the Greek and means
"white violet."

Color photo on page 132

Leucojum aestivum

This "nostalgia plant" with pretty white flowers and attractive foliage hails from France, but has now become an entrenched Southerner.

How to Grow
The snowflake adapts well to any well-drained site without a lot of bed preparation. Companion plants, however, may require something very different. Go ahead and prepare the bed by incorporating 3 to 4 inches of organic matter and 3 pounds of a slow-release 5-10-5 fertilizer per 100 square feet and till to a depth of 8 to 10 inches. Plant the bulbs 3 to 4 inches deep and space 3 to 6 inches apart. Water after planting and apply a layer of mulch.

Companion Planting
Plant in bold clumps with other spring-flowering bulbs like narcissus. Plant around beds of azaleas where the white flowers will be seen against their vibrant colors. They make an exceptional border plant for spring beds. In October, plant blue 'Crown' or 'Crystal Bowl' pansies, or Johnny Jump-ups, in front of snowflakes.

Care and Maintenance
Give a light sidedressing of the above fertilizer in the spring when new growth appears. The snowflake is close to being maintenance-free. Trim back in midsummer when the foliage turns yellow. Clumps will appreciate dividing every 3 to 5 years after the foliage has yellowed.

Recommended Varieties
'Gravetye Giant' is a variety that grows larger than the species. *L. vernum*, called 'Spring Snowflake', is not as showy or as hardy.

Spider Lily

Lycoris radiata

This is the great plant with spidery red blooms and no leaves you see blooming right after school has started.

How to Grow

Plant bulbs in the spring. Choose a site in full sun to filtered light. Stick the bulbs in any well-drained location and they will naturalize. If you want to include them in the perennial garden, prepare soil by incorporating 3 to 4 inches of organic matter like fine pine bark and compost, tilling to a depth of 8 to 10 inches. Plant 3 to 4 inches deep and 6 to 8 inches apart.

Companion Planting

If you are fortunate enough to have areas between trees with a ground cover like ivy, then you can develop a naturalized area interplanted with red spider lilies. With planning, you can give them defined areas in the perennial garden where their September blooms match nicely with gold lantana or blue salvia.

Care and Maintenance

Water while in bloom to keep them going as long as possible. Do not cut foliage until it turns yellow and dies. After blooming, side-dress with a light application of a 12-6-6 slow-release fertilizer. Divide your spider lily clumps every 4 or 5 years, soon after foliage dies in the spring.

Recommended Varieties

L. radiata has red forms, and it also has *L. radiata* var. *alba*, a white form. *L. aurea* is a yellow-gold type that blooms in summer. *L. squamigera* has pink flowers and a purple form (these are the ones most often called "Naked Ladies").

Other Names:
Resurrection Flower,
Hurricane Lily,
Naked Ladies,
School House Lily

Light Needs:

Added Benefit:

Zones: 7 to 9

Bloom Time:
September

Bloom Color:
Red, yellow, white

Height: 12 to 15 in.

Spacing: 6 to 8 in.

Water Needs:
Low/moderate

Soil:
Moist, well drained

Uses: Perennial garden, natural areas

Did You Know?

Lycoris is named for the beautiful actress and mistress of Mark Anthony.

Color photo on page 132

GRASSES

As the carpet is the foundation of the living room indoors, the grass is the foundation of the landscape.

Since the home lawn is such an important element of a pleasing landscape, it is essential to do it right from the start—which means proper selection of a turfgrass. Our choices of lawn grass that will grow in Mississippi can be listed pretty quickly. Factor in sunlight or shade conditions, and the list shortens further.

Bermudagrass forms a dense, attractive sod. It is the most widely grown lawn grass in Mississippi because of its adaptation to our climate and soil types. It spreads primarily through stolon growth, although rhizomes do play a part in its aggressive growth habits. Its aggressiveness makes Bermudagrass the best grass for areas of high traffic, since it can spread quickly to cover damaged areas. The major factor limiting Bermudagrass growth is the amount of sunlight it requires. The grass does not thrive in heavy shade and can really only tolerate partial shade for half a day. It is best to have full sun for a lawn of the highest quality .

> The first thing that visitors see when they pull in to the driveway is your lawn.

Centipedegrass is one of the most popular choices because of its low maintenance requirements. It is a joy to those who want an acceptable-quality turf with the least amount of effort. It is a slow-growing, naturally lime-green, somewhat coarse turfgrass adapted to acid sandy soils. It has poor wear tolerance and recovers slowly from injury. Its shade tolerance is better than that of Bermudagrass, but not as good as St. Augustinegrass.

St. Augustinegrass is a popular choice for lawns in south and central Mississippi. Outstanding shade tolerance makes this grass the overwhelming favorite for lawns under the stately live oaks of the Gulf Coast as well as the tall pines midstate. Winter damage occurs in lawns in zone 7a and the northern reaches of zone 7b, and severe winters may cause damage as far south as the northern reaches of zone 8a. St. Augustinegrass is the most cold-sensitive of all of the lawn grasses grown in Mississippi.

Zoysiagrass (*Zoysia* species) is gaining popularity as a choice for lawns in the central and northern portions of the state. The zoysiagrasses have the best cold tolerance and are not as likely to sustain winter damage. Zoysiagrasses form dense, thick sods of high quality. They have more shade tolerance than Bermudagrass, and many think they form a finer, more attractive lawn than St. Augustinegrass or centipedegrass.

If the grass you mow is the only one you grow, you are missing a landscape winner. Here in the States, in the South in particular, we have thought of grass as something for the cows to eat. In European gardens, particularly in those of Great Britain, ornamental grasses have long played a prominent role in the flower border.

Several new grasses have appeared over the past few years, such as Muhly grass. Muhly grass, a native, is a clumping type grass that has an interesting leaf texture followed by gorgeous pink cotton candy–like blooms in the fall. Other grasses new to our market are the golden Japanese sweet flag, Japanese sedge, and Japanese silver grass.

Ornamental grasses are low-maintenance plants that can be used as specimen plantings or groupings, both tall and dwarf. Simply plant one and plant your favorite flowers around it, and you will look like a design pro.

Whether you are using turf or ornamental grasses, the planting area or bed has to be well prepared, just as for any other plant.

> Gardeners are finally realizing that they do not have to go to design school to be taught how to use ornamental grasses.

Bermuda

Cynodon species and hybrids

Bermudagrass, the choice for high-traffic full-sun areas, is easy to establish.

How to Grow

Remove debris and rocks from the new lawn area. Apply a nonselective herbicide to kill existing grasses and weeds. Apply fertilizer and lime if needed, as prescribed by your Mississippi State University Extension Service soil test. Till to a depth of 4 inches. Rake the soil smooth. Plant at the rate of $1/2$ pound seed per 1000 square feet, or lay sod using 330 squares per 1000 square feet. Squares of sod can be cut into 2-by-2-inch plugs and planted 12 inches apart. Keep watered during establishment.

Landscape Merit

Bermuda is aggressive and recovers quickly from wear and tear. Although it is the most adaptive grass in the state, it does not tolerate shade. It has an attractive texture and blue-green color.

Care and Maintenance

Apply recommended preemergent herbicides in the fall to control winter weeds. Make another application in late winter to control spring and summer weeds. Feed with a 3-1-2 ratio fertilizer. The numbers on the bag reflect the percentage of product in the mixture. Apply 4 pounds (6 in zone 8b) of actual nitrogen per 1000 square feet in split applications, 1 pound per month starting in April. Cut Bermudagrass $3/4$ to 1 inch high (hybrids: $1/2$ to 1 inch high).

Recommended Varieties

'Princess', 'Savanna', 'Sultan', and 'Sunstar' are improved seeded types. 'MS-Choice' and 'MS-Pride', developed by Mississippi State University, are sod-only types, but they are superior, producing few seedheads.

Other Name:
Wiregrass

Light Needs:

Zones: 7 to 9

Texture: Fine

Wear Resistance:
Good

Water Needs: Less

Soil:
Slightly acid/neutral

Did You Know?
Even though it's "common," it originated in Africa.

Centipede

Eremochloa ophiuroides

Centipede is becoming a popular grass due to its low maintenance needs and its tolerance of partial shade.

How to Grow

Remove rocks and debris from the new lawn area. Apply a nonselective herbicide, killing existing grasses and weeds. Apply fertilizer according to your Mississippi State University Extension Service soil test. Till to a depth of 4 inches. Rake the soil smooth. Plant at the rate of 4 ounces seed per 1000 square feet, or lay sod using 330 squares per 1000 square feet. Squares of sod can be cut into 2-by-2-inch plugs and planted 12 inches apart. Keep watered during establishment

Landscape Merit

Centipede has a yellow-green color and has the lowest maintenance needs of the grasses. Its slow-growing nature means it is also slower to establish or recover from injury. It has more shade tolerance than Bermuda, but less than St. Augustinegrass.

Care and Maintenance

Apply recommended preemergent herbicides in fall to control winter weeds. Make another application in late winter to control spring and summer weeds. Feed with a 3-1-2 ratio fertilizer. The numbers on the bag reflect the percentage of product in the mixture. Apply 1 pound (2 in zone 8b) of actual nitrogen per 1000 square feet in spring, except in southern Mississippi, where you should apply in April and August. Cut centipede $1^{1}/_{2}$ to 2 inches high.

Recommended Varieties

'Oklawn' and 'Tennessee Hardy' have shown more cold tolerance.

Light Needs:

Zones: (7), 8, 9

Texture: Medium

Wear resistance: Low/poor

Water Needs: Moderate/frequent

Soil: Moist, acidic

Did You Know?

Iron will help give a darker green to the centipede.

Dwarf Sweet Flag

Acorus gramineus

The sweet flags, with their fanlike leaves, are some of the prettiest ornamental grasses for the landscape. They are underused.

How to Grow

Plant nursery-grown transplants into well-prepared beds. Soil should be rich in organic matter, so incorporate 3 to 4 inches of peat or compost to improve drainage and aeration. While tilling, add 2 pounds of 12-6-6 slow-release fertilizer per 100 square feet. Plant at the same depth they were growing in the containers, placing the crown of the plant slightly above the soil line. Add a good layer of mulch after planting.

Landscape Merit

Sweet flag works well in wet or dry sites, and the golden variegated foliage of varieties like 'Ogon' are striking. They are exceptional plants for water gardens, and look great tucked into rock gardens. They can be used for ground covers.

Care and Maintenance

Feed in late winter with a light application of the above fertilizer. Sweet flags become aggressive in moist soil, but are easily divided. They spread similarly to an iris spreading from rhizome tips. The foliage remains pretty for a long time. When it does turn brown, cut to the ground in late winter as you would liriope. Keep well mulched in summer and going into winter.

Recommended Varieties

'Ogon' with bright gold leaves is the most striking; 'Variegatus' with creamy white stripes is also worthy.

Other Name:
Sweet Flag

Light Needs:

Zones: 7, 8, (9)

Bloom Time:
Spring

Bloom Color:
Inconspicuous

Height: 10 to 14 in.

Spacing:
12 to 14 in.

Water Needs:
Moderate

Soil:
Moist, slightly acidic

Did You Know?

The species *A. calamus* is the source of the herbal Oil of Calmus.

Chinese Pennisetum

Pennisetum alopecuroides

When you grow fountain grass, you look as if you have "arrived" in the world of gardening.

How to Grow

Plant nursery-grown transplants into well-prepared beds. Beds should be rich in organic matter, so incorporate 3 to 4 inches of peat or compost to improve drainage and aeration. While tilling, add 2 pounds of 12-6-6 slow-release fertilizer per 100 square feet. Plant at the same depth they were growing in the containers, placing the crown of the plant slightly above the soil line. Add a good layer of mulch after planting.

Landscape Merit

The 3-foot-tall clumps with arching leaves and striking pink to purple plumes are perfect as part of the perennial garden. Use in beds at the entrance to the home. Combine with your favorite flowers of compatible colors. They look handsome when grown adjacent to water features.

Care and Maintenance

Trim foliage back to 6 inches above the ground in late winter. In early spring, feed with a light application of the above fertilizer. Maintain a 3-inch layer of mulch to conserve moisture and deter competition from weeds.

Recommended Varieties

'Hameln', compact and 24 to 30 inches tall, is a well-known favorite. 'Moudry' has black 12-inch plumes on 24-inch-tall plants. *P. setaceum* fountain grass is one of the most beautiful, treated as an annual in all but the coastal counties.

Other Name:
Swamp Foxtail

Light Needs:

Added Benefits:

Zones: 7 to 9

Bloom Time:
Summer

Bloom Color:
Pink, bronze-purple, black

Height: 3 to 4 ft.

Spacing:
18 to 24 in.

Water Needs:
Moderate/frequent

Soil:
Moist, well-drained

Did You Know?

Pennisetum comes from the Latin word meaning "feather-bristle."

Japanese Sedge

Carex morrowii

The sedges open up a new world in grass growing with their unique colors and striped foliage.

Other Name:
Japanese Variegated Sedge

Light Needs:

Zones: 7 to 9

Bloom Time:
Summer

Bloom Color:
No ornamental value

Height: 10 to 12 in.

Spacing:
12 to 18 in.

Water Needs:
Frequent

Soil:
Moist, well-drained

Did You Know?

The Japanese sedge has a distinguished relative . . . nut grass!

How to Grow
Plant nursery-grown transplants into well-prepared beds. Beds should be rich in organic matter, so incorporate 3 to 4 inches of peat or compost to improve drainage and aeration. While tilling, add 2 pounds of 12-6-6 slow-release fertilizer per 100 square feet. Plant at the same depth they were growing in the containers, placing the crown of the plant slightly above the soil line. Add a good layer of mulch after planting.

Landscape Merit
The Japanese sedge excels in partially shady borders, rock gardens, water gardens, and edgings. They are useful when planted in bold drifts. Plant in front of large hostas. Try some in containers on the patio or deck.

Care and Maintenance
In late winter, cut the foliage back to 4 to 6 inches above the ground. In early spring, side-dress with a light application of the above fertilizer. Keep mulched and watered throughout the summer and you will find happiness with these plants. When clumps get crowded, divide in very early spring. Keep a good layer of mulch applied to conserve moisture and keep weeds in check.

Recommended Varieties
'Goldband' golden variegation and 'Variegata' silver and white variegation are the most readily available. Others to try are 'Silk Tassel' and 'Hime-kansuge'. Try also *C. elata* and *C. conica*.

Liriope

Liriope muscari

Liriope, which is in the lily family, is one of our best choices for small clump-forming grasses.

How to Grow
Plant nursery-grown transplants in well-prepared beds. Beds should be rich in organic matter, so incorporate 3 to 4 inches of peat or compost to improve drainage and aeration. While tilling, add 2 pounds of 12-6-6 slow-release fertilizer per 100 square feet. Plant at the same depth they were growing in the containers, placing the crown of the plant slightly above the soil line. Mulch after planting.

Landscape Merit
Liriope excels as a border plant or massed as a ground cover, and is a staple of the shade garden. Grow along a path or in-between stepping stones. Don't overlook the beautiful lilac flowers tall enough for cutting for the vase.

Care and Maintenance
In late winter, cut the foliage to about 3 to 4 inches above the ground. Side-dress with a light application of the fertilizer above in early spring. Liriope responds well to dividing in early spring to spread around the landscape. Keep a layer of mulch to conserve moisture and help deter weeds. There are effective over-the-top herbicides to control grasses that encroach on the liriope planting.

Recommended Varieties
'Big Blue' (12 to 15 inches), 'Majestic' (15 to 18 inches), 'Silvery Sunproof' (white variegation, 12 to 15 inches), and 'Variegata' (yellow variegation, 10 to 15 inches) are the leading varieties. Coastal gardeners should try 'Evergreen Giant', which gets over 2 feet tall.

Other Name:
Lily Turf

Light Needs:

Added Benefit:

Zones: 7 to 9

Bloom Time:
Summer

Bloom Color:
Lilac, purple, white

Height: 12 to 18 in.

Spacing:
12 to 18 in.

Water Needs:
Moderate/frequent

Soil:
Moist, well-drained

Did You Know?
Liriope spicata is a creeping lily turf—read about it in the Ground Cover chapter.

Maiden Grass

Other Name:
Eulalia Grass

Light Needs:

Added Benefits:

Zones: 7 to 9

Bloom Time:
Summer and fall

Bloom Color:
White, pink, silver

Height: 5 to 6 ft.

Spacing: 4 to 6 ft.

Water Needs:
Moderate/frequent

Soil:
Moist, well-drained

Did You Know?

The name *miscanthus* comes from the Greek word meaning "flower stalk."

Miscanthus sinensis

The tall, billowy plumes of maiden grass create some of the prettiest displays in the landscape.

How to Grow

Plant nursery-grown transplants into well-prepared beds. Beds should be rich in organic matter, so incorporate 3 to 4 inches of peat or compost to improve drainage and aeration. While tilling, add 2 pounds of 12-6-6 slow-release fertilizer per 100 square feet. Plant at the same depth they were growing in the containers, placing the crown of the plant slightly above the soil line. Add a good layer of mulch after planting.

Landscape Merit

Maiden grass can be planted as an accent or specimen, but is made to be included in the perennial flower border. The flowers are great for the vase. Maiden grass is at home with flowers like black-eyed Susans, purple coneflowers, and taller blue salvias. Annuals like the old-fashioned zinnia planted in single colors is striking, as is the tough standard, 'New Gold' lantana.

Care and Maintenance

In late winter, cut miscanthus back to the ground. Side-dress with an application of the fertilizer above in early spring and midsummer. Keep the bed well mulched and watered during the summer. Propagate by dividing in early spring.

Recommended Varieties

M. sinensis 'Variegata' (Japanese Silver Grass) is superior—look for the varieties 'Silverfeder', 'Cabaret', and 'Cosmopolitan'. *M. sinensis* 'Zebrinus' (Zebra Grass) with creamy-yellow horizontal bands of variegation, is much-loved in the South. 'Purpurescens' is known for red foliage that turns purple-red in the summer.

Muhlygrass

Muhlenbergia capillaris

The pink and billowy cotton candy–like blossoms of this new grass has caught the attention of gardeners all over the Mississippi.

How to Grow
Plant nursery-grown transplants into well-prepared beds. Beds should be rich in organic matter, so incorporate 3 to 4 inches of peat or compost to improve drainage and aeration. While tilling, add 2 pounds of 12-6-6 slow-release fertilizer per 100 square feet. Plant at the same depth they were growing in the containers, placing the crown of the plant slightly above the soil line. Add a good layer of mulch after planting.

Landscape Merit
The spiky texture of the leaves warrants growing this plant as an accent in the perennial border. In September, magic happens as the 2-foot-tall plants form large pink blossoms that appear like a mound of cotton candy, reaching 4 feet. The flowers last until the first freeze. Grow as a specimen or small clumps anywhere in the garden. The blooms are attractive blowing in the wind.

Care and Maintenance
In late winter, cut the plant back to the ground and side-dress with a light application of the above fertilizer. Feed again in midsummer. Keep mulched, and water during prolonged dry periods. The clump can be divided in the spring to thin or add more plants.

Recommended Varieties
Muhlygrass is sold generic and sells quickly.

Other Name:
Purple Muhly

Light Needs:

Added Benefit:

Zones: 7 to 9

Bloom Time:
Late summer and fall

Bloom Color:
Pink, rose

Height: 2 to 4 ft.

Spacing:
24 to 36 in.

Water Needs:
Low/moderate

Soil:
Slightly moist, well drained

Did You Know?
Muhlygrass is native in the coastal areas of the South.

St. Augustine

Light Needs:

Zones: 8, 9

Texture: Coarse

Wear Resistance:
Moderate

Water Needs:
Moderate/frequent

Soil: All soil, moist

Did You Know?
St. Augustinegrass is native to the Gulf Coast.

Stenotaphrum secundatum

St. Augustine is the lushest of all turfgrasses, enticing you to lie down and take a nap on a warm sunny day.

How to Grow

Remove rocks and debris from the new lawn area. Apply a nonselective herbicide, killing existing grasses and weeds. Apply fertilizer and lime according to your Mississippi State University Extension Service soil test. Till to a depth of 4 inches. Rake the soil smooth. St. Augustinegrass is established by laying sod, using 330 squares per 1000 square feet. Squares of sod can be cut into 2-by-2-inch plugs and planted 12 inches apart. Keep watered during establishment.

Landscape Merit

St. Augustine has the best shade tolerance of all the turfgrasses but is the most cold sensitive. It is much more vigorous than centipede and recovers quickly from injury. It does not tolerate drought well. It has a deep dark-green color for months.

Care and Maintenance

Apply recommended preemergent herbicides in fall to control winter weeds. Make another application in late winter to control spring and summer weeds. Feed with a 3-1-2 ratio fertilizer. The numbers on the bag reflect the percentage of product in the mixture. Apply 2 pounds (3 in zone 8b) of actual nitrogen per 1000 square feet in split applications, 1 pound every 2 months starting in April.

Recommended Varieties

'Raleigh', 'Palmetto', and 'Delmar' are the leading varieties because of resistance to the virus "St. Augustine decline."

Zoysia

Zoysia species and hybrids

Zoysiagrass is gaining in popularity because of its finer texture and superior cold tolerance.

How to Grow

Remove rocks and debris from the new lawn area. Apply a nonselective herbicide, killing existing grasses and weeds. Apply fertilizer according to your Mississippi State University Extension Service soil test. Till to a depth of 4 inches. Rake soil smooth. Zoysia is best established by laying sod, using 330 squares per 1000 square feet. Squares of sod can be cut into 2-by-2-inch plugs and planted 12 inches apart, but this is much less satisfactory with zoysia. Keep watered during establishment.

Landscape Merit

Zoysia is shade tolerant, cold tolerant, and drought tolerant, has few pests, and forms dense growth, choking out competition from weeds. It does, however, have tendencies toward thatch. Reel mowers work better than rotary on zoysia.

Care and Maintenance

Apply recommended preemergent herbicides in fall to control winter weeds. Make another application in late winter to control spring and summer weeds. Feed with a 3-1-2 ratio fertilizer. The numbers on the bag reflect the percentage of product in the mixture. Apply 4 pounds (6 in zone 8b) of actual nitrogen per 1000 square feet, but in split applications (1 pound per month starting in April). Mow to maintain 1 to $1\frac{1}{2}$ inches in height.

Recommended Varieties

Z. *tenuifolia* (zones 8 and 9), Z. *matrella*, and Z. *japonica* are three species that perform in Mississippi. Z. *japonica* varieties 'Meyer' and 'Emerald' are improved selections.

Light Needs:

Zones: 7 to 9

Texture: Fine

Wear Resistance: Good

Water Needs: Moderate/frequent

Soil: All soil, moist

Did You Know?

Zoysia spreads by stolons and rhizomes.

GROUND COVERS

Ground covers have finally hit the mainstream. It seems as if everyone's using them, and with great success. Not only can we plant them where there isn't enough sunlight for turf to survive, we can also use them on steep slopes where mowing can be difficult, even dangerous. Most important, we have learned to use them as a transition between shrubs and lawn. Just like turf or any other landscape shrub, they give that feeling of green lushness, yet they tend to be much easier to maintain and water

Ground covers add a finished professional look to a landscape.

A well-chosen ground cover can provide cooling for your home, year-round color, and additional leaf texture. It will spread by itself, have a compact growth habit, and be dense enough to keep out weeds. Many have a fibrous root system, making them excellent for erosion control on slopes.

Those dense shady areas where bare soil is an eyesore would be a prime location for one of the trailing periwinkles, *Vinca major* or *Vinca minor*. Asian jasmine, English ivy, liriope, or mondo grass are all well suited for full or partial shade.

There are at least a dozen ferns that look exotic or tropical in tough, shady areas. Look for one of the *Dryopteris* species such as the autumn fern or southern wood fern.

One of my favorite ground covers is the ajuga. The *Ajuga reptans* 'Bronze' is the fastest-growing variety and has purple-bronze foliage. The variety 'Burgundy Glow' is another good one, with a reddish purple cast. They both produce small, attractive blue flowers.

The sunny areas of the landscape are well suited to some of the trailing junipers that are among the most attractive ground covers available. The lowest-growing of them all is *Juniperus horizontalis* 'Wiltonii' or 'Blue Rug'. *Juniperus conferta* 'Blue Pacific' reaches a height of 15 inches and has a spread of 6 to 8 feet. There are close to a dozen different junipers that make excellent ground covers. These are not recommended for areas of poor drainage.

One of my top ground cover picks is the creeping phlox (*Phlox subulata*) which has absolutely striking flower color during the time of azalea bloom. There are varieties in pink, lavender, blue, and a shade of red. This plant is a ground-hugging 6-inch-tall mass of needlelike foliage during the rest of the year.

Prepare the soil for ground covers just as you would any other shrub bed. Apply a total-kill herbicide seven to ten days before planting. Till the soil with organic matter to improve drainage and aeration. Since many ground covers spread by roots, loose organic soil is needed.

Mississippians can choose from a huge selection of ground covers.

If you are planting under trees where grass will not grow, you will find it difficult to work the soil. Make an effort to avoid severing the roots of the trees. A spade fork may help loosen the soil. Two to three inches of a light, highly organic mix can be brought in to raise the soil line and allow you a little more room to work.

If you anticipate walking through an area of planted ground cover, items like steppingstones or brick should be placed before planting. Most ground covers will not tolerate heavy foot traffic. If you are working with a slope, it is best not to disturb the soil because of erosion possibilities. Maintaining adequate moisture and light cultivation around existing plants will help the newly planted ground cover become established and spread, too!

Ajuga

Ajuga reptans

Striking foliage, intense blue-violet flowers, and a quick-spreading nature are just a few appealing traits of this easy-to-grow ground cover.

How to Grow

Ajuga has the ability to grow under any light conditions and spread if there has been good soil preparation. Spread 3 to 4 inches of organic matter like fine pine bark or compost, and till to a depth of 8 to 10 inches. Incorporate 2 pounds of slow-release 12-6-6 fertilizer per 100 square feet. Space nursery-grown transplants 8 to 10 inches apart.

Landscape Merit

Ajuga looks good as a border plant for other ground covers like liriope and juniper, as well as by itself or adjacent to dwarf shrubs like yaupon hollies. The metallic-looking leaves of Ajuga are exceptional with rocks or between steppingstones.

Care and Maintenance

A light springtime application of the above fertilizer will be appreciated. Good drainage is a must or root rot will occur. Ajuga spreads by runners and will go where it is not wanted, but it is easy to keep edged or trimmed back. After the blooms have faded, use a string trimmer or lawn mower to deadhead. If the patch should thin in the middle, work soil gently, divide from the outer area, and replant.

Recommended Varieties

'Bronze' (fast spreading with reddish bronze leaves), 'Burgundy Glow' (green and pink leaves with white and blue flowers), 'Rosea' (pink flowers), and 'Variegata' (leaves edged in light yellow) are some of the easier-to-find selections. Several green varieties are also sold.

Other Names:
Bugle Weed,
Carpet Bugle

Light Needs:

Zones: 7 to 9

Bloom Time:
Spring, summer

Bloom Color:
Blue-violet, pink, white

Height: 2 to 6 in.

Spacing: 8 to 10 in

Water Needs:
Moderate

Soil:
Moist, well drained

Did You Know?

Not too many plants have such wide adaptability—zones 4 to 10, sun or shade!

Color photo on page 132

Asian Jasmine

Trachelospermum asiaticum

This is one of the best ground covers, forming a thick mass of lush green foliage that gives the landscape a professional appearance.

How to Grow

Asian jasmine is adaptable to sun or shade. For quicker, healthier coverage, prepare a bed: Spread 3 to 4 inches of organic matter like fine pine bark or compost, tilling to a depth of 8 to 10 inches, incorporating 2 pounds of slow-release 12-6-6 fertilizer per 100 square feet. Plant gallon-sized plants 18 to 24 inches apart, 4-inch-container plants 8 to 12 inches. Water frequently until established; apply mulch.

Landscape Merit

This is one of the best transition plants for evergreen shrubs and turf. It's great as a border plant for sidewalks and non-turf areas where pine straw is used under groups of trees. If you have a sloping area that is hard or dangerous to mow, use Asian jasmine as a ground cover.

Care and Maintenance

In spring and midsummer, feed with a light application of the above fertilizer. In late winter, shear back to 6 inches—in the northern regions of the state, this will be mandatory for many years because of winter burn. After shearing you will be rewarded with lush new growth. Trim to keep in bounds and out of nearby shrubs. Water during dry periods.

Recommended Varieties

Asian jasmine is most often sold generic. There are named varieties and a variegated form ('Variegatum'). 'Nortex' has smaller leaves with silvery-gray veins. 'Asia Minor' is a more compact dwarf selection.

Other Name:
Japanese Star Jasmine

Light Needs:

Zones: (7), 8, 9

Bloom Time:
Grown for foliage

Bloom Color:
Yellow

Height: 10 to 12 in.

Spacing: 8 to 24 in.

Water Needs:
Moderate

Soil:
Moist, well drained

Did You Know?

The 'Confederate Jasmine' is a close relative.

Color photo on page 132

'Bath's Pink' Dianthus

Other Name:
Cheddar Pinks

Light Needs:

Added Benefit:

Zones: 7, 8, (9)

Bloom Time:
Early spring

Bloom Color:
Pink

Height:
6 in. foliage,
15 to 18 in. in flower

Water Needs:
Moderate

Soil:
Moist, well drained

Did You Know?

'Bath's Pink', a carnation relative, was found by Jane Bath of Stone Mountain, Georgia.

Color photo on page 132

Dianthus gratianopolitanus

Garden visitors often exclaim over the beautiful foliage and showy flowers of 'Bath's Pink'.

How to Grow

The ideal site is in morning sun and afternoon shade (full sun or filtered light is also suitable). Prepare soil by adding 3 to 4 inches of organic matter, like fine pine bark or compost, along with 2 pounds of slow-release 12-6-6 fertilizer per 100 square feet, tilling to a depth of 8 to 10 inches. Space gallon-sized plants 18 to 24 inches apart, 8 to 12 inches for smaller sizes. Keep watered until established; add a layer of mulch to moderate temperatures.

Landscape Merit

The blue-gray-green spreading foliage is beautiful. The tall pink flowers in spring are equally attractive. A good ground cover and fine cottage-garden perennial, it is useful for lower-level plantings by antique roses draped over a picket fence. Place rocks or statuary in the middle of the patch. The foliage really stands out against a backdrop of junipers.

Care and Maintenance

Feed after bloom with a light application of the above fertilizer. Deadhead flowers to keep a tidy look. 'Bath's Pink' will spread easily. You'll want some elsewhere, and they are easy to propagate by division. Water during dry periods.

Recommended Varieties

'Bath's Pink' is by far the best variety and usually the only one available. Others for consideration are 'Spotty', 'Tiny Rubies', and 'Little Joe'.

Common Periwinkle

Vinca minor

Though grown for foliage, the periwinkle gives flowers in various shades. This is a spreading ground cover that can mask unsightly tree roots.

How to Grow

Filtered light or partial shade is ideal. If you want to develop a professional-looking bed in the shortest amount of time, don't skimp on soil preparation. Incorporate 3 to 4 inches of organic matter and till to a depth of 8 to 10 inches. Include 2 pounds of slow-release 12-6-6 fertilizer per 100 square feet. Space gallon-sized plants 12 inches apart, 4-inch containers 8 inches. Water thoroughly and mulch.

Landscape Merit

The periwinkle has deep-green glossy foliage that is handsome in large beds under the filtered light of pines. Plant with narcissus for spring bloom and red spider lily for late-summer bloom. The pretty periwinkle blooms enhance the bed. It is another excellent choice for shady slopes where it is nearly impossible to mow, or to get grass to grow.

Care and Maintenance

Watch the moisture level of new beds during the first summer; from then on they are fairly drought tolerant. Shear or prune to increase branching. Shearing in early spring also stimulates new growth. Trim to keep within the confines of allotted space.

Recommended Varieties

There are many varieties available to your garden center, and your demand will bring even more choices. Ask for 'Alba' (white), 'Bowles' (superior-blooming blue), 'Rosea' (violet pink), 'Purpurea' (burgundy), and 'Variegata' (green and cream leaves, blue flowers).

Other Name:
Vinca

Light Needs:

Zones: 7 to 9

Bloom Time:
Spring

Bloom Color:
Blue, white, violet, burgundy

Height: 4 to 6 in.

Spacing: 4 to 12 in.

Water Needs:
Low/moderate

Soil:
Slightly moist, well drained

Did You Know?

The summer annual periwinkle used to be known as *Vinca rosea* but is now *Catharanthus roseus*.

Color photo on page 132

Creeping Phlox

Other Names:
Moss Pink, Thrift

Light Needs:

Added Benefit:

Zones: 7 to 9

Bloom Time:
Early spring

Bloom Color:
Blue, pink, red, white

Height: 6 to 12 in.

Spacing: 8 to 12 in.

Water Needs:
Low/moderate

Soil:
Slightly moist, well
drained

Did You Know?
The Southern garden
can have a perennial
phlox blooming for
7 to 8 months.

Color photo on page 132

Phlox subulata

Brilliant iridescent flowers completely cover this plant during the early spring at the same time azaleas and narcissus are in bloom.

How to Grow
Plant in full sun to bright filtered light. Loose, well-drained soil is necessary, so spread a 2- to 3-inch layer of organic matter like fine pine bark or compost with an inch of sand, tilling to a depth of 8 to 10 inches. Incorporate 2 pounds of slow-release 12-6-6 fertilizer per 100 square feet of bed space. Space 12 to 18 inches apart, water thoroughly, and mulch.

Landscape Merit
This phlox gives life to rock gardens and slopes with its gorgeous flowers and evergreen foliage. White dogwood blossoms, pink redbud blooms, and the ground-hugging 'Blue Emerald' phlox make the springtime garden a living picture. If not used as a ground cover, it deserves to be in the perennial garden.

Care and Maintenance
After bloom, shear back by half and feed with a light application of the above fertilizer. Creeping phlox may creep past the area you desire. In this case, divide clumps, layer, or take cuttings in the fall. Keep the soil moist for quick rooting.

Recommended Varieties
The most popular blue is 'Blue Emerald'. Consider also 'Blue Hills' and 'Emerald Cushion Blue'. Choice pink varieties are 'Emerald Cushion Pink', 'Apple Blossom', and 'Perfection'. For red varieties, ask for 'Crackerjack' and 'Scarlet Flame'. For white, consider 'Snowflake' and 'White Delight'.

English Ivy

Hedera helix

Where grass is hard to grow, English ivy's dark evergreen foliage gives a lush garden look.

How to Grow

Choose a site in partial to full shade. Determine up front if you mind pruning to keep it from climbing nearby walls or trees. If so, you might consider another ground cover or site. English ivy prefers well-prepared and -drained, organic-material-rich beds. Container-grown plants can be planted anytime, requiring a little more care in summer. Space gallon-sized plants 18 to 24 inches apart, smaller sizes 10 to 12 inches.

Landscape Merit

English ivy looks good year 'round and is among the best choices for slope areas that are impossible to mow, hard to get things to grow on, and plagued by erosion. Shady areas under trees where grass can no longer grow are no problem for this trooper. If you have a waist-high wall that you would like draped in green, this is your plant.

Care and Maintenance

Feed with a light application of slow-release 12-6-6 in late winter. Fight fungal leaf spotting by picking infected leaves, watering in early morning, and avoiding overfertilization. Established plantings can grow until stems build up to a thatchlike quality. When this occurs, mow down in early spring and new growth will quickly cover.

Recommended Varieties

'Hahn's Self Branching', 'Baltica', 'Needlepoint', 'Gold Heart', and 'Buttercup' are a few samples of a list that is longer than you would ever guess (considering that generic is still widespread).

Other Name:
Common Ivy

Light Needs:

Zones: 7 to 9

Bloom Time:
Grown for foliage

Bloom Color:
Inconspicuous

Height: 6 to 10 in.

Spacing:
10 to 24 in.

Water Needs:
Moderate

Soil:
Moist, well drained

Did You Know?

This ivy is great to use for a topiary.

Color photo on page 132

Juniper

Juniperus species

Other Name:
Trailing Juniper

Light Needs:

Zones: 7 to 9

Bloom Time:
Grown for foliage

Bloom Color:
Inconspicuous

Height: 4 to 24 in.

Spacing: 2 to 4 ft.

Water Needs:
Moderate

Soil:
Moist, well drained

Did You Know?
With junipers you will always have a little greenery for the vase.

Color photo on page 133

The juniper family gives us not only great trees and shrubs, but also superior evergreen ground covers.

How to Grow
Select a site in full sun (partial shade is tolerated). Prepare soil deeply by spreading a 3- to 4-inch layer of organic matter, like fine pine bark or compost, along with 2 pounds per 100 square feet of 5-10-5 fertilizer. Till to a depth of 8 to 10 inches. Plant nursery-grown plants at the same depth they were growing in the container and space as recommended for their variety, some as far apart as 4 feet. Water well and apply a layer of mulch. Watch moisture during the first summer.

Landscape Merit
Trailing junipers give a forest fragrance to the landscape. Since they are woody ornamentals, they offer a texture different from that of herbaceous ground covers. Try them gently cascading over a rock wall. Use in a layered look: taller evergreens like hollies, a middle layer of red-leafed Japanese barberries, and the lower-level trailing junipers.

Care and Maintenance
Feed with a light application (1 pound per 100 square feet) of an 8-8-8 in early spring. Selectively hand-prune any yellowing, dieback, or unwanted growth. Maintain mulch to conserve moisture and prevent weeds. Watch for spider mites and treat early if needed.

Recommended Varieties
There are four species of junipers with scores of good spreading varieties used as ground covers. Some of the better choices are *J. chinensis* 'Sargentii' and 'Sea Spray'; *J. conferta* 'Blue Pacific' and 'Emerald Sea'; *J. horizontalis* 'Bar Harbor', 'Emerald Isle', and 'Wiltonii'; and *J. procumbens* 'Greenmound'.

Liriope

Liriope spicata

Part of the lily family, liriope's grassy-leafed texture makes for an excellent easy-to-grow ground cover for large areas.

How to Grow

Prepare the planting bed to obtain fastest coverage. Spread a 3- to 4-inch layer of organic material, like fine pine bark or compost, tilling to a depth of 8 to 10 inches. Incorporate 2 pounds of slow-release 12-6-6 fertilizer. Container-grown plants can be planted anytime, though in summer they will require more water. Space gallon-sized plants 12 to 15 inches apart, 4-inch-container-grown plants 6 inches. Gallon-sized plants can be divided and planted at a closer spacing. Water thoroughly and apply a layer of mulch.

Landscape Merit

Creeping lily turf excels where there is not enough light for a good stand of St. Augustine or centipede-grass. The taller grassy leaf texture will provide a layered look between turf and trees or shrubs. It is great at choking out competing weeds.

Care and Maintenance

Keep newly planted beds watered during the summer. Feed established beds with light applications of the above fertilizer in early spring and midsummer. If foliage looks ragged in late winter, mow or trim back to ground level before new growth emerges in the spring. Keep a good layer of mulch around plants until the bed is full.

Recommended Varieties

Creeping lily turf comes in green and a variegated form called 'Silver Dragon'. *Liriope muscari* is clump-forming, but can be mass-planted to cover. Read about it in the Grasses chapter.

Other Name:
Creeping Lily Turf

Light Needs:

Zones: 7 to 9

Bloom Time:
Summer

Bloom Color:
Lilac and white

Height: 8 to 15 in.

Spacing:
6 to 15 in.

Water Needs:
Moderate

Soil:
Moist, well drained

Did You Know?

Liriope is called lily turf because it is in the lily family.

Color photo on page 133

Monkey Grass

Other Name:
Mondo Grass

Light Needs:

Zones: 7 to 9

Bloom Time:
Summer

Bloom Color:
Lilac, white

Height: 4 to 12 in.

Spacing: 6 to 8 in.

Water Needs:
Low/moderate

Soil:
Slightly moist,
well drained

Did You Know?

Ophiopogon comes from the Greek and means "serpent's beard."

Color photo on page 133

Ophiopogon japonicus

This is the true "monkey grass," the best grass substitute for those impossible areas around the landscape. It is suitable to both large and small spaces.

How to Grow

Choose a site in partial shade to shade and prepare the bed well. Spread a 3- to 4-inch layer of organic material like fine pine bark or compost along with a slow-release 12-6-6 fertilizer at 2 pounds per 100 square feet. Till to a depth of 8 to 10 inches. Space plants 6 to 8 inches apart, water thoroughly, and apply mulch.

Landscape Merit

This is a superb ground cover under trees and between rocks in a stone path, and can be used to effectively stop erosion. Mondo grass is a particularly nice plant for triangular areas, corners, or other tight places not reachable with the lawn mower. Established plantings block out competitive weeds.

Care and Maintenance

Keep well watered during the first summer, and maintain a good layer of mulch. Established plantings block out weeds, but you will need to assist with weed removal until plants grow together. Feed in early spring and midsummer with a light application of the above fertilizer. Established plantings should be mowed in late February to remove ragged-looking tips. New spring growth will quickly emerge, looking lush and healthy.

Recommended Varieties

In addition to generic, you may find 'Nanus', which is dwarf, and 'Silver Mist', a variegated selection.

Wood Ferns

Dryopteris species

No plant gives a lush jungle or tropical look as do ferns. Wood fern is one of the easiest to get established and is a staple in the woodland garden.

How to Grow

Choose a site that is partial shade to shade, though a little morning sun is tolerated. Prepare soil by adding 3 to 4 inches of organic matter like fine pine bark or compost. Till the bed to a depth of 8 to 10 inches. Set out plants in mid- to late spring, 18 to 24 inches apart. Water well and apply a layer of mulch.

Landscape Merit

The fronds of ferns provide nice contrast between the woodland floor and tall trees and shrubs. Ferns give you the feeling of walking in a prehistoric garden. They are suited for serving as lower-level plants to shade-loving shrubs like hydrangeas and camellias.

Care and Maintenance

Ferns are tough, but they will need supplemental watering during the drier times of summer. Keep them well mulched. When the ferns die back in winter, prune the branches for a tidy look. Many gardeners are unaccustomed to looking on the underside of the fronds. It is not uncommon for the leaves to form hundreds of spores, the fern's reproductive system. The spores' presence usually means your ferns are happy in the environment you have provided.

Recommended Varieties

D. marginalis 'Leather Wood Fern', *D. erythrosora* 'Autumn Fern', and *D. ludovichiana* 'Southern Shield Fern' are all good choices, as are those of the *Thelypteris* species.

Other Names:
Shield Fern, Male Fern

Light Needs:

Zones:
7 to 9

Bloom Time:
Grown for foliage

Bloom Color:
None

Height: 2 to 5 ft.

Spacing: 18 to 24 in.

Water Needs:
Moderate/frequent

Soil:
Moist, well drained

Did You Know?

Dryopteris comes from the Greek and means "oak fern."

Color photo on page 133

HERBS

Many people seem determined to associate herbs with a 1970s hippie adventure in the garden. The truth is, herb gardening is riding on a new wave of popularity, and the value of herbs has been known for centuries. They have been used for flavorings in foods and as medicines for ailments.

I recently spent $5.95 for one tiny bottle of an herb I could have grown! After buying this and other expensive herbs and spices, I felt as if I needed to take two St. John's Wort tablets to cheer me up. (St. John's Wort, an herb, is one of the hot sellers in the health and vitamin area. Users claim that it will improve your outlook on life.)

> Consider planting an herb garden this year.

Basils are as attractive as coleus in the landscape, work great in containers, and are a delight in the kitchen. In recent years, All-America Selections has given its prestigious award to two basils—'Siam Queen' and 'Sweet Dani', a lemon basil. Basil is also excellent as a container plant.

Most herbs thrive in well-drained soil that has a pH of 6.0 to 6.8 for optimum growth. The growing area should be tilled to a depth of 8 to 12 inches. Although herbs are somewhat drought tolerant, adequate soil moisture is required for normal growth.

Annual herbs require more soil moisture than perennial herbs. Adding organic matter such as compost, peat moss, and pine bark will help the moisture-holding capacity of your soil.

A proper nutritional balance is important for proper growth. Overfertilization causes succulent or weak growth. Succulent growth dilutes the essential oils, thus limiting the flavor and aroma of herbs. Use a complete fertilizer with a 1-2-2 or 1-2-1 ratio such as a 5-10-10 or 5-10-5. Fertilize perennial herbs in early spring, using about one-fourth to one-half the amount used on vegetables. Annual herbs benefit from a light application of a complete fertilizer after each harvest.

To obtain foliage with the maximum amount of oil, harvest in the early morning after the dew has dried. As the sun warms the foliage, the oil becomes diluted by internal water movement via transpiration. To allow adequate time for regrowth of perennial herbs, do not harvest rigorously after late summer.

Herbs are great when mixed with vegetables in the garden—but I would encourage you to plant an herb garden that has its own identity. Because of their diverse habits, colors, and textures, herbs can create wonderful artistic and geometric designs.

Some herbs grow tall and need to be placed in the back of the garden. Others are short and spreading, perfect for the low border. Try using creeping thymes between steppingstones.

While basils give an ornamental look to the garden, plants like artemisias and santolina lend a Mediterranean flair with their gray color. Santolina can be hung in closets as a moth deterrent.

Every spring, most garden centers offer a broad selection of herbs for immediate planting in the garden. Select healthy and vigorous plants. The roots should be white to greenish white.

Some herbs that I am rarely without are rosemary, oregano, thyme, cilantro, chives, and mints. While I don't grow sages for culinary purposes, I do grow salvias for their aromatic foliage for tying and hanging in the kitchen and their gorgeous flowers suitable for the vase.

In addition to their culinary and medicinal purposes, many herbs are great landscape plants.

Artemesia

Artemesia species

In a world dominated by green, it's nice to have some plants with gray leaves. When they are fragrant, it's extra special.

How to Grow

Plant in full sun to partial shade. Though tolerant of poor soil, good drainage is a must. If drainage is less than perfect, incorporate 3 to 4 inches of organic matter to help loosen the soil and provide aeration. Apply 1 pound of slow-release 5-10-5 fertilizer per 100 square feet. Set nursery-grown transplants out at the same depth they were growing in containers.

Companion Planting

Artemesias are as much at home in a perennial garden as in an herb garden. In the perennial garden, choose plants that tolerate the dryness artemesia prefers. Trailing purple *Lantana montevidensis* is a good choice. In the herb garden, santolina, thyme, oregano, and rosemary are nice companions.

Care and Maintenance

Artemisia fertilizer requirements are low. Prune to shape, and watch for unwanted spreading. Artemesia may need to be dug up and divided every three or four years. The aromatic foliage can be harvested in early morning and used in a number of ways, from repelling moths to making potpourris, sachets, and wreaths.

Recommended Varieties

Hybrid 'Powis Castle' is known for endurance in our heat and humidity. 'Silver King' *A. ludoviciana albula* has striking lacy foliage, making it ideal for arrangements. Another variety of the same species is 'Silver Queen', which is not as large, but has a finer foliage. *A. abrotanum* (southernwood) is a wonderful plant with great fragrance, but is green.

Other Names:
Wormwood,
Southernwood

Light Needs:

Added Benefits:

Zones:
7 to 9 (varies by species)

Bloom Time:
Summer (grown primarily for foliage)

Bloom Color:
Yellow-gray

Height: 2 to 5 ft.

Spacing: 1 to 3 ft.

Water Needs: Low

Soil: Well drained, slightly moist

Uses:
Perennial gardens, herb gardens

Did You Know?

Artemesia provides the flavor for Vermouth.

Color photo on page 133

Basil

Ocimum basilicum

What could be better than walking out to your own basil patch and harvesting some for pesto? Many varieties have pretty flowers, too.

How to Grow

Plant in full sun. Spread 3 to 4 inches of organic matter and 1 pound per 100 square feet of slow-release 5-10-5 fertilizer, tilling to a depth of 8 to 10 inches. Basil is direct-seeded, or seedlings are available at garden centers. Seedlings emerge in 7 to 10 days. Transplants may be set out a little deeper than they grew in containers—they will root along the stem. Water, then mulch.

Companion Planting

Basil, an annual herb, looks good in flower, vegetable, and herb gardens. Purple-leafed types combine with yellow flowers like lantana and marigolds, or pink flowers like verbenas. Lime-green varieties look great with purples like gomphrena. Basil can be grown with herbs like cilantro or parsley, or crops like leaf lettuce.

Care and Maintenance

Keep basil watered and harvested and flower buds pinched. Harvest just as the flower buds are forming for the most concentrated oils, flavor, and fragrance. Apply a light application of the above fertilizer every 4 to 6 weeks, or after harvest. It is easy to produce a fall crop.

Recommended Varieties

Thai basils like 'Siam Queen' have deep maroon-tinged leaves on purple stems and a concentrated anise flavor. 'Sweet Dani', an All-America Selections winner, has a lemon flavor. 'Purple Ruffles' is as pretty as any coleus yet yields wonderful basil leaves. All are easy to grow.

Other Name:
Sweet Basil

Light Needs:

Added Benefits:

Grown as Annual

Bloom Time:
Summer (grown mostly for foliage)

Bloom Color: Pink, Lavender, purple, white

Height: 1 to 3 ft.

Spacing: 12 to 15 in.

Water Needs:
Moderate

Soil:
Moist, well drained

Uses: Flower beds, herb and vegetable gardens, containers

Did You Know?
Ocimum comes from the Greek word for "fragrance," basil from the Greek for "kingly."

Color photo on page 133

Borage

Other Names:
Tail Wort, Star Flower

Light Needs:

Added Benefits:

Grown as Annual

Bloom Time:
Summer

Bloom Color: Blue
to pink to lavender

Height: 1 to 3 ft.

Spacing: 12 to 14 in.

Water Needs:
Moderate

Soil:
Moist, well drained

Uses:
Flower or herb garden

Did You Know?
Borage comes from the Celtic word meaning "courage."

Color photo on page 133

Borago officinalis

Borage is an easy-to-grow plant with edible gray-green leaves that taste like cucumbers. The pretty flowers are edible, too!

How to Grow
Choose a site in full sun to partial shade. Prepare soil by incorporating 3 to 4 inches of organic matter, like fine pine bark or compost, along with 1 pound of a slow-release 5-10-5 fertilizer per 100 square feet, and till to a depth of 8 to 10 inches. Borage comes in transplants in the herb section of your garden center, or it can be direct-seeded.

Companion Planting
Borage should be in the section of the herb garden reserved for plants that require regular watering, like basil, cilantro, and parsley. The bluish-purple blooms look good combined with your favorite yellow or pink flowers.

Care and Maintenance
Borage is one of those wonderful annuals that acts like a perennial by reseeding—and quite prolifically. Thin the ones you do not want, or give them away. Pruning throughout the season will encourage a bushier, tidier look. Apply a layer of mulch to conserve moisture and limit the seedling population. The immature leaves are most suitable for fresh eating. Young tender leaves are also used for teas. The flowers are harvested and frozen in ice cubes, or candied for garnish.

Recommended Varieties
Borage is generic. The cucumber-flavored leaves are high in potassium and calcium.

Catmint

Nepeta species

These beautiful lavender-blue flowers, produced abundantly in spring and summer, look like a rolling sea in the wind. Your cat may just have to go and nibble from time to time.

How to Grow

The ideal site is morning sun and afternoon shade. The plants prefer well-drained beds, so soil preparation is vital. Incorporate 3 to 4 inches organic matter like fine pine bark and peat, along with 1 pound of slow-release 5-10-5 fertilizer. Set out transplants 1 to 2 feet apart at the same depth they were growing in containers. Water and mulch after planting. The plants will develop into a perennial ground cover.

Companion Planting

From a distance the catmint looks like a sea of flowers. Plant in front of fountain or maiden grass or Indian Summer rudbeckia. Try placing an orange or apricot-colored gazing-globe in the middle of the bed.

Care and Maintenance

Cut back after blooming and feed with a water-soluble fertilizer, or side-dress with time-release granules. A new flush of growth and flowers often occurs. Plants can become vigorous and spread over or out of boundaries; prune as needed.

Recommended Varieties

The most common, and many think the prettiest, is the 'Six Hills Giant' catmint. The dark-violet flowers (called racemes) are often 10 to 12 inches long, and are borne on plants 2 to 3 feet tall. 'Dropmore Hybrid' is smaller, but not as easy to find. 'Porcelain' has attractive light-blue flowers with blue-gray foliage.

Other Name:
Catnip

Light Needs:

Added Benefits:

Zones: 7 to 9

Bloom Time:
Summer, fall

Bloom Color: Blue, lavender, purple, white

Height: 2 to 3 ft.

Water Needs:
Moderate

Soil: Well drained, slightly moist

Uses:
Ground cover, herb garden, perennial garden

Did You Know?

Catnip is in the mint family.

Color photo on page 133

Chives

Allium schoenoprasum

What more could a gardener want than this perennial that can be used as edging, bears pretty flowers, is delicious, and produces more with every harvest?

How to Grow

Chives are in your garden for the long haul, so give them a proper home. Plant in full to partial shade, preparing the soil well. Apply a 3- to 4-inch layer of organic matter like fine pine bark or compost, along with 1 pound of slow-release 5-10-5 fertilizer per 100 square feet, tilling to a depth of 8 to 10 inches. Set out container-grown plants in early spring at the same depth they were growing in the containers, and 12 to 18 inches apart.

Companion Planting

Chives need to be planted with other plants that require regular watering, like basil, cilantro, and parsley. Chives work in almost the same situation as liriope. Though they are perennial, plant chives in the center of a container with 'Purple Wave' or other trailing-type petunias cascading over the edge.

Care and Maintenance

In early spring, side-dress with a light application of slow-release 12-6-6 fertilizer. Even though chives like moist, rich soil, they don't like soggy conditions, so don't overwater. As you harvest leaves, cut them as far down as possible so as not to leave a wound showing. Deadhead old flowers as needed. Clumps will probably need dividing every 3 or 4 years.

Recommended Varieties

The most commonly grown are onion chives, *Allium schoenoprasum*. More robust and a little hotter are the garlic chives, *Allium tuberosum*.

Other Name:
Chinese Chives

Light Needs:

Added Benefits:

Zones: 7 to 9

Bloom Time:
Spring

Bloom Color:
Light purple, white

Height: 18 to 24 in.

Spacing: 12 to 18 in.

Water Needs:
Moderate

Soil:
Moist, well drained

Uses:
Herb, vegetable, and perennial gardens; containers

Did You Know?
Chives are in the lily family.

Color photo on page 133

Cilantro

Coriandrum sativum

Fresh cilantro is the key to Mexican food flavor. It is easy to grow throughout the long season.

How to Grow

Cilantro likes well-drained beds rich in organic matter in full sun to partial shade. Apply a 3- to 4-inch layer of organic matter, along with 1 pound of slow-release 5-10-5 fertilizer per 100 square feet, tilling to a depth of 8 to 10 inches. Cilantro is available at garden centers each spring in very limited quantity. Plant at the same depth they were growing in their container, or direct-seed by sowing ¹/₂ inch deep. Cilantro can be grown through the winter in most of the state.

Companion Planting

Cilantro can be grown in rows or spot-planted around the herb or vegetable garden. It is so flavorful in cooking you may want to keep some in pots with flowers, tucked in the perennial garden. It does require moisture, so put it with other herbs of the same water requirement, like basil or parsley.

Care and Maintenance

Cilantro is grown for fresh leaves, so it is advisable to sow multiple crops. As the summer temperatures rise, cilantro quickly goes to flower, ending the good leaf production. Harvest the tender leaves from the top and cut several inches down, which will bring on new growth. Prune the central stalk as it develops, stalling flower formation. Keep the plants watered and mulched.

Recommended Varieties

Cilantro is sold generic.

Other Name:
Coriander

Light Needs:

Added Benefits:

Zones: 7 to 9

Bloom Time:
Early spring, summer

Bloom Color:
Pink, white, mauve

Height: 18 to 24 in.

Spacing: 10 to 12 in.

Water Needs:
Moderate

Soil:
Moist, well drained

Uses:
Herb, vegetable, and perennial garden; containers

Did You Know?

The seeds of cilantro become the spice called coriander.

Color photo on page 133

Dill

Light Needs:

Added Benefits:

Zones: 7 to 9

Bloom Time:
Spring, summer

Bloom Color:
Yellow

Height: 24 to 36 in.

Spacing: 12 to 18 in.

Water Needs:
Moderate

Soil:
Moist, well drained

Uses:
Herb, vegetable, and butterfly gardens; large containers

Did You Know?
Dill comes from a word meaning "to lull" and it was given to babies with colic.

Color photo on page 133

Anethum graveolens

What would a pickle be without dill? Dill is used in salads, in fish and poultry dishes, and to season other vegetables. The tall, feathery leaves are an important food for butterfly larvae.

How to Grow
Plant in full sun in well-drained soil. Incorporate 3 to 4 inches of organic matter like fine pine bark or compost, along with 1 pound per 100 square feet of a slow-release 5-10-5 fertilizer. Dill is an excellent fall and winter crop. Sow multiple crops in the spring and thin to 12 inches. Dill will quickly bolt with very hot temperatures.

Companion Planting
Dill is the most needed herb for delicious pickles, and the gorgeous flowers are the key. Dill looks quite at home in the perennial garden, with its feathery foliage and yellow flowers. Grow in the herb garden with fennel, which has similar leaves. Both plants make outstanding choices for the butterfly or herb garden. Plant a bunch behind 'Biloxi Blue' or 'Homestead Purple' verbena.

Care and Maintenance
Keep watered and well mulched during the summer. Harvest dill when the flowers are open, but before seeds have formed. Immature leaves can be harvested as flavoring for sour cream, meat, and fish. Dill seeds are good to use fresh or dried in salads.

Recommended Varieties
Dill is mostly sold generic. 'Tetra', a selection known for more heat tolerance, is a little shorter in height.

Fennel

Foeniculum vulgare

Tall, feathery foliage on this easy-to-grow perennial is loved by Europeans and swallowtail caterpillars; we need to grow and use it, too!

How to Grow

Plant in full sun to partial shade. Good drainage is essential, so add 3 to 4 inches of organic matter like fine pine bark or compost. Apply 1 pound of slow-release 5-10-5 fertilizer per 100 square feet, tilling to a depth of 8 to 10 inches. Nursery-grown transplants are frequently available in the herb section of the garden center, but you can try growing from seed. Fennel reaches 3 to 5 feet in height, so place it at the back of the garden. Common *Foeniculum vulgare* is perennial and should last for several years.

Companion Planting

Fennel and dill combine nicely. The feathery foliage is good combined with cosmos, which has a similar look. Lantanas of your favorite color look perfect surrounding fennel. Your garden may turn out to be one-stop shopping for swallowtails!

Care and Maintenance

Fennel is drought-tolerant, but it appreciates water during dry periods. Cut tender leaves for fish dishes. Cut stems and lay on fish while grilling. After seed have been harvested, cut back to about 1 inch and new growth will quickly emerge. Feed with a light application of the above fertilizer at this time.

Recommended Varieties

Foeniculum vulgare 'Purpurascens' is a bronze-leafed type that is hardy and beautiful. *Foeniculum vulgare* var. *azoricum*, or Florence fennel, is an annual, but well worth growing. Its bulb is cooked like a vegetable.

Other Name:
Sweet Fennel

Light Needs:

Added Benefits:

Zones: 7 to 9

Bloom Time:
Spring, summer

Bloom Color:
Yellow

Height: 3 to 5 ft.

Spacing: 2 to 3 ft.

Water Needs:
Low/moderate

Soil: Slightly moist, well drained

Uses: Herb, vegetable, and butterfly garden

Did You Know?

Fennel is used in the flavoring of several liqueurs.

Color photo on page 133

Lemon Balm

Melissa officinalis

Other Names:
Melissa, Bee Balm

Light Needs:

Added Benefits:

Zones: 7 to 9

Bloom Time:
Summer, fall

Bloom Color:
Lilac

Height: 18 to 24 in

Spacing: 24 to 36 in.

Water Needs:
Moderate

Soil:
Moist, well drained

Uses:
Herb gardens,
containers

Did You Know?
Melissa is Greek
for bees—which it
does attract.

Color photo on page 134

Lemon balm is a great easy-growing perennial with lemon-scented leaves. The variegated form is one of the prettiest plants in the herb garden.

How to Grow
Plant with morning sun and afternoon shade, or high filtered light. It can be grown in full sun, although it adds a little more stress to the plant. Prepare soil by incorporating 3 to 4 inches of organic matter and 1 pound of slow-release 5-10-5 fertilizer per 100 square feet, tilling to a depth of 8 to 10 inches. Transplants are usually found in the herb section of your garden center, but lemon balm is easily grown from seed. This is a spreading plant, so set plants at least 24 to 36 inches apart.

Companion Planting
Place lemon balm in the section of the herb garden containing plants that need regular watering. The variegated type looks striking when planted in a partially shady area with lavender or purple impatiens. Try growing a large clump of lemon balm flanked by hostas.

Care and Maintenance
Keep watered during the summer months. Shear back to remove unwanted growth and dead growth from winter. This plant is vigorous; additional feeding should not be necessary for some time. Keep the plants mulched during summer. Harvest tender leaves to use in drinks, salads, poultry and fish recipes, potpourri, or sachets.

Recommended Varieties
Mostly sold generic except for 'Aurea', which has a golden variegation, a similar one called 'Golden', and 'All Gold'.

Oregano

Origanum vulgare

Oregano is the staple of Italian dishes. This upright easy-to-grow perennial is a pleasure to harvest from your own herb garden for use.

How to Grow

Prepare soil by adding 3 to 4 inches of organic matter like fine pine bark or compost, along with 1 pound of slow-release 5-10-5 fertilizer per 100 square feet, tilling to a depth of 8 to 10 inches. Transplants are available in the herb section of your garden center, or it can be direct-seeded. Set out transplants at the same depth they were growing in their containers. Space plants 2 feet apart.

Companion Planting

Oregano prefers a more Mediterranean climate with less water. Plant with rosemary, thyme, and santolina. The vibrant colors of the moss rose are beautiful additions for this type of garden.

Care and Maintenance

The drought tolerance mentioned above occurs only after establishment, so watch the soil's moisture level until then. Harvest young tender leaves in the early morning to use in dishes, or dry and store them for later use. Prune out dead areas and shear occasionally to generate growth. Oregano roots easily from cuttings, so trade varieties with friends. The flowers dry attractively for arrangements.

Recommended Varieties

Origanum vulgare is the common oregano and is mostly sold generic at the garden center. There are many varieties available through culinary garden mail-order catalogs. *O. vulgare* subs. *hirtum*, called Greek oregano, is also much utilized.

Other Name:
Wild Marjoram

Light Needs:

Added Benefits:

Zones: 7 to 9

Bloom Time:
Summer, fall

Bloom Color:
Purple, white

Height: 2 to 3 ft.

Spacing: 1 to 2 ft.

Water Needs:
Low/moderate

Soil: Slightly moist, well drained

Uses:
Herb gardens, containers

Did You Know?

Origanum comes from the Greek word meaning "mountains" and the Greek word meaning "joy."

Color photo on page 134

Parsley

Petroselinum crispum

Other Name:
French Parsley

Light Needs:

Added Benefits:

Zones: 7 to 10

Bloom Time:
Grown for foliage

Bloom Color:
Yellow

Height: 10 to 24 in.

Water Needs:
Moderate

Soil:
Moist, well drained

Uses:
Edgings, borders, herb gardens, butterfly gardens, containers

Did You Know?

Parsley will freshen your breath. Is that why it is on my plate?

Color photo on page 134

You know parsley as that little garnish that shows up on your plate at restaurants, and it is put to good use finely chopped in all sorts of sauces, salads, and vegetable dishes.

How to Grow

Plant in full sun to partial shade. Parsley prefers well-drained soil rich in organic matter. Add a layer of 3 to 4 inches of fine pine bark or compost, along with 1 pound of slow-release 5-10-5 fertilizer per 100 square feet, tilling to 8 to 10 inches. Transplants are readily available at the herb section of your garden center. You can direct-sow, but first soak the hard-coated seeds for 24 hours in warm water.

Companion Planting

Plant parsley with other plants that need regular watering, like basil and cilantro. Parsley looks good as an edging or border plant, or grown in flower beds. It is among the better butterfly garden plants.

Care and Maintenance

If your parsley is harvested often, side-dress monthly with a light application of a high-nitrogen fertilizer such as 12-6-6. As soon as plants are 6 to 8 inches high, leaves can be harvested. When you harvest, cut back to the base or crown of the plant. Parsley is a biennial and usually comes through the winter fine. It blooms the second year, at which time it should be removed.

Recommended Varieties

Two main types are Italian parsley (*Petroselinum crispum* var. *neapolitanum*) and curly or French parsley (*Petroselinum crispum* var. *crispum*).

Pineapple Sage

Salvia elegans

Pineapple sage is extra special, with fragrant leaves that give off the aroma of fresh crushed pineapple. The red flowers attract hummingbirds.

How to Grow

Plant in full sunlight to partial shade. Prepare soil deeply by adding 3 to 4 inches of organic matter such as fine pine bark or compost. Incorporate 1 pound of slow-release 5-10-5 fertilizer per 100 square feet, working to a depth of 8 to 10 inches. If growing in the northern third of the state, plant in a well-drained protected area, treat as an annual, or bring indoors during the winter.

Companion Planting

If you ever wanted to plant a garden for humming-birds, the pineapple sage would make a great foundation. Red salvias, lobelia or cardinal flower, shrimp plant, salvia 'Indigo Spires', and blue anise sage combine to make a hummingbird paradise. Pineapple sage also deserves to be in the herb garden.

Care and Maintenance

Side-dress with a light application of a higher-nitro-gen fertilizer like a 12-6-6 every 6 to 8 weeks through August. Keep well watered and mulched throughout the summer. When winter approaches, add an extra layer of mulch and root a few stems in water just in case the winter turns severe. Harvest leaves to give a pineapple flavor to drinks, cheese spreads, poultry dishes, and jellies.

Recommended Varieties

The pineapple sage is usually sold generic, but 'Frieda Dixon' is a salmon-colored variety.

Other Name:
Houseplant Sage

Light Needs:

Added Benefits:

Zones: (7, 8), 9

Bloom Time:
Summer

Bloom Color:
Red, salmon

Height: 3 to 4 ft.

Spacing: 2 to 3 ft.

Water Needs:
Moderate

Soil:
Moist, well drained

Uses:
Herb gardens, hummingbird gardens

Did You Know?

Pineapple sage roots easily in water or by cuttings.

Color photo on page 134

Rosemary

Rosmarinus officinalis

Rosemary's fragrant foliage gives as much pleasure as just about any plant. For a long-lasting dried bouquet, tie a few sprigs in the kitchen with Mexican bush sage flowers and cinnamon sticks.

How to Grow

Rosemary prefers well-drained, slightly dry soil. Add 3 to 4 inches of organic material, like fine pine bark or compost, with 1 pound of slow-release fertilizer, like a 5-10-5, per 100 square feet, tilling to a depth of 8 to 10 inches. Rosemary is available at your garden center. Larger 1- and 2-gallon sizes are a good buy, providing more cold hardiness. Plant at the same depth they were growing in their containers. In the northern part of the state, plant in a protected area or in containers, giving winter protection.

Companion Planting

In the herb garden, group rosemary with plants that like it dry, like artemesia, oregano, and santolina. In the flower garden, rosemary grows three feet tall and looks exceptional with groundcover-type lantanas, 'Victoria' blue salvia, purple gomphrena, and 'Purple Heart'.

Care and Maintenance

Keep watered until established. Rosemary should not need any more fertilizer. Control growth by frequent tip pruning. You see tip-pruned, Christmas tree–shaped rosemary for sale during the holidays, and you can do the same. Rosemary leaves are used in pork, poultry, and lamb dishes, and to make herbal baths.

Recommended Varieties

'Arp' and 'Hardy Hill' are among the most hardy; 'Tuscan Blue' and 'Old Salem' are another couple of good choices. Don't be surprised to see rosemary sold generic at your garden center.

Other Name:
Sea Dew

Light Needs:

Added Benefits:

Zones: (7), 8, 9

Bloom Time:
Summer

Bloom Color:
Lavender

Height: 3 to 4 ft.

Spacing: 2 to 3 ft.

Water Needs:
Low/moderate

Soil: Slightly moist, well drained

Uses: Herb gardens, flower beds, and large containers

Did You Know?

Greek scholars wore rosemary garlands to stimulate the brain.

Color photo on page 134

Scented Geranium

Pelargonium species

With many intense fragrances, these flowers are treats for the nose.

How to Grow

Scented geraniums are best grown in containers in all but extreme coastal Mississippi. They can be planted as annuals or border plants, or dug up and brought indoors. If growing in the garden, make sure soil is well drained and in full sunlight. If growing in containers, choose a potting mixture that is light, airy, and well drained. Scented geraniums thrive in the heat and develop a "woodiness" that gives them durability.

Companion Planting

Try growing upright rosemary in a large container with two or three scented geraniums cascading off in different directions. Locate in the garden with plants that are on the drier side.

Care and Maintenance

Harvest leaves for fresh use in beverages, teas, jams, and jellies. The flowers are edible and are useful as garnish. When leggy, prune to induce new growth and bushiness. When growing in containers, you will most likely need to water every day, which also means weekly applications of a water-soluble fertilizer or feeding with time-release granules. When brought indoors for the winter, monitor water closely. Water only when soil is dry to the touch. Place in a bright area and pinch to maintain bushiness.

Recommended Varieties

What is your favorite fragrance? *P. quercifolium* (almond), *P. odoratissimum* (apple), *P. scabrum* (apricot), and *P. crispum* (lemon) are just a few.

Other Name:
Pelargonium

Light Needs:

Added Benefits:

Zones: 9 to 10

Bloom Time:
Summer

Bloom Color:
White and rose

Height: 1 to 3 ft.

Spacing: 18 to 24 in.

Water Needs:
Low/moderate

Soil:
Slightly moist, well drained

Uses:
Herb garden borders, mixed containers, baskets

Did You Know?

Scented geraniums root easily by tip cuttings.

Color photo on page 134

Thyme

Other Names:
Garden Thyme,
Mother of Thyme

Light Needs:

Added Benefits:

Zones: 7 to 10

Bloom Time:
Spring, summer

Bloom Color: Pink,
purple, lilac, white

Height: 2 to 16 in.

Spacing: 12 to 18 in.

Water Needs:
Low/moderate

Soil: Slightly moist,
well drained

Uses: Herb garden
borders, rock gardens,
mixed containers

Did You Know?
The word "thyme"
comes from the Greek
word for perfume.

Color photo on page 134

Thymus species

Thyme is a wonderfully fragrant spreading plant that is ideal to grow in the herb garden or between cracks or crevices in a walkway or on a wall.

How to Grow
Choose a site in full sun, though some shade will be tolerated. Good drainage is an essential ingredient of your success. Add a 3- to 4-inch layer of organic matter like fine pine bark or compost, along with 1 pound of slow-release fertilizer such as 5-10-5 per 100 square feet, tilling to a depth of 8 to 10 inches. Thyme is easy to find in the herb section of your garden center. Plant it at the same depth it was growing in the container and apply water.

Companion Planting
Thyme needs to be planted in a section of the herb garden that will remain on the dry side. Plant with rosemary, oregano, and santolina. Creeping thymus should be grown as a border plant, while upright thyme can be planted in the middle of the garden.

Care and Maintenance
With spring growth, feed with a light application of 12-6-6 fertilizer. Avoid watering from overhead sprinklers. Keep thymus lightly and regularly sheared for tender growth. Harvest leaves anytime to use fresh or dry. Layering by pegging is an easy way to propagate new plants.

Recommended Varieties
Thymus vulgaris is the common thyme. Other good ones to try are *Thymus × citriodorus* (lemon thyme) and *Thymus pseudolanuginosus* (woolly thyme). There are many more to choose from.

Yarrow

Achillea millefolium

Yarrow is one of the easiest-grown perennial herbs, and is among the most sought after for its successfully drying flowers.

How to Grow

Plant in full sun for best flower performance. Yarrow needs well-drained, average soil. If yours is not well drained, raise the bed by incorporating 3 to 4 inches of organic matter, like fine pine bark or compost. Use 1 pound of slow-release 5-10-5 fertilizer per 100 square feet, tilling to a depth of 8 to 10 inches. Set out nursery-grown transplants, or direct-seed in the spring.

Companion Planting

Yarrows need to be placed with plants requiring less water. It also works well in the perennial garden when planted in front of drought-tolerant plants like lantanas and verbenas. Purple gomphrenas look exceptional with a yarrow like 'Coronation Gold'.

Care and Maintenance

Harvest yarrow while still in bloom and before any flowers start to turn brown. Hang them upside-down in a well-ventilated room until dry. After spring bloom, cut flowers back to the ground to encourage new growth and fall bloom. Yarrow is a prolific spreader; remove unwanted plants and deadhead before flowers have a chance to reseed. Division is best done in the fall in crowded areas.

Recommended Varieties

A. millefolium, or common yarrow, is available in varieties like 'Fire King', 'Debutante' (which has almost a dozen colors), and 'Summer Pastels', an All-America Selections winner series from 1990. 'Cerise Queen' with its cherry-red blooms is still one of the most popular. 'Coronation Gold' is a superior variety of *A. filipendula*.

Other Name: Milfoil

Light Needs:

Added Benefits:

Zones: 7 to 9

Bloom Time: Spring, summer, fall

Bloom Color: Varied

Height: 12 to 42 in.

Spacing: 18 to 24 in.

Water Needs: Low/moderate

Soil: Slightly moist, well drained

Uses: Perennial gardens, herb gardens

Did You Know?

In France, yarrow is called "Carpenter's Herb" in the belief it has healing properties when used on the hands of working people.

Color photo on page 134

PERENNIALS

Garden centers now see a huge demand for perennials that will bloom the first year. If you are not on the perennial bandwagon yet, you might want to get in tune with the rest of the country!

Perennials range from the old cottage garden favorites to new improved varieties to new species of plants that are being brought to us by modern-day plant explorers. Perennials are easy to care for. The most important rule in selecting a perennial is to make sure it is appropriate for the site you have in mind. Because it is a perennial, it will occupy that space for some time.

Gardeners are rediscovering perennials, the plants that return year after year.

Make sure the site is appropriate for the plant's height, light requirements, soil type, and hardiness for your area. Consider whether or not it will be a good companion plant in color and maintenance for flowers nearby.

Soil preparation for perennials is about the same as for annuals. Think about the length of time you are expecting the plants to be there: proper soil preparation is essential. Making major corrections can be virtually impossible without completely redoing a bed.

Many Mississippians work with a soil that takes a pickaxe to break apart, and soil compaction can quickly become a problem. Working in four inches of organic matter like compost, peat, humus, or pinebark will allow for water and nutrient penetration and oxygen to get to the roots of those plants. Not all gardeners are plagued with tight clay. Some have sandy soils with a tendency to dry quickly, and the same organic matter is needed to help hold in water and keep nutrients from leaching out.

Adding a two- or three-inch layer of mulch after planting will help keep the soil moderate in temperature, conserve soil moisture, and prevent weeds and further compaction.

Perennials look best when grown in a border, whether it borders a fence, wall, or driveway. When creating your perennial border, plant in large bold drifts of color. In other words, plant in groups. One shasta daisy here, another there, doesn't have the same impact as a dozen shastas in an oblong oval, planted next to a drift of black-eyed Susans, next to a dozen indigo spire salvias. Do you get the drift?

A mixed border of annuals, perennials, and woody evergreens is one of the best styles for gardeners in urban neighborhoods. Woody evergreens, like hollies, serve as the foundation of the border. The bed will look good in winter. Very few perennials bloom for the entire summer and annuals can give quick, immediate, and long-lasting color as perennials come and go with their bloom.

Gardeners will fall in love with the ability to divide and multiply perennials to place in other parts of the landscape or give to friends and neighbors. A general rule of "green thumb" is to divide the perennials during the time opposite their season of bloom. Plants like daylilies, phlox, black-eyed Susans, purple coneflowers, and shasta daisies are easy to clump-divide. Other plants like verbenas, salvias, and lantana are easy to root from cuttings for additional plants.

Mississippi is a state with a rich gardening history, from large antebellum homes with formal gardens to cottages that contain plantings that would make a botanical garden cry in envy. These gardens have one thing in common: they would not be complete without perennials playing a prominent role.

> Perennials look best when grown in a border.

Black-Eyed Susan

Other Name:
Orange Coneflower

Light Needs:

Added Benefits:

Zones: 7 to 9

Bloom Time:
Summer, fall

Bloom Color:
Golden yellow

Height: 24 to 30 in.

Spacing: 12 to 15 in.

Water Needs:
Low/moderate

Soil:
Moist, well drained

Uses:
Cottage gardens,
middle of the border

Did You Know?
The black and brown cones are useful in arrangements.

Color photo on page 134

Rudbeckia fulgida 'Goldsturm'

'Goldsturm' was the 1999 Perennial Plant of the Year. This is the most reliable perennial black-eyed susan, with gorgeous 3- to 4-inch flowers.

How to Grow
Choose a site in full sun for best flowering, although some shade is tolerated. 'Goldsturm' cannot tolerate wet feet, so prepare the bed by adding 3 to 4 inches of organic matter (like fine pine bark or compost), tilling to a depth of 8 to 10 inches. Incorporate 2 pounds of a slow-release 12-6-6 fertilizer. Set your plants out at the same depth they were growing in their containers and mulch.

Companion Planting
'Goldsturm' is at home in a cottage garden, grouped with salvias like blue anise sage, 'Indigo Spires', and 'Victoria'. Perennial verbenas like 'Biloxi Blue' and 'Homestead Purple' look great as understory plants. Surround a purple or plum-colored buddleia with several of these rudbeckias. 'Hilo Princess' angelonia is wonderful massed adjacent to 'Goldsturm'.

Care and Maintenance
Use the above fertilizer for sidedressing every 6 to 8 weeks during the growing season. Keep flowers deadheaded for a tidy look and to encourage blooming. After the plants finish blooming in late summer, cut flower stalks and a new taller fall flush will develop. 'Goldsturm' is vigorous and may need dividing in two years.

Recommended Varieties
Rudbeckia fulgida 'Goldsturm' is the leading perennial rudbeckia. There are some other good choices, such as *Rudbeckia triloba*, which was a Georgia Gold Medal winner, *Rudbeckia lanciniata* 'Golden Glow', and 'Autumn Sun'.

Blue Anise Sage

Salvia guaranitica

The deepest blue flowers of all are produced for months on plants that reach four feet high. This plant was a Georgia Gold Medal winner, and thrives in Mississippi, too!

How to Grow

Choose a site in full sun for best flowering. This plant is winter hardy throughout the state, but only with good drainage. Add 3 to 4 inches of organic matter like fine pine bark or compost, tilling to a depth of 8 to 10 inches. Incorporate 2 pounds of a 12-6-6 slow-release fertilizer. Plant in spring after the soil has warmed, at the same depth it was growing in the container. Mulch.

Companion Planting

Blue anise sage is great among yellow and golden flowers like the black-eyed susan 'Goldsturm', or behind a layer of 'New Gold' lantana. The deep blue also looks good behind perennial pink verbenas like 'Port Gibson' and 'Temari'.

Care and Maintenance

This is an easy-care plant. Deadhead as needed and do not be afraid to cut back for better branching. Should the plant look a little tired in midsummer, give a little pick-me-up with a light application of the above fertilizer. The plant will probably need dividing in three years. Make sure it goes into winter with an added layer of mulch. Like many salvias, this one is easy to propagate by cuttings.

Recommended Varieties

This salvia is usually sold generic, but selections like 'Costa Rica Blue' and 'Purple Splendour' are seen from time to time.

Other Name:
Brazilian Sage

Light Needs:

Added Benefits:

Zones: 7 to 9

Bloom Time:
Summer, fall

Bloom Color:
Shades of blue

Height: 4 to 5 ft.

Spacing:
24 to 30 in.

Water Needs:
Moderate

Soil:
Moist, well drained

Uses:
Cottage gardens, middle to back of border

Did You Know?

It is called anise for the licorice fragrance of the leaves.

Color photo on page 134

Butterfly Weed

Other Name:
Indian Paintbrush

Light Needs:

Added Benefits:

Zones: 7 to 9

Bloom Time:
Summer

Bloom Color:
Orange, yellow,
yellow with red

Height: 2 to 3 ft

Water Needs:
Low/moderate

Soil: Well drained,
slightly moist

Uses: Perennial and
butterfly gardens

Did You Know?

Asclepios was the god
of medicine in
Greek mythology.

Color photo on page 134

Asclepias tuberosa

The bright gold-orange flowers of this plant in the milkweed family are not only good as cutflowers, but are the passion of the monarch butterfly.

How to Grow

Good drainage is a necessity with asclepias. Incorporate 3 to 4 inches of organic matter like fine pine bark or humus. Plants are few and far between at nurseries, but they can be grown from seed. If the seed is harvested from the wild, it will need a cold treatment in the refrigerator. *Asclepias curassavica* is readily available at garden centers; it blooms longer but is reliably perennial only in zone 9.

Companion Planting

Asclepias is a staple in the perennial garden geared toward butterflies. Locate with other such plants like 'Biloxi Blue' verbena, lantanas, buddleias, and salvias like 'Victoria', 'Indigo Spires', and blue anise sage.

Care and Maintenance

Mulch plants to conserve moisture and keep weeds in check. Asclepias is not only loved by the monarch for its flowers, but also as a host plant for their offspring. Don't panic: the kids will love watching the caterpillar grow and devour the plant to become a butterfly. The leaves and flowers will return.

Recommended Varieties

The *Asclepias tuberosa* is sold generically by plant and seed; 'Gay Butterflies' and 'Hello Yellow' can be found. If you don't mind growing as an annual, look for *Asclepias curassavica* (the blooms are actually prettier, and it blooms in summer and fall). Varieties you may find are 'Red Butterfly' and 'Silky Gold'.

Coreopsis

Coreopsis species

The showy flowers in shades of yellow and orange give a bright, bold look to the Southern cottage garden or the modern perennial border. The flowers are great for cutting and bringing indoors.

How to Grow
Well-drained soil is a must. High fertility, on the other hand, is not recommended. Improve drainage by adding 3 to 4 inches of organic matter, tilling to a depth of 8 to 10 inches. Set out nursery-grown transplants after the last frost. Plant at the same depth they were growing in their containers and apply mulch.

Companion Planting
'Early Sunrise' and 'Sunray' varieties of coreopsis grandiflora look great adjacent to tall shasta daisies and 'Victoria' blue salvia or 'Indigo Spires'. One of the most beautiful combinations of pastels occurs when the 'Moonbeam' variety of *Coreopsis verticillata* is planted with Russian Sage (*Perovskia atriplicifolia*).

Care and Maintenance
Deadheading old flowers may be more important with these plants than with just about any other. Not only will you get more flowers and make them look tidy, but you'll be preventing the old flowers from getting infected and spreading the infection to the rest of the plant. Clumps can be divided in spring or fall as they get crowded.

Recommended Varieties
'Early Sunrise', an All-America Selections winner from 1989, 'Sunburst', and 'Sunray' are among the best of the *Coreopsis grandiflora*. 'Baby Sun' and 'Sundancer' are recognized performers of *Coreopsis lanceolata*. 'Moonbeam' (the Perennial Plant of the Year for 1992) and 'Zagreb' are both good *Coreopsis verticillata*.

Other Name:
Tickseed

Light Needs:

Added Benefits:

Zones: 7 to 9

Bloom Time:
Spring, summer

Bloom Color:
Yellow, orange

Height: 20 to 36 in.

Spacing: 12 to 15 in.

Water Needs:
Low/moderate

Soil: Well drained, slightly moist

Uses: Cottage gardens, modern perennial borders

Did You Know?
Coreopsis means "buglike."

Color photo on page 134

Daylily

Other Names:
Hemerocallis hybrids

Light Needs:

Added Benefit:

Zones: 7 to 9

Bloom Time:
Late spring, summer, fall

Bloom Color:
All shades except blues

Height: 18 to 36 in.

Spacing: 18 to 24 in.

Water Needs:
Low/moderate

Soil: Well drained, slightly moist

Uses:
Daylily gardens, perennial gardens, flower beds

Did You Know?
The flowers are reportedly edible.

Color photo on page 135

Hemerocallis hybrids

They bloom only for a day, but each scape has loads of buds that open up to glorious flowers over weeks—even months, for some varieties.

How to Grow
Choose a site with at least six hours of sun. For the necessary well-drained beds, add 3 to 4 inches of organic matter, tilling to a depth of 8 to 10 inches. Incorporate 2 pounds of 1-2-2 ratio slow-release fertilizer per 100 square feet. Set out plants so that the crowns are resting on the soil line. Space plants to allow for good air circulation.

Companion Planting
Nothing captures the imagination like a garden dedicated to daylilies. Every day colors and appearances change. Daylilies are well suited to having bold clumps in perennial gardens. Daylilies like 'Stella d'Oro' are best for massing like annuals; try masses adjacent to a large area of purple heart, or planted in front of 'Victoria' blue salvia.

Care and Maintenance
Keep daylilies deadheaded for a tidy appearance. Unless growing for seed, remove pods as they form. Daylilies are drought tolerant, but you should provide supplemental water during dry periods. Feed with a light application of the above fertilizer in September. Most daylilies will need dividing every three years. Keep beds mulched going into winter.

Recommended Varieties
There are thousands and thousands of daylilies, thanks to hybridizers everywhere. Visit a daylily garden near you and get acquainted with your local Hemerocallis Society. For landscape purposes 'Stella d'Oro' is hard to beat.

Hibiscus

Hibiscus species and hybrids

No flower is as showy or big as the perennial hibiscus.

How to Grow

Choose a site in full sun to partial shade with wind protection. This is one plant that doesn't require absolutely perfect drainage—but no swamps. If the soil is tight and compact, till in 3 to 4 inches of organic matter and a light application of a 12-6-6 fertilizer. Set out transplants in late spring, or direct-seed. Plant at the same depth they were growing in the containers.

Companion Planting

The *Hibiscus moscheutos* (or giant rose mallow) hybrids look great planted in front of bananas and upright elephant ears for a tropical look, or as understory plants for palm trees. They look romantic planted with summer phlox against a white picket fence in a cottage garden.

Care and Maintenance

Be prepared to give supplemental water during the summer months. Established plants will need a light application of the above fertilizer at spring emergence, and about every 6 to 8 weeks through the growing season. Lightly prune to maintain shape if needed. In late fall, cut back stems to just above the ground. Go into winter with a good layer of mulch.

Recommended Varieties

One of the showiest hybrids is 'Moy Grande', with red-magenta flowers reaching 12 inches across. 'George Riegel', with ruffled pink blooms, and 'Lord Baltimore', with deep-red flowers, are considered two of the prettiest. Well-known seed types include 'Disco Belle', 'Frisbee', and 'Rio Carnival'. *Hibiscus coccineus* 'Texas Star', with red star-shaped flowers, is gaining in popularity in the Southeast.

Other Name:
Rose Mallow

Light Needs:

Added Benefits:

Zones: 7 to 9

Bloom Time:
Summer

Bloom Color:
Pink, red, white, blends

Height: 24 to 60 in.

Spacing: 15 to 36 in.

Water Needs:
Moderate

Soil: Moist, loose

Uses:
Tropical gardens,
cottage gardens

Did You Know?

The confederate rose is actually *Hibiscus mutabilis*.

Color photo on page 135

Hostas

Hosta species and hybrids

Other Name:
Plantain Lily

Light Needs:

Added Benefits:

Zones: 7, 8, (9)

Bloom Time:
Summer; mostly grown for foliage

Bloom Color:
Lavender, white

Height: 1 to 3 ft.

Spacing: 1 to 3 ft.

Water Needs:
Moderate

Soil:
Moist, well drained

Uses: Shade gardens, background and border plants

Did You Know?
Some varieties have an intoxicating fragrance.

Color photo on page 135

No plant does as well in the shade as hosta, which is why there are now thousands of varieties.

How to Grow
Plant from nursery-grown transplants in early spring so they will get acclimatized before hot summer temperatures appear. Incorporate 3 to 4 inches of peat or compost to improve drainage and aeration. While tilling, add 2 pounds of 12-6-6 slow-release fertilizer per 100 square feet. Plant at the same depth they were growing in containers, placing the plant's crown slightly above the soil. Add a layer of mulch after planting.

Companion Planting
Hostas look tropical and combine well with bananas, elephant ears, and gingers. They make great border plants for woodland trails. Masses of impatiens or caladiums work nicely around hostas planted in groups of three.

Care and Maintenance
Hostas need to be watered during dry periods. Feed with light applications of the above fertilizer every 6 to 8 weeks. Slugs and snails seem to be the main pests, so treat with baits or sprays as needed. Clumps can be divided in the spring as growth resumes.

Recommended Varieties
'August Moon' (chartreuse leaves, white flowers), 'Blue Angel' (blue-green leaves white flowers), 'Blue Wedgwood' (blue-green leaves, lavender flowers), 'Chartreuse Wriggles' (chartreuse and gold leaves with lavender flowers), and 'Hadspen Blue' (oval blue leaves and lavender flowers) are a tiny sampling. A few known for fragrance are 'Fragrant Bouquet', 'Heaven Scent', and 'Invincible'.

Indigo Spires

Salvia farinacea × S. longispicata

Tall blue-flowered spikes are produced all summer, spiraling in the air. Flower color intensifies in fall.

How to Grow
Salvia 'Indigo Spires' is a tender perennial. Well-drained soil is needed for spring return. In the northern third of the state, plant in a protected area with full sun. Add 3 to 4 inches of organic matter. Incorporate 2 pounds of a 12-6-6 fertilizer per 100 square feet of bed space. Plant in spring from nursery-grown transplants. Set out at the same depth they were growing in the containers. Don't plant under street lights—they are daylength-sensitive.

Companion Planting
They give that wonderful spiky texture that works well behind flowers like 'Goldsturm' or 'Indian Summer' rudbeckia. Try orange and gold lantanas in front of or around either. Blooms of lantanas and indigo spires will attract bees and butterflies.

Care and Maintenance
Keep salvias mulched through summer and winter. 'Indigo Spires' responds to midsummer pruning to encourage bushiness. They make great cutflowers. Cut them and hang upside-down to dry indoors. Tie the flowers with sprigs of rosemary and a couple of cinnamon sticks, using ribbon. This will be pretty for months. Cut stalks to about 6 inches and mulch after they freeze.

Recommended Varieties
These are sold generically. Try also *Salvia leucantha*, *Salvia coccinea*, *Salvia greggii*, and *Salvia superba*, or your garden won't be complete.

Other Name:
Sage

Light Needs:

Added Benefits:

Zones: 7 to 8 (protected), 9

Bloom Time: Summer, fall

Bloom Color: Blue, purple, pink

Height: 3 to 4 ft.

Spacing: 2 to 3 ft.

Water Needs: Low to moderate

Soil: Well drained, slightly moist

Uses: Cottage gardens, middle to back of border

Did You Know?
Salvia comes from a Latin word meaning "to save or heal."

Color photo on page 135

Lantana

Other Name:
Ham and Eggs

Light Needs:

Added Benefits:

Zones: (7), 8, 9

Bloom Time:
Spring, summer, fall

Bloom Color:
All shades and blends except blue.

Height: 2 to 6 ft.

Spacing: 2 to 4 ft.

Water Needs:
Low/moderate

Soil: Well drained, slightly moist

Uses: Butterfly gardens, cottage gardens, baskets, containers

Did You Know?
The lantana is closely related to the verbena.

Color photo on page 135

Lantana × hybrida

No group of plants offers the colors, heat tolerance, and length of bloom of lantanas. Watch butterflies and hummingbirds go for the nectar.

How to Grow
Plant in full sun. Prepare beds, incorporating 3 to 4 inches of organic matter and tilling to a depth of 8 to 10 inches. Apply 2 pounds of slow-release 12-6-6 fertilizer per 100 square feet. Lantanas are so happy here that they grow with a vigor many underestimate, so space plants accordingly. Water and mulch after planting.

Companion Planting
Plant a group around a buddleia of a complementary color. Add some zinnias for a butterfly garden all summer. The 'New Gold' lantana is excellent with perennial blue salvia, red 'Dreamland' zinnias, and 'Japanese Silver Grass'. Try planting with perennial verbenas like 'Biloxi Blue' or 'Tapien Violet'.

Care and Maintenance
Prune during the year to keep in bounds or to stimulate new growth and bloom. Water during periods of drought. Give a light application of the above fertilizer in midsummer. If your lantana is a heavy seed producer, keep seeds picked off. They drain the plant's energy and are poisonous if ingested. Plants will probably freeze to the ground; add a layer of mulch to encourage spring return.

Recommended Varieties
'New Gold' lantana was the 1996 Mississippi Medallion winner and is still the best for continuous bloom and few seeds. 'Lemon Drop' and 'Silver Mound' are highly rated. For bright reds and oranges, look for 'Radiation' and 'Spreading Sunset'. 'Sonrise' (magenta, yellow, and orange) has proven itself, too.

Liatris

Liatris spicata

This native wildflower produces long, purple, spiky flowers that are well suited to the vase. Whether in the garden or field, they will catch your eye.

How to Grow
Choose a site in full sun. Prepare beds by incorporating 3 to 4 inches of organic matter, along with 2 pounds of slow-release 12-6-6 fertilizer per 100 square feet. Liatris may be direct-seeded in September and October for bloom next summer, or planted in spring from readily available nursery-grown transplants. Thin or space plants 12 to 15 inches apart, water, and mulch.

Companion Planting
The liatris is at home next to a white picket fence and grown as an understory plant with plants like the 'Goldsturm' rudbeckia, purple coneflower, or any colors of narrowleaf zinnia. 'Moonbeam' coreopsis creates a unique and appealing look with the liatris.

Care and Maintenance
As growth emerges in the spring, side-dress with a light application of the above fertilizer. Thin or move out competing plants to allow the liatris to thrive. Cut back the flower spikes after they have finished their bloom. As the clump ages, you may want to divide in early spring. Dust with a fungicide before returning to the soil.

Recommended Varieties
Liatris spicata is the most widely seen species at the garden center. The varieties are 'Floristan White', 'Floristan Purple', and 'Kobold' (violet-pink). Wildflower catalogs, and sometimes the seed racks, offer the native *Liatris elegans*, which blooms later in the season.

Other Names:
Blazing Star, Gay Feather

Light Needs:

Added Benefits:

Zones: 7, 8 (9)

Bloom Time:
Summer

Bloom Color:
Pink, purple, white

Height: 16 to 36 in.

Spacing: 12 to 18 in.

Water Needs:
Moderate

Soil: Well drained, slightly moist

Uses: Cottage gardens, cutflower gardens, perennial borders

Did You Know?
This is one of the few flowers that opens from the top down.

Color photo on page 135

Louisiana Phlox

Phlox divaricata

For about two months these flowers can stop traffic with their psychedelic blue color. They are fragrant; the early butterflies love them and you will, too!

How to Grow

Plant in morning sun and afternoon shade, or filtered light. Prepare soil by incorporating 3 to 4 inches organic matter, like humus or fine pine bark, along with 2 pounds of a slow-release 12-6-6 fertilizer per 100 square feet. Till to 8 to 10 inches. Plants are available at garden centers in the early spring. Plant at the same depth they were growing in the containers, water, and mulch.

Companion Planting

This phlox blooms at the most wonderful time of year in the South—when azaleas, dogwoods, and many narcissus are blooming. Use them as a border plant. Their color combines well with almost any other spring-blooming plant, depending on how bold you are. They look exceptional around newly leafed-out Japanese maples with red leaves.

Care and Maintenance

After bloom is finished, cut back tops and foliage by about half. This is an excellent time to drop in a caladium bulb every 12 inches; phlox tolerates this summer companion just fine. New growth will emerge, which is pretty nondescript until next spring. When spring growth emerges, side-dress with a light application of the above fertilizer. Divide plantings as needed in early spring.

Recommended Varieties

Usually sold generically, but 'Chattahoochee', a *Phlox pilosa* hybrid, lavender-blue with a red eye, is gaining popularity. 'Louisiana Purple', 'Laphamii', and 'London Grove' are occasionally seen.

Other Name:
Wild Sweet William

Light Needs:

Added Benefits:

Zones: 7 to 9

Bloom Time:
Spring

Bloom Color:
Blue, lavender, pink

Height:
12 to 15 in.

Water Needs:
Moderate to frequent

Soil:
Moist, well-drained

Uses:
Spring gardens as border plant, and natural areas

Did You Know?
These phlox root easily from cuttings.

Color photo on page 135

Purple Coneflower

Echinacea purpurea

Echinacea is not just an herbal remedy for colds, but is one of the prettiest flowers in the garden, with loads of morning fragrance and visiting butterflies.

How to Grow

Choose a site in full sun. Prepare soil, incorporating 3 to 4 inches of organic matter, along with 2 pounds of slow-release 12-6-6 fertilizer per 100 square feet. Till 8 to 10 inches deep. Purple coneflowers can be direct-seeded in fall for bloom next year, but the easiest way may be to buy 4-inch green transplants in early spring. Those not yet budded will continue to put out leaves, making themselves at home in your garden. Space plants 2 to 3 feet apart at the same depth they were in containers. Water in and mulch. Thin and transplant seedlings 2 to 3 feet apart as well.

Companion Planting

Purple coneflowers are a staple of the Southern cottage garden and look great in bold drifts with shasta daisies, 'Goldsturm' rudbeckias, or 'Victoria' blue salvia, or planted around buddleias like 'Plum Delight' or 'Empire Blue'.

Care and Maintenance

In early spring, side-dress with a light application of the above fertilizer, and again in midsummer. Established clumps are best divided in fall, but can be carefully divided in early spring. Deadhead spent flowers for increased bloom. These heads can be dried and used in arrangements and as bird food.

Recommended Varieties

'Magnus' was the Perennial Plant of the Year in 1998. Another big favorite is 'Bravado', with wonderful morning fragrance. 'Bright Star' is also acclaimed. 'White Swan' is a standard white variety.

Other Name: Coneflower

Light Needs:

Added Benefits:

Zones: 7 to 9

Bloom Time: Summer, fall

Bloom Color: Light purple, pink, rose, white

Height: 2 to 4 ft.

Spacing: 2 to 3 ft.

Water Needs: Low/moderate

Soil: Slightly moist, well drained

Uses: Cottage gardens, cutflower gardens, perennial gardens

Did You Know?

Echinacea is Greek for "hedgehog" or "sea urchin."

Color photo on page 135

Purple Heart

Tradescantia pallida

Deep-purple vining foliage graces this plant that is tough as nails as long as it has good drainage. The persistent foliage looks striking for months, disappearing in winter and returning in spring.

How to Grow

'Purple Heart' is drought tolerant and thrives in poorer soils if well drained. Companion plants may not appreciate such a rugged environment. Prepare beds as if for them—'Purple Heart' will thrive there, too! Incorporate 3 to 4 inches of organic matter, along with 2 pounds of slow-release 12-6-6 fertilizer per 100 square feet. Space 12 to 14 inches apart, planting at the same depth they were growing in the containers. Water deeply; mulch.

Companion Planting

If you ever thought you might not have a green thumb, plant 'Purple Heart' in front of a group of 'New Gold' lantana, and behind the lantana plant a clump or two of purple fountain grass. This will make your neighbors jealous of your apparent expertise. Other good companion plants are melampodium, narrowleaf zinnias, and pink verbenas like 'Port Gibson' and 'Temari'.

Care and Maintenance

Remove dead foliage after it freezes, and apply a layer of protective mulch. Tip-prune during the year to increase bushiness. In early spring when growth emerges, feed with a light application of the above fertilizer. Stems are easy to root for additional plants around the landscape.

Recommended Varieties

'Purple Heart' has been called "setcreasea," and is still sometimes sold by that name. Other related *Tradescantias* perform well, such as spiderwort *Tradescantia virginiana* and the not-so-hardy 'Wandering Jew' *Tradescantia fluminensis*.

Other Name:
Setcreasea

Light Needs:

Zones: 7 to 9

Bloom Time:
Grown for foliage

Bloom Color: Blue

Height: 12 to 18 in.

Spacing: 12 to 14 in.

Water Needs:
Low/moderate

Soil:
Slightly moist,
well-drained

Uses:
Borders, rock gardens,
baskets, containers

Did You Know?

The 'Purple Heart' is native to the Yucatan.

Color photo on page 135

Russian Sage

Perovskia atripilicifolia

'Russian Sage' was the 1995 Perennial Plant of the Year, with blue spiky flowers and olive gray-green foliage. The foliage and flowers look good in vase arrangements.

How to Grow

Choose a site in full sun. Prepare beds by adding 3 to 4 inches of organic matter (like fine pine bark or compost), along with 2 pounds of slow-release 12-6-6 fertilizer per 100 square feet, tilling to a depth of 8 to 10 inches. Set out nursery-grown transplants 24 inches apart and at the same depth they were growing in the containers. Water and mulch.

Companion Planting

'Russian Sage', with its light-blue flowers, looks great planted behind 'Moonbeam' coreopsis. Try growing behind 'Lemon Drop' lantana or 'Port Gibson' verbena. The 'Purple Heart' looks good as an understory plant. Low-growing pink ground-cover roses like 'Baby Blanket' look good in front of 'Russian Sage'.

Care and Maintenance

'Russian Sage' should be cut back in winter or early spring to stimulate a new flush of growth and blooms. After cutting back, side-dress with a light application of the above fertilizer. Some complain that it gets leggy during the growing season, but light pruning will keep it bushy and blooming, and will encourage it to bloom right through fall. It can be propagated by cuttings or division. Flowers are good for cutting and drying.

Recommended Varieties

In Mississippi it is still found mostly as a generic plant, but occasionally 'Blue Haze', 'Blue Mist', and 'Filagran' are seen.

Light Needs:

Added Benefits:

Zones: 7 to 9

Bloom Time: Summer, fall

Bloom Color: Shades of blue

Height: 3 to 4 ft.

Spacing: 2 ft.

Water Needs: Low/moderate

Soil: Slightly moist, well-drained

Uses: Cottage gardens, back of the perennial border

Did You Know?

The 'Russian Sage' isn't a sage, and it isn't from Russia. Its home is Pakistan.

Color photo on page 135

Stokes Aster

Other Name:
Cornflower Aster

Light Needs:

Added Benefits:

Zones: 7 to 9

Bloom Time: Summer

Bloom Color: Blue, purple, white

Height: 1 to 2 ft.

Spacing: 12 to 18 in.

Water Needs: Moderate

Soil: Moist, well drained

Uses: Sunny borders of perennial gardens

Did You Know?
These cutflowers have a long vase life.

Color photo on page 135

Stokesia laevis

Large 3- to 4-inch-wide blue flowers adorn this plant from late spring through summer. This wonderful plant is native and can be seen growing along our highways.

How to Grow
Choose a site in full sun for best bloom; partial shade is tolerated. Make sure beds are well drained, incorporating 3 to 4 inches of organic matter like fine pine bark, humus, or compost. Till to a depth of 8 to 10 inches and add 2 pounds of a slow-release 12-6-6 fertilizer. Plant from nursery-grown transplants in the spring and set out at the same depth they were growing in the containers. Complete the job by watering deeply and applying mulch.

Companion Planting
Plant in bold drifts adjacent to large marigolds like 'Antigua' or 'Marvel'. Lantanas like 'Lemon Drop' or 'Silver Mound' also look good with the 'Stokes Aster'. Pink-colored verbenas or petunias make another nice combination.

Care and Maintenance
When growth emerges in the spring, feed with a light application of the above fertilizer, and again in midsummer. When stalks have finished blooming, cut them back to the base, even with the plant. They sometimes rest in summer to bloom again in the fall. They form large clumps that are easy to divide in early spring. Go into the winter tidy, with a protective layer of mulch.

Recommended Varieties
Generic seems to be most prevalent, but varieties like 'Blue Danube' (lavender blue), 'Bluestone' (blue) and 'Klaus Jelitto' (light blue), 'Wyoming' (purple), and 'Silver Moon' (white) are most worthy of purchase.

Summer Phlox

Phlox paniculata

Tall, fragrant, rich-colored flowers make the summer phlox an old-fashioned beloved perennial. Great for cutting, they bloom for months!

How to Grow

Plant in plenty of sun, with a little afternoon shade protection. Prepare beds by adding 3 to 4 inches of organic matter like fine pine bark and incorporating 2 pounds per 100 square feet of a slow-release 12-6-6 fertilizer. Till 8 to 10 inches deep. Plant as soon as they are available at garden centers, or divide clumps in early spring when growth has resumed. Plant at the same depth they were growing in the containers. Space plants to allow good air circulation. Water deeply and mulch.

Companion Planting

Plant magenta, pink, and purple summer phlox to the back of the border with black-eyed Susans in front or adjacent. Phlox and old garden roses, or groundcover roses, combine for an "Old Southern" look. Try planting 'Stella d'Oro' daylilies massed in front.

Care and Maintenance

In spring, side-dress with a light application of the above fertilizer, and again in midsummer. Keep them deadheaded and you will have flower production longer than you expect. Stake for support if they get tall. Should powdery mildew occur, spray with a recommended fungicide. Clumps will have to be divided every three years. Be a good neighbor and give some away.

Recommended Varieties

'Eva Collum' (pink with a dark eye), 'Franz Schubert' (lilac with a dark eye), 'Blue Boy' (lavender-blue), 'Pinafore Pink' (pale pink), and 'Starfire' (red) are commonly seen. Old-fashioned magentas are still among the best.

Other Name:
Perennial Phlox

Light Needs:

Added Benefits:

Zones: 7 to 9

Bloom Time: Summer, fall

Bloom Color: Pink, white, magenta, blue, red

Height: 2 to 4 ft.

Spacing: 12 to 24 in.

Water Needs: Moderate

Soil: Moist, well drained

Uses: Cottage gardens, back of the perennial border

Did You Know?

Phlox drummondii is an old-fashioned garden annual

Color photo on page 135

Verbena

Other Name:
Garden Verbena

Light Needs:
☼

Added Benefits:

Zones: 7 to 9

Bloom Time:
Spring, summer, fall

Bloom Color:
Many shades and blends, none yellow

Height: 6 to 18 in.

Spacing: 12 to 24 in.

Water Needs:
Low/moderate

Soil:
Moist, well-drained

Uses: Cottage gardens, edging and middle of the perennial border, baskets, containers

Did You Know?
The verbena family includes lantana, vitex tree, and clerodendrons.

Color photo on page 136

Verbena × hybrida

Verbenas are one of the most colorful, long-blooming, useful landscape plants, treasured by gardeners and butterflies.

How to Grow
Plant in full sun. Verbenas thrive in deep well-drained beds rich in organic matter. Spread 3 to 4 inches of fine pine bark or compost, along with 2 pounds of slow-release 12-6-6 fertilizer, tilling to a depth of 8 to 12 inches. Verbenas are spreading plants, so space accordingly. Some are upright, reaching 18 inches, others much shorter. Set out plants at the same depth they were growing in the container, then water and mulch.

Companion Planting
Mass-plant for the best show. 'Homestead Purple', 'New Gold' lantana, and 'Plum Delight' buddleia not only look good but create butterfly heaven. Verbenas like 'Biloxi Blue', 'Temari Violet', and 'Homestead Purple' look great with black-eyed Susans. Pair pink verbenas like 'Port Gibson' and 'Temari Patio Pink' with 'Purple Wave' petunias.

Care and Maintenance
Side-dress with a light application of the above fertilizer at spring growth, and every four to six weeks during the growing season. Deadhead to keep flowers coming. In midsummer, cut back by one-third to renew growth and blooms. Water during dry periods and maintain a good layer of mulch.

Recommended Varieties
Biloxi Blue was a 1999 Mississippi Medallion winner, growing 18 inches tall and spreading. 'Homestead Purple' (a Georgia Gold Medal and Louisiana Select winner), 'Port Gibson' (pink and white), 'Tiger Rose' (light purple and blue), 'Rose King' (light purple), 'Taylortown Red', 'Temari' series, and 'Tapien' series are all good. Look for 'Babylon', and 'Tortuga' series in 2000.

Victoria

Salvia farinacea

This is one of the prettiest easy-to-grow blue flowers. It is not uncommon to see the flower spike reaching three feet in height, buzzing with bees or butterflies.

How to Grow

Choose a site in full sun with well-drained soil. Prepare the bed deeply, spreading a 3- to 4-inch layer of organic matter, along with 2 pounds of slow-release 12-6-6 fertilizer per 100 square feet, tilling to a depth of 8 to 10 inches. Plant nursery-grown transplants after the soil has warmed. Set out at the same depth they were growing in the containers, water deeply, and add a layer of mulch.

Companion Planting

'Victoria' looks great massed with 'New Gold', 'Radiation', or 'Spreading Sunset' lantanas. It also looks exceptionally nice planted with 'Pink Wave' or 'Rose Wave' petunia. Melampodiums are great companions for 'Victoria'. Try massing 'Burgundy Sun' coleus with 'Victoria' planted in front.

Care and Maintenance

When growth emerges in the spring, side-dress with a light application of the above fertilizer, and again in May and July. Keep deadheaded, and don't hesitate to prune back to generate new growth or bushiness. Victoria is perennial most winters. Add a protective layer of mulch in the fall, as temperatures of 10 degrees Fahrenheit or below usually prove fatal. It is a great plant, even treated as an annual.

Recommended Varieties

'Victoria' was a 1998 Mississippi Medallion winner and will always be a standout performer. 'Blue Bedder' (medium-blue), 'Porcelain' (gray-white), and the All-America Selections winner 'Strata' (blue and gray) are other choices.

Other Names:
Mealycup Sage

Light Needs:

Added Benefits:

Zones: (7), 8, 9

Bloom Time:
Spring, summer, fall

Bloom Color: Blue

Height: 18 to 36 in.

Spacing: 12 to 24 in.

Water Needs:
Moderate

Soil:
Moist, well drained

Uses: Cottage gardens, middle of the perennial border

Did You Know?
The mealycup sage is native to Texas.

Color photo on page 136

*Mississippi is a state with
a rich gardening history, from
large antebellum homes
with formal gardens to small
cottage gardens with plantings
that would make a botanical
garden cry in envy . . .*

Ageratum
Ageratum houstonianum

Angelonia
Angelonia angustifolia

Begonia
Begonia semperflorens–Cultorum Hybrids

Black-Eyed Susan
Rudbeckia hirta

Blue Daze
Evolvulus pilosus

Celosia
Celosia argentea

Cleome
Cleome hassleriana

Coleus
Coleus × hybridus

Cosmos
Cosmos sulphureus

Dianthus
Dianthus chinensis

Flowering Kale and Cabbage
Brassica oleracea

Geranium
Pelargonium × hortorum

Gomphrena
Gomphrena globosa

Impatiens
Impatiens wallerana

Marigold
Tagetes species

Melampodium
Melampodium paludosum

Mexican Heather
Cuphea hyssopifolia

MillionBells
Calibracoa × hybrida

Narrow-Leaf Zinnia
Zinnia angustifolia

Ornamental Sweet Potato
Ipomoea batatas

Pansy
Viola wittrockiana

Periwinkle
Catharanthus roseus

Petunia
Petunia × hybrida

Portulaca
Portulaca grandiflora

Salvia
Salvia splendens

Scaevola
Scaevola aemula

Snapdragon
Antirrhinum majus

Sunflower
Helianthus annuus

Viola
Viola cornuta

Zinnia
Zinnia elegans

Amaryllis
Hippeastrum species and hybrids

Bearded Iris
Iris × germanica

Caladium
Caladium bicolor

Canna
Canna × generalis

Crinum
Crinum species and hybrids

Gladiolus
Gladiolus × hortulanus

Louisiana Iris
Iris species and hybrids

Monbretia
Crocosmia × crocosmiiflora

Narcissus
Narcissus species

Siberian Iris
Iris sibirica × I. Sanguinea hybrids

Snowflake
Leucojum aestivum

Spider Lily
Lycoris radiata

Ajuga
Ajuga reptans

Asian Jasmine
Trachelospermum asiaticum

'Bath's Pink' Dianthus
Dianthus gratianopolitanus

Common Periwinkle
Vinca minor

Creeping Phlox
Phlox subulata

English Ivy
Hedera helix

Juniper
Juniperus species

Liriope
Liriope spicata

Monkey Grass
Ophiopogon japonicus

Wood Ferns
Dryopteris species

Artemesia
Artemesia species

Basil
Ocimum basilicum

Borage
Borago officinalis

Catmint
Nepeta species

Chives
Allium schoenoprasum

Cilantro
Coriandrum sativum

Dill
Anethum graveolens

Fennel
Foeniculum vulgare

Lemon Balm
Melissa officinalis

Oregano
Origanum vulgare

Parsley
Petroselinum crispum

Pineapple Sage
Salvia elegans

Rosemary
Rosmarinus officinalis

Scented Geranium
Pelargonium species

Thyme
Thymus species

Yarrow
Achillea millefolium

Black-Eyed Susan
Rudbeckia fulgida 'Goldsturm'

Blue Anise Sage
Salvia guaranitica

Butterfly Weed
Asclepias tuberosa

Coreopsis
Coreopsis species

Daylily
Hemerocallis hybrids

Hibiscus
Hibiscus species and hybrids

Hostas
Hosta species and hybrids

Indigo Spires
Salvia farinacea × *S. longispicata*

Lantana
Lantana × *hybrida*

Liatris
Liatris spicata

Louisiana Phlox
Phlox divaricata

Purple Coneflower
Echinacea purpurea

Purple Heart
Tradescantia pallisa

Russian Sage
Perovskia atripilicifolia

Stokes Aster
Stokesia laevis

Summer Phlox
Phlox paniculata

Verbena
Verbena × hybrida

Victoria
Salvia farinacea

Antique and Species Roses
Rosa species and hybrids

Climbing Rose
Rosa × hybrida

Floribunda Rose
Rosa × hybrida

Grandiflora Rose
Rosa × hybrida

Groundcover Rose
Rosa × hybrida

Hybrid Tea Rose
Rosa × hybrida

Miniature Rose
Rosa × hybrida

Shrub Rose
Rosa × hybrida

Boxwood
Buxus microphylla

Chinese Holly
Ilex cornuta

Chinese Juniper
Juniperus chinensis

False Holly
Osmanthus species

Holly Hybrids
Ilex × species

Japanese Aucuba
Aucuba japonica

Japanese Barberry
Berberis thunbergii

Japanese Fatsia
Fatsia japonica

Japanese Ligustrum
Ligustrum japonicum

Japanese Ternstroemia
Ternstroemia japonica

Japanese Viburnum
Viburnum japonicum

Japanese Yew
Podocarpus macrophyllus

Mahonia
Mahonia species

Nandina
Nandina domestica

Wax Myrtle
Myrica cerifera

Possumhaw Holly
Ilex decidua

Azalea
Rhododendron species

Bottlebrush Buckeye
Aesculus parviflora

Bridal Wreath Spiraea
Spiraea × vanhouttei

Butterfly Bush
Buddleia davidii

Camellia
Camellia japonica and *sasanqua*

Flowering Quince
Chaenomeles speciosa

Forsythia
Forsythia × intermedia

Gardenia
Gardenia jasminoides

Glossy Abelia
Abelia × grandiflora

Hydrangea
Hydrangea macrophylla

Indian Hawthorn
Rhaphiolepis indica

Loropetalum
Loropetalum chinense var. rubrum

Mock Orange
Philadelphus coronarius

Oakleaf Hydrangea
Hydrangea quercifolia

Rose-of-Sharon
Hibiscus syriacus

Virginia Sweetspire
Itea virginica

American Holly
Ilex opaca

Bald Cypress
Taxodium distichum

Chinese Pistache
Pistacia chinensis

Eastern Red Cedar
Juniperus virginiana

Ginkgo
Ginkgo biloba

Japanese Maple
Acer palmatum

Lacebark Elm
Ulmus parvifolia

Red Maple
Acer rubrum

River Birch
Betula nigra

Shumard Oak
Quercus shumardii

Spruce Pine
Pinus glabra

Southern Live Oak
Quercus virginiana

Sweetgum
Liquidambar stryaciflua

Willow Oak
Quercus phellos

Crape Myrtle
Lagerstroemia indica × *L. fauriei* hybrids

Dogwood
Cornus florida

Golden Raintree
Koelreuteria paniculata

Grancy Graybeard
Chionanthus virginicus

Japanese Magnolia
Magnolia soulangiana

Ornamental Pear
Pyrus calleryana

Redbud
Cercis canadensis

Southern Magnolia
Magnolia grandiflora

Taiwan Flowering Cherry
Prunus campanulata

Vitex
Vitex agnus-castus

Allamanda
Allamanda cathartica

Banana
Musa species

Bougainvillea
Bougainvillea species

Butterfly Ginger
Hedychium coronarium

Chinese Hibiscus
Hibiscus rosa-sinensis

Citrus
Citrus species

Crepe Ginger
Costus speciosus

Croton
Codiaeum variegatum

Hidden Ginger
Curcuma petiolata

Mandevilla
Mandevilla species

Night Jasmine
Cestrum nocturnum

Scarlet Ginger
Hedychium coccineum

Variegated Shell Ginger
Alpinia zerumbet variegata

Yellow Shrimp Plant
Pachystachys lutea

Black-Eyed Susan Vine
Thunbergia alata

Carolina Jessamine
Gelsemium sempervirens

Clematis
Clematis species and hybrids

Coral Honeysuckle
Lonicera sempervirens

Coral Vine
Antigonon leptopus

Crossvine
Bignonia capreolata

Hyacinth Bean
Lablab purpureus

Moon Vine
Ipomea alba

Trumpet Vine
Campsis radicans

Wisteria
Wisteria sinensis

Many Mississippians consider the camellia the "Queen" of flowering shrubs.

COLOR WHEEL FOR
SELECTING COMPANION PLANTS

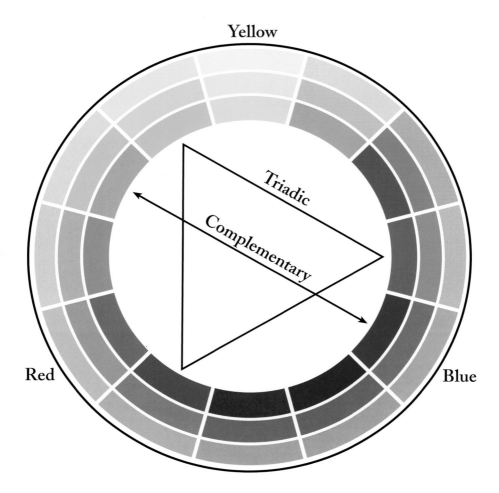

1. The most basic color scheme is **monochromatic**, in which all the flowers are the same color, or lighter or darker shades of the same color.

2. When you use colors next to each other on the color wheel, you are using an **analogous** color scheme, in which the colors have similar tones that visually tie them together.

3. When you use colors directly opposite each other on the color wheel, you are using the attractive **complementary** color scheme.

4. Use three or four colors that are equal distances apart on the color wheel, and you have created a scheme or harmony called **triadic** or **quadratic** (depending on the number of colors used).

The shade provided by trees in Mississippi is one of life's memorable pleasures . . .

ROSES

The Greek poetess Sappho proclaimed the rose the Queen of Flowers. Ronald Reagan signed a proclamation making the rose our National Flower. Indeed, it is a rare gardener who hasn't longed for a rose garden and basketfuls of cut roses.

Nurseries, garden centers, and even catalogs sell roses that can be planted successfully with a little careful consideration. Roses are graded, with 1 being the best, so look for those that are graded 1 to $1^1/2$ to ensure getting a rose that will give you extended pleasure.

Whether your plantings are bare root or container grown, much of your success will depend on soil preparation before planting. Improve the existing soil by adding large amounts of organic matter like peat, compost, or humus. Good drainage is essential, so plant in raised beds.

Before planting bare-root roses, soak the roots overnight. Trim off any broken roots, and prune the tips of any branches which may have been damaged.

Roses need five to six hours of direct sun each day. Morning sun is essential, but afternoon shade is tolerated. Good air movement helps the dew and rain dry quickly, thus discouraging disease.

Avoid planting under eaves or gutters where bushes can be damaged by falling water. Plant your roses where they are easy for you to watch, enjoy, and be aware of any insect or disease problems.

Dig the planting hole large enough and deep enough to accommodate all the roots without crowding them. Mound soil in the bottom of the hole to form the shape of a cone. Spread the roots carefully over the firmed cone of soil. If you are planting a container-grown rose, make a flat mound in the center of the hole to hold the rootball.

Fill in with a mixture of equal parts organic matter and soil, packing the medium gently but firmly around the roots. Make sure the bud union (where the top of the plant was grafted to

> There is sure to be a rose that will fit your style.

the rootstock) is at least one inch above the soil level to allow for settling.

Water the plant thoroughly to eliminate any air pockets in the soil. Watering with a soaker hose or drip irrigation during the growing season will keep foliage dryer and help in disease control.

There are some great roses available—from the hybrid teas and grandifloras that require a little vigilance, to floribundas where the disease pressure is lighter. Thousands of miniature roses have hit the market since the 1980s and can be used as perennials. Landscapers are now using shrub roses and groundcover roses as they would azaleas. The roses of yesteryear, or antique roses, have captured the imagination of today's gardeners with their beauty, form, and fragrance, as they surely did for our grandparents. You may choose a formal rose garden or decide to incorporate these beauties into an existing landscape. Pruning is usually done from mid-February to early March. Each class of rose calls for a specific pruning method determined by the rose's form and whether or not it repeats bloom. Pruning techniques for each class will be given on the following pages.

The fertilization of roses should be based on a soil test. Normal application times are at bud break, at formation of first rosebuds, and then every six weeks until two months before the first fall frost.

Tree roses are gaining wide acceptance by home gardeners for their elegant and statuesque appearance in both landscape and container. It is not uncommon to find hybrid teas, grandifloras, floribundas, and miniatures in tree form also called "standards."

> If you are looking for vigor and fragrance, try one of the David Austin English Roses.

Antique and Species Roses

Rosa species and hybrids

Light Needs:

☀

Added Benefits:

Zones: 7 to 9

Bloom Time:
Spring, summer, fall

Bloom Color:
Pink, purple, white,
yellow, red, and blends

Height: 4 to 20 ft

Water Needs:
Moderate

Soil:
Moist, well drained

Uses:
Rose gardens, cottage
gardens, climbers

Did You Know?

The largest rose in the
world is a 'Lady Banks'
in Tucson, Arizona.

Color photo on page 136

If you remember a fragrant rose growing outside grandmother's porch, you may be pleasantly surprised to discover that very rose is available today.

How to Grow

Choose a site in full sun, and plant on raised organically amended beds (refer to planting technique in chapter introduction on pages 146–147).

Care and Maintenance

Fertilize in late winter and every 6 weeks with a light application of 12-6-6 slow-release fertilizer, finishing in August. Leaves are most susceptible to disease in their first two weeks of growth—an ideal time (along with the conclusion of rainy period) to apply fungicide. Water roses from underneath with a wand, soaker hose, or drip system.

Pruning

Remove dead and diseased canes. Cut back vigorous canes by one-third. One-time bloomers should be pruned after they bloom.

Recommended Varieties

'Mutablis' (1896), the butterfly rose, is easy to grow and changes colors. 'The Fairy' (1932), a polyantha rose, and species roses like 'Lady Banks' (*R. banksiae*) and the 'Chestnut Rose' (*R. roxburghii*) are disease resistant. 'Mrs. B.R. Cant', is a fragrant 1901 tea rose. Favorite fragrant bourbon roses are 'Souvenir de la Malmaison' (1843), 'Madame Isaac Periere' (1881), and the thornless climber 'Zephirine Drouhin' (1868). Some hybrid perpetuals, which are not perpetual, but are drop-dead gorgeous, have fragrance too!

Climbing Rose

Rosa × hybrida

Climbing roses don't really climb, but will adorn a picket fence, arbor, or trellis like no other plant.

How to Grow

Choose a site in full sun, and plant on raised beds rich in organic matter. See planting technique in chapter introduction (pages 146–147).

Care and Maintenance

Feed in late winter with a light application of a 12-6-6 fertilizer, then every six weeks through August. With the first spring growth, apply a coating of systemic fungicide. Spray after rainy periods and with each new flush of growth.

Pruning

Train climbers to a support structure. After planting, long canes will form, but don't prune during the first two years other than to remove dead wood or make the training cuts. The goal is to develop long, bendable canes. Tie one or two along the fence or trellis. As the canes are tied outward, lateral buds will form, eventually forming lateral branches that will perform like regular roses growing out of the ground. In February, prune back these lateral branches to within three buds of the long cane. When deadheading, cut back to a five- or seven-leaf leaflet to encourage new growth and blooms. Prune by one-third in August for superior fall bloom. Climbers that bloom only once should be pruned afterward. At some point old, woody, unproductive canes will have to be removed to make way for new vigorous ones.

Recommended Varieties

'Blaze' (red) is one of the best; 'Altissimo' and 'Don Juan' are also highly rated among natural climbers. Sports of other classes have yielded climbers such as 'Climbing Double Delight' and 'Climbing Queen Elizabeth'.

Other Name:
Ramblers

Light Needs:

Added Benefits:

Zones: 7 to 9

Bloom Time:
Spring, summer, and fall

Bloom Color:
Many colors and blends

Height: 10 to 20 ft.

Water Needs:
Moderate/frequent

Soil:
Moist, well drained

Uses:
Trellis, arbor, pergola, tower, fence

Did You Know?

A sport is a mutation, or a change in growth pattern such as when a hybrid tea sends out a climbing cane.

Color photo on page 136

Floribunda Rose

Rosa × hybrida

Floribundas are among the most beautiful flowers in the world, with many clusters of blooms opening at once.

How to Grow
Choose a site in full sun on raised beds rich in organic matter. Spread a 3- to 4-inch layer of organic matter like fine pine bark and peat, and till to a depth of 8 to 10 inches, incorporating 3 pounds of a slow-release 5-10-5 fertilizer per 100 square feet. Refer to planting techniques in chapter introduction (pages 146–147), spacing 3 to 4 feet apart.

Care and Maintenance
Floribundas get blackspot but show some tolerance. Keeping the leaves dry is important. Water from underneath, and space plants for maximum air circulation. Young leaves going through expansion are most susceptible. Spray after rainy periods and with each flush of growth. Apply light applications of a slow-release 12-6-6 fertilizer every six weeks through August.

Pruning
Prune floribundas hard in mid-February, cutting back by at least 50 percent. Remove dead and diseased wood, and twiggy interior growth, leaving six to eight good canes about 14 to 18 inches tall. Top cuts should be at a 45-degree angle just above an outward-facing bud. When deadheading, cut just above a leaflet that has five or more leaves.

Recommended Varieties
'Sunsprite' and 'Sun Flare', both yellow and beautiful, are recommended for novice growers. 'Livin' Easy' (orange), 'Apricot Nectar' (pink apricot, gold blend), 'Bill Warriner' (coral), and 'Showbiz' (red) are other good choices.

Light Needs:

☼

Added Benefits:

Zones: 7 to 9

Bloom Time:
Spring, summer, fall

Bloom Color:
Many colors and blends

Height: 2 to 4 ft.

Water Needs:
Moderate/frequent

Soil:
Moist, well drained

Uses:
Formal rose garden, accent, flower bed, containers

Did You Know?
A floribunda is a cross between a hybrid tea and a polyantha.

Color photo on page 136

Grandiflora Rose

Rosa × hybrida

Grandifloras, with their huge flowers, have the best traits of hybrid teas and floribundas.

How to Grow

Choose a site in full sun. Build the bed up above the soil line, adding a 3- to 4-inch layer of organic matter like fine pine bark, compost, or humus. Till to a depth of 8 to 10 inches. Incorporate 3 pounds of slow-release 5-10-5 per 100 square feet. Refer to techniques in chapter introduction (pages 146–147), spacing plants 4 to 6 feet apart.

Care and Maintenance

After pruning, feed with a light application of 12-6-6 fertilizer every six weeks, ending in August. With the first growth, apply a coating of systemic fungicide. Spray after rainy periods and with each flush of growth. When deadheading, cut back to a five- or seven-leaf leaflet to encourage new growth and blooms.

Pruning

Grandiflora maintenance is similar to that of hybrid teas, except for pruning. Prune in mid- to late February, removing at least 50 percent of the plant. Remove all dead and diseased wood and internal twiggy growth. The goal is to leave six to eight thick canes cut back to 18 inches. The top cuts should be at a 45-degree angle just above an outward-facing bud. Pruning by one-third is also done in August for superior fall bloom.

Recommended Varieties

'Gold Medal' (yellow), 'Arizona' (orange and yellow blend), 'Shreveport' (orange), 'Tournament of Roses' (pink), 'Caribbean' (orange and yellow blend), 'Queen 'Elizabeth' (pink), and 'Candelabra' (coral-orange) are well-respected grandifloras.

Light Needs:

Added Benefits:

Zones: 7 to 9

Bloom Time: Spring, summer, fall

Bloom Color: All shades, colors and blends

Height: 4 to 6 ft.

Water Needs: Moderate/frequent

Soil: Moist, well drained

Uses: Formal rose garden, flower garden, accent

Did You Know?

The grandiflora class made its debut in 1954 with the rose 'Queen Elizabeth'.

Color photo on page 136

Groundcover Rose

Rosa × hybrida

Roses have been used for a long time as ground covers, but the term "groundcover rose" has just now become popular. Many of these roses are the easiest and showiest to grow.

How to Grow

Prepare your groundcover rose bed by incorporating 3 to 4 inches of organic matter, along with 3 pounds of a slow-release 5-10-5 fertilizer per 100 square feet, tilling to a depth of 8 to 10 inches. Groundcover roses reach 3 feet in height and spread. Plant your roses according to the technique described in chapter introduction (pages 146–147), spacing them 3 to 4 feet apart. Water after planting, and apply a good layer of mulch.

Care and Maintenance

Feed with a light application of slow-release 12-6-6 fertilizer after pruning, and side-dress every six weeks through August. Many of the groundcover roses require minimal spraying. Apply a fungicide with the first new flush of growth and after rainy periods. Monitor roses often to know when to spray.

Pruning

Pruning the groundcover rose is quite easy. Remove any dead or diseased wood. When pruning, reduce size by about 50 percent, maintaining the natural shape. Removing old canes will eventually be necessary to generate lush new growth and blooms. To encourage a better fall bloom, lightly prune again in mid-August by 10 or 15 percent.

Recommended Varieties

'The Fairy' is an old-fashioned polyantha that serves well as a ground cover. Other good choices are 'Nearly Wild', 'Flower Carpet', 'Rosey Carpet', and 'Baby Blanket'.

Light Needs:

Added Benefits:

Zones: 7 to 9

Bloom Time:
Spring, summer, fall

Bloom Color:
Pink, white, red, yellow

Height: 2 to 3 ft.

Water Needs:
Moderate/frequent

Soil:
Moist, well drained

Uses: Ground cover, low hedge

Did You Know?
There are over 15,000 known varieties of roses.

Color photo on page 136

Hybrid Tea Rose

Rosa × *hybrida*

The first hybrid tea, 'La France', made its debut in 1867.

How to Grow

Prepare beds by incorporating 3 to 4 inches of organic matter like fine pine bark, compost, or humus, along with 3 pounds of a slow-release 5-10-5 fertilizer per 100 square feet. Till to a depth of 8 to 10 inches. Set out according to the technique in chapter introduction (pages 146–147). Space plants to allow maximum air circulation (4 ft apart). Water deeply and mulch.

Care and Maintenance

Fungicides control blackspot—the lush post-pruning growth is especially susceptible. Spray after rainy periods and with each new flush of growth. During the summer, apply water only beneath the plants. Feed with a light application of 12-6-6 fertilizer after pruning, then every six weeks through August.

Pruning

Prune in mid-February. Remove diseased and dead wood, and internal twiggy growth, cutting the plant back by at least 50 percent and leaving four to six good canes at 12 to 14 inches. The top cuts should be at a 45-degree angle just above an outward-facing bud. In August, prune by one-third to generate bloom for fall. When deadheading, cut to just above a leaflet with five to seven leaves.

Recommended Varieties

Fragrant 'Mr. Lincoln' (red) and 'Double Delight' (red and white) remain highly popular. Pristine (white-pink blend), 'Touch of Class' (orange-pink blend), and 'Rio Samba' (orange-red-yellow blend) are personal favorites.

Light Needs:

Added Benefits:

Zones: 7 to 9

Bloom Time: Spring, summer, fall

Bloom Color: Many colors and blends

Height: 3 to 6 ft.

Water Needs: Moderate/frequent

Soil: Moist, well drained

Uses: Formal rose garden, perennial garden

Did You Know?

The hybrid tea is a cross between the tea rose and the hybrid perpetual.

Color photo on page 136

Miniature Rose

Added Benefits:

Zones: 7 to 9

Bloom Time:
Spring, summer, fall

Bloom Color:
Many colors and blends

Height: 12 to 24 in.

Water Needs:
Moderate/frequent

Soil:
Moist, well drained

Uses:
Edging for formal rose
garden, perennial
garden, containers

Did You Know?

It is estimated that
there have been over
2,000 miniatures
hybridized since 1980.

Color photo on page 136

Rosa × hybrida

Miniature roses look just like tiny hybrid teas or floribundas, and act like perennials in the garden. You will love them.

How to Grow

Grow miniatures as edging for rose gardens, perennial gardens, and spot plantings. Prepare your miniature rose bed by incorporating 3 to 4 inches of organic matter and tilling to a depth of 8 to 10 inches. Apply 3 pounds of a slow-release 5-10-5 per 100 square feet of bed space. Plant according to the technique in the chapter introduction (pages 146–147). Space plants 18 to 24 inches apart and water deeply. Apply mulch.

Care and Maintenance

Feed with a light application of 12-6-6 fertilizer after pruning, and every six weeks thereafter through August. Unfortunately, miniatures are susceptible to the same diseases as their larger cousins. Apply a fungicide spray with the first flush of growth after pruning, after rainy periods, and with each flush of growth after deadheading. Water from underneath with a wand or soaker hose to keep leaves dry. Watch for spider mites!

Pruning

Prune miniatures as you do hybrid teas, floribundas, and grandifloras by removing dead and diseased wood and internal twiggy growth. Reduce the plant by 50 percent, leaving four to six good canes. Dispose of all pruned material. Prune by one-third in August to generate more blooms for fall.

Recommended Varieties

There are some outstanding selections. 'Minnie Pearl' (pink), 'Starina' (orange-red), 'Rainbows End' (orange-yellow blend), and 'Hot Tamale' (orange-yellow blend) are just a few.

Shrub Rose

Rosa × hybrida

These are landscape-quality roses that don't need as much pampering as do other classes. Try growing them and you will look like a rose expert.

How to Grow

Good drainage is crucial. Prepare soil by working in 3 to 4 inches of organic matter like composted pine bark and humus. Apply 3 pounds of slow-release 5-10-5 fertilizer per 100 square feet. Till in to a depth of 8 to 10 inches. Plant as instructed in the chapter introduction (pages 146–147), spacing plants 6 to 8 feet apart. After planting, water deeply and apply a layer of mulch.

Care and Maintenance

Feed with light applications of a 12-6-6 fertilizer after pruning and every six weeks through August. Shrub roses are more tolerant of blackspot than hybrid teas, but they still can show signs of the disease's presence. Apply a fungicidal spray with the first spring growth and after unusually heavy rains. The group of shrub roses is growing, and some are more disease susceptible than others. Roses need water during the summer; apply underneath the foliage canopy. Conserve moisture by mulching.

Pruning

Always prune off dead or diseased wood. Shrub roses are usually thinned and shaped to keep the natural form. The most vigorous canes should have about one-third their length removed to generate new growth and blooms.

Recommended Varieties

'Pink Simpliciy', 'Carefree Delight', and 'Carefree Beauty' are outstanding choices. Some of the finest, fragrant and vigorous, are David Austin's English Roses that now total in the hundreds. The Meidiland roses are also widely acclaimed for tough landscape quality.

Light Needs:

Added Benefits:

Zones: 7 to 9

Bloom Time:
Spring, summer, fall

Bloom Color:
All colors and blends

Height: 4 to 8 ft.

Water Needs:
Moderate/frequent

Soil:
Moist, well drained

Uses:
Landscape beds,
rose garden

Did You Know?

The fruit of the rose is the hip. It's high in vitamin C and good for jam, and birds love it.

Color photo on page 136

SHRUBS

One of my favorite landscape architects taught me that we should strive to make our landscape look good in January. If it looks good in the winter, the likelihood increases that it will look good the rest of the year. This cannot be accomplished without shrubs at the center of the plan.

At one time shrubs were used to hide the ugly foundations of a house. While that may still be necessary in some cases, new homes have changed. In today's landscape, shrubs often work better when used to frame other plantings or when used en masse to create a thicket appearance. They lead us toward a path, create a backdrop, or serve to contrast with the color of the flower border.

Gardeners make some common mistakes when using shrubs in the landscape. One is called the "Noah's Ark Syndrome." Somehow gardeners get the urge to plant two of everything. Two shrubs are planted here and two over there, and this is repeated all over the landscape. Perhaps they think a specimen holly might be lonely, so they get two. This leads to design problems. Design possibilities improve when we work with odd numbers such as 3, 5, 7, and 9 when planning the shrub bed.

Another common problem is the "Straight Line Syndrome." Many gardeners feel that everything should be planted in a row. Certainly this formal design has some historical roots, but the landscapes that grab your attention today are those that have bold sweeping curves.

Gardens with curves are reminiscent of Sunday drives in the country, when you think about turning around to go home but drive on to see what is around the next curve. Curves in the landscape hold mystery. Perhaps there is a bench or statue around the corner or some wonderful blooming shrub. Planting in a straight line takes away the mystery.

> We should strive to make our landscapes look good in January.

Landscape designers use a tool called a French Curve to draw curves on paper. You can use a long flexible garden hose in the landscape to shape beds with bold sweeping curves around the corners of your home.

Just as we prepare a bed to sleep in at night, we should prepare a bed for the life of our shrubs, one where weeds and grass have been removed and organic matter has been added to allow for good drainage. Many homeowners find it easiest to have a truckload of specially prepared landscape mixes delivered for the new beds. There are so many shrubs to choose from that it can seem overwhelming. If there were only one group I was permitted to encourage gardeners to plant, it would be hollies. Hollies are real troopers when it comes to taking our climate of extremes. They are tough in our high Mississippi heat and humidity, and they are the ones left standing after record low temperatures. Some of my favorites are the 'Mary Nell', 'Nellie R. Stevens', 'Foster's', and 'Burford' hollies. A new group of 'Mary Nell' seedlings called the 'Red Holly Hybrids' are gaining wide acceptance in Mississippi. They have elegant form and produce berries.

Design possibilities improve when we work with odd numbers such as 3, 5, 7, and 9.

Container-grown shrubs can be planted at just about any time, though spring and fall are the best choices. Dig the planting hole three to five times as large as the rootball but no deeper. Gently tease the roots to break their circular pattern. Should the shrubs be potbound, separate the roots, making three vertical cuts through the root system with a knife. Mulch those beds after planting!

Boxwood

Color photo on page 136

Buxus microphylla

Boxwood has glossy evergreen foliage that is very attractive. It is suitable for use as a specimen or in groups and hedges.

How to Grow

Incorporate 3 to 4 inches of organic matter, along with 2 pounds of 5-10-5 fertilizer per 100 square feet, tilling deeply. Dig the planting hole three to five times as wide as the rootball, but no deeper. Place the plant in the hole and backfill to two-thirds. Tamp the soil firmly and water to settle. Add the remaining backfill, repeat the process, and apply mulch.

Landscape Merit

Use boxwoods as a living wall to border rose gardens, herb gardens, or water features. Use as informal hedges or in small groups of three as a middle layer between a crape myrtle and ground cover. Try boxwoods in decorative containers framing the entrance to your home.

Care and Maintenance

Watch the moisture level during the first year and water deeply when required. Feed four weeks after transplanting with a slow-release balanced fertilizer (like an 8-8-8) at 1 pound per 100 square feet. In beds that are less than three years old, feed as above in March and August, and feed established plantings in March. Light pruning can be done anytime. Make major prunings in late winter.

Recommended Varieties

'Compacta' (less than 24 inches), 'Green Beauty' (3 to 5 ft.), and 'Winter Green' (2 to 4 ft.) are considered some of the best. The English boxwood *B. sempervirens* also has great landscape value.

Other Name:
Littleleaf Boxwood

Light Needs:

Zones: 7 to 9

Flower:
Inconspicuous but fragrant

Height: 2 to 4 ft.

Spacing: 2 to 3 ft.

Water Needs:
Moderate

Soil:
Moist, well drained

Uses:
Specimen, small hedges, formal gardens

Did You Know?

Buxus comes from the Latin term for "box tree."

Chinese Holly

Ilex cornuta

The dark-green glossy foliage and bright-red berries of Chinese holly make the winter landscape come alive.

How to Grow

Plant in full sun to partial shade. Prepare beds by incorporating 3 to 4 inches of organic matter, along with 2 pounds of a 5-10-5 fertilizer per 100 square feet, tilling deeply. Dig the planting hole three to five times wider than the rootball, but no deeper. Place the plant in the hole and backfill to two-thirds. Tamp the soil and water to settle. Add the remaining backfill, repeat, and apply mulch.

Landscape Merit

Chinese hollies have one thing in common: the ability to tolerate our climate. Selections like 'Burford' may grow to 20 feet tall and look great as a tree. As a screen, it's the perfect backdrop for azaleas, the elegant Japanese maple, or summer color. Dwarf selections like 'Dwarf Burford' and 'Carissa' work as specimen plantings and hedges.

Care and Maintenance

Moisture is especially important the first year; water deeply when required. Feed four weeks after transplanting with a slow-release balanced fertilizer like an 8-8-8, at 1 pound per 100 square feet. Feed mature plantings in April and August. Hollies with heavy berry crops need this last application. Make major prunings in late winter, light prunings anytime. Use a dormant oil to control scale.

Recommended Varieties

'Burfordii' (15 to 20 ft.), 'Dwarf Burford' (6 to 8 ft.), 'Carissa' (3 to 4 ft.), 'Needlepoint' (8 to 10 ft.), and 'Rotunda' (3 to 4 ft.) are the leading varieties.

Other Name:
Horned Holly

Light Needs:

Added Benefit:

Zones: 7 to 9

Bloom Time:
Inconspicuous

Bloom Color:
(Red berries)

Height: 3 to 20 ft.

Spacing: 4 to 10 ft.
(variety dependent)

Water Needs:
Moderate

Soil:
Moist, well drained

Did You Know?
Much of the holly's climate toughness comes from a thick, waxy cuticle on the leaf.

Color photo on page 136

Chinese Juniper

Juniperus chinensis

Light Needs:

Zones: 7 to 9

Bloom Time:
Grown for foliage

Bloom Color:
Inconspicuous

Height: 3 to 12 ft.

Spacing: 2 to 10 ft.
(variety dependent)

Water Needs:
Moderate

Soil:
Moist, well drained

Did You Know?

The *Juniperus chinensis* group has ground covers, shrubs, and trees.

Color photo on page 137

Of all the conifers, junipers play the most important role in landscape beautification.

How to Grow

Incorporate 3 to 4 inches of organic matter, along with 2 pounds of 5-10-5 fertilizer per 100 square feet, tilling deeply. Dig the planting hole three to five times as wide as the rootball, but no deeper. Place the plant in the hole and backfill with soil up to two-thirds the depth. Tamp the soil and water to settle. Add the remaining backfill, repeat the process, and apply mulch.

Landscape Merit

Junipers are some of our toughest plants, with the ability to take cold, heat, and drought. Their needle-like foliage and evergreen scent are welcome in the landscape. Many have a blue-green foliage that stands out when planted against dark evergreens. The red leaves of barberry combine wonderfully with junipers. Junipers in the 3- to 5-foot range are excellent choices for framing crape myrtles.

Care and Maintenance

Moisture is especially important the first year; water deeply when required. Feed four weeks after transplanting with a slow-release balanced fertilizer like an 8-8-8, at 1 pound per 100 square feet. Feed established plantings every 8 weeks through September. Watch for spider mites and bagworms, and treat early.

Recommended Varieties

'Armstrongii' (3 to 4 ft.), 'Blue Point' (7 to 8 ft.), 'Hetzii' (10 to 12 ft.), 'Pfitzeriana' (4 to 5 ft.), 'Plumosa' (3 to 4 ft.), and 'Shimpaku' (4 to 5 ft.) are just a few good selections of about a hundred.

SHRUBS

False Holly

Osmanthus species

Tall plants with hollylike foliage and a delightful fragrance make this group worthy of a place in your landscape.

How to Grow
Plant in full sun to partial shade. Plant the fragrant tea olive in a protected area in zones 7 and 8. Prepare soil, incorporating 3 to 4 inches of organic matter, along with 2 pounds of a 5-10-5 fertilizer per 100 square feet, tilling deeply. Dig the planting hole three to five times as wide as the rootball, but no deeper. Place the plant in the hole and backfill to two-thirds. Tamp the soil and water to settle. Finish and apply mulch.

Landscape Merit
Osmanthus offers us the look of a holly, some with bold, striking variegation and others with enticing fragrance. Some are ideal as filler plants between shrubs like azaleas or hydrangeas. The fragrant tea olive, or devilwood, looks great when surrounded by hollies or junipers, and makes excellent screens.

Care and Maintenance
Moisture is especially important the first year; water deeply when required. Feed four weeks after transplanting with a slow-release balanced fertilizer like an 8-8-8, at 1 pound per 100 square feet. In beds less than three years old, feed as above in March and August, and feed established plantings in March. Make major prunings in late winter, light prunings anytime.

Recommended Varieties
Try *O. heterophylus* 'Holly Osmanthus' (8 to 15 ft.), 'Gulftide', 'Goshiki', and 'Variegatus'. Look for *O. fragrans* (fragrant tea olive, 8 to 10 ft.), *O. americanus* (devilwood, 15 to 30 ft.), and *O. × fortunei* (15 to 20 ft.).

Light Needs:

Added Benefit:

Zones:
7 to 9 (varies with species)

Bloom Time:
Spring and summer or fall and winter

Bloom Color:
White

Height: 10 to 20 ft.

Spacing: 4 to 8 ft.

Water Needs:
Moderate

Soil:
Moist, well drained

Did You Know?
The *O. americanus* (also known as American wild olive) has been in cultivation since 1758.

Color photo on page 137

Holly Hybrids

Light Needs:

☀ ◑

Added Benefit:

Zones: 7 to 9

Bloom Time:
Spring

Bloom Color:
Inconspicuous
(red berries)

Height: 6 to 25 ft.

Spacing: 8 to 15 ft.
(variety dependent)

Water Needs:
Moderate

Soil:
Moist, well drained

Did You Know?

The United States National Arboretum plays an important role in releasing new plants such as hollies, hybrid crape myrtles, and many others.

Color photo on page 137

Ilex × species

Hybrids, with their glossy leaves, berries, and conical form, are among the hollies most prized by landscapers.

How to Grow

Incorporate 3 to 4 inches of organic matter, along with 2 pounds of 5-10-5 fertilizer per 100 square feet, tilling deeply. Dig the planting hole three to five times as wide as the rootball, but no deeper. Place the plant in the hole and backfill to two-thirds. Tamp the soil and water to settle. Add the remaining backfill, repeat the process, and apply mulch.

Landscape Merit

The natural shape of many holly hybrids offers a look that is unmatched: glossy green leaves and berries on tall Christmas tree–like shrubs. Try three triangular clusters of three surrounded by azaleas, with redbuds or dogwoods between the groups. Use at corners to naturally lengthen the front of your home.

Care and Maintenance

Moisture is especially important the first year; water deeply when required. Feed four weeks after transplanting with a slow-release balanced fertilizer like an 8-8-8, at 1 pound per 100 square feet. Feed established plantings in April and August. Hollies with heavy berry crops need this last application. Make major prunings in late winter, light prunings anytime. Use dormant oil for scale.

Recommended Varieties

Look for 'Fosters' *I.* × *attenuata* (20 to 25 ft.), 'Mary Nell' (6 to 12 ft.), and 'Nellie R. Stevens' (10 to 15 ft.). Try some of the new Red Holly Hybrids: 'Little Red' (10 ft.), 'Robin' (14 ft.), 'Festive' (12 ft.), 'Cardinal' (14 ft.), 'Oakleaf' (14 ft.), 'Patriot' (12 ft.), and 'Liberty' (14 ft.).

Japanese Aucuba

Aucuba japonica

Aucuba often has brightly colored leaf variegation and will give life to shady spots around your home. It is easier to grow than you may think.

How to Grow
Plant in partial to full shade. Incorporate 3 to 4 inches of organic matter, and 2 pounds of a 5-10-5 fertilizer per 100 square feet, tilling deeply. Dig the planting hole three to five times as wide as the root-ball, but no deeper. Place the plant in the hole and backfill to two-thirds. Tamp the soil and water to settle. Add the remaining backfill, repeat the process, and apply mulch.

Landscape Merit
Aucuba is the best shrub for giving year-round color to shady areas of the landscape. Bold, brightly variegated foliage makes the plants wonderful as accents. Plant groups around fatsia for a tropical look. Fuchsia impatiens look nice in front of the more brightly variegated forms.

Care and Maintenance
Moisture is especially important the first year; water deeply when required. Feed four weeks after transplanting with a slow-release balanced fertilizer like an 8-8-8, at 1 pound per 100 square feet. In beds less than three years old, feed as above in March and August, and feed established plantings in March. Light pruning can be done anytime to improve. Make your cut just above a leaf. Watch for mealybugs and spider mites and treat early.

Recommended Varieties
'Picturata', 'Sulphur', 'Serratifolia', and 'Variegata' (all 6 to 10 ft.) are the most common varieties, though often sold generic as Gold Dust Aucuba.

Other Name:
Spotted Laurel

Light Needs:

Zones: 7 to 9

Bloom Time:
Spring

Bloom Color:
Maroon (followed by berries)

Height: 6 to 8 ft.

Spacing: 3 to 4 ft.

Water Needs:
Low/moderate

Soil:
Slightly moist, well drained

Did You Know?
If your aucuba doesn't produce berries, it may be because it is a male plant.

Color photo on page 137

Japanese Barberry

Berberis thunbergii

This tough shrub offers the home landscape colorful foliage and a virtually pest-free nature.

How to Grow

Plant in full sun to partial shade. Incorporate 3 to 4 inches of organic matter, along with 2 pounds of a 5-10-5 fertilizer per 100 square feet, tilling deeply. Dig the planting hole three to five times as wide as the rootball, but no deeper. Place the plant in the hole and backfill to two-thirds. Tamp the soil and water to settle. Add the remaining backfill, repeat the process, and apply mulch.

Landscape Merit

In a world of green, red-leafed Japanese barberries are worth their weight in gold. The deep-red leaves serve all summer as a colorful contrast between seas of green. No burglar would survive trying to get through one to a window. Summer flowers look exceptionally good against the red backdrop.

Care and Maintenance

Moisture is especially important the first year; water deeply when required. Feed four weeks after transplanting with a slow-release balanced fertilizer like an 8-8-8, at 1 pound per 100 square feet. In beds less than three years old, feed as above in March and August, and feed established plantings in March. Prune in late winter to encourage dense growth. Remove old woody canes in the center of the plant.

Recommended Varieties

The red-leafed varieties *B. thunbergii* var. *atropurpurea* are the most popular, some of the most notable being 'Crimson Pygmy' (2 ft.), 'Crimson Giant' (4 to 5 ft.), 'Crimson Velvet' (4 to 5 ft.), and 'Rose Glow' (5 to 6 ft.).

Light Needs:

Zones: 7 to 9

Bloom Time: Spring

Bloom Color: Yellow

Height: 4 to 6 ft.

Spacing: 3 to 4 ft.

Water Needs: Moderate

Soil: Moist, well drained

Did You Know?

The nandina and mahonia are in the barberry family.

Color photo on page 137

Japanese Fatsia

Fatsia japonica

Large palmate leaves make this plant seem Hawaiian.

How to Grow

Choose a site in partial to full shade. Plant in a protected area in north zone 8, and in containers to be brought indoors in zone 7. Incorporate 3 to 4 inches of organic matter, along with 2 pounds of a 5-10-5 fertilizer per 100 square feet, tilling deeply. Dig the planting hole three to five times as wide as the rootball, but no deeper. Place the plant in the hole and backfill to two-thirds. Tamp the soil and water to settle. Add the remaining backfill, repeat the process, and apply mulch.

Landscape Merit

Fatsia is one of the best shrubs for imparting a tropical feeling. Its leaves have the look of a philodendron, yet fatsia is hardy. Its giant leaves were made for the pool, water garden, or large atrium. Grow as understory plants to banana trees. Ferns combine well from underneath.

Care and Maintenance

Moisture is especially important the first year; water deeply when required. Feed four weeks after transplanting with a slow-release balanced fertilizer like an 8-8-8, at 1 pound per 100 square feet. In beds less than three years old, feed as above in March and August, and feed established plantings in March. Light annual prunings will keep plants shapely. Remove old stalks to encourage young shoots.

Recommended Varieties

It is most often sold generic. Varieties include 'Aurea' (golden variegation), 'Variegata' (white variegation), and 'Moseri' (compact).

Other Name:
Japanese Aralia

Light Needs:

Added Benefits:

Zones: (7), 8, 9

Bloom Time:
Fall or winter

Bloom Color:
Creamy white

Height: 5 to 8 ft.

Spacing: 4 to 5 ft.

Water Needs:
Moderate/frequent

Soil:
Moist, well drained

Did You Know?

Fatshedera is a cross between English ivy and fatsia.

Color photo on page 137

Japanese Ligustrum

Ligustrum japonicum

This old-fashioned staple is still one of the best values for the landscape dollar.

How to Grow

Plant in full sun to partial shade. Incorporate 3 to 4 inches of organic matter, along with 2 pounds of a 5-10-5 fertilizer per 100 square feet, tilling deeply. Dig the planting hole three to five times as wide as the rootball, but no deeper. Place the plant in the hole and backfill to two-thirds. Tamp the soil and water to settle. Add the remaining backfill, repeat the process, and apply mulch.

Landscape Merit

Ligustrums have taken a bad rap because of the kudzulike nature of their rowdy cousins, the wild privets. Ligustrums work as screens, hedges, and specimens, and are among the best for shaping into small multitrunked trees. The fragrance of the blossoms is sweet, though sometimes overpowering.

Care and Maintenance

Moisture is especially important the first year; water deeply when required. Feed four weeks after transplanting with a slow-release balanced fertilizer like an 8-8-8, at 1 pound per 100 square feet. In beds less than three years old, feed as above in March and August, and feed established plantings in March. Make major prunings in late winter; light pruning can be done anytime.

Recommended Varieties

Several variegated varieties, such as 'Howardii', 'Variegatum', and 'Silver Star', are in the trade. 'Recurvifolium' has leaf curl. I still prefer the old-fashioned generic.

Other Name:
Japanese Privet

Light Needs:

Added Benefits:

Zones: 7 to 9

Bloom Time:
Late spring, early summer

Bloom Color:
White

Height: 10 to 12 ft.

Spacing: 5 to 8 ft.

Water Needs:
Moderate

Soil:
Moist, well drained

Did You Know?

Ligustrum sinense 'Variegata' is one of our best variegated shrubs, with light-green-and-cream foliage.

Color photo on page 137

Japanese Ternstroemia

Ternstroemia japonica

The cleyera (really Japanese ternstroemia) is a shrub that should play a vital role in all Southern landscapes. It excels where pittosporum and photinia often fail.

How to Grow

Plant in full sun to partial shade. Incorporate 3 to 4 inches of organic matter, along with 2 pounds of a 5-10-5 fertilizer per 100 square feet, tilling deeply. Dig the planting hole three to five times as wide as the rootball, but no deeper. Place the plant in the hole and backfill to two-thirds. Tamp the soil and water to settle. Add the remaining backfill, repeat the process, and apply mulch.

Landscape Merit

Cleyera looks as though it has had a coat of polish, as it literally shines in the garden. The new growth is a shiny copper or bronze, making it a perfect substitute for the disease-plagued red tip photinia. It is great as a specimen, or accent. Try grouping small azaleas or wood ferns around cleyera.

Care and Maintenance

Moisture is especially important the first year; water deeply when required. Feed four weeks after transplanting with a slow-release balanced fertilizer like an 8-8-8, at 1 pound per 100 square feet. In beds less than three years old, feed as above in March and August, and feed established plantings in March. Light pruning to shape can be done anytime.

Recommended Varieties

This plant is often sold as cleyera japonica. Varieties are still hard to find. Look for 'Burgundy', 'Burnished Gold', and 'Dodd Littleleaf'.

Other Name:
Japanese Cleyera

Light Needs:

Zones: 7 to 9

Bloom Time:
Late spring, early summer

Bloom Color:
Inconspicuous, yellow, fragrant

Height: 8 to 10 ft.

Spacing: 5 to 8 ft.

Water Needs:
Moderate

Soil:
Moist, well drained

Did You Know?

The ternstroemia is in the tea family with the camellia.

Color photo on page 137

Japanese Viburnum

Other Name:
Wax Leaf Viburnum

Light Needs:

Added Benefits:

Zones: 7 to 9

Bloom Time: Spring

Bloom Color: White

Height: 10 to 20 ft.

Spacing: 6 to 8 ft.

Water Needs: Moderate

Soil: Moist, well drained

Did You Know?
The *V. dentatum*, or arrowwood, is a deciduous native and has great fall color.

Color photo on page 137

Viburnum japonicum

High-gloss leathery leaves make this one of the showiest green plants in the landscape.

How to Grow
Plant in full sun to partial shade. Incorporate 3 to 4 inches of organic matter, along with 2 pounds of a 5-10-5 fertilizer per 100 square feet, tilling deeply. Dig the planting hole three to five times as wide as the rootball, but no deeper. Place the plant in the hole and backfill to two-thirds. Tamp the soil and water to settle. Add the remaining backfill, repeat the process, and apply mulch.

Landscape Merit
The Japanese viburnum is unbelievably beautiful and has huge, glossy leaves. It is like a holly without the points or needles. Recommended as a hedge and screen, I prefer it as a specimen pruned to a pyramidal shape and combined with a layer of lower-level shrubs such as junipers or barberry. The spring flowers are slightly fragrant.

Care and Maintenance
Watch the moisture the first year and water deeply when required. Feed four weeks after transplanting with a slow-release balanced fertilizer like an 8-8-8, at 1 pound per 100 square feet. In beds less than three years old, feed as above in March and August, and feed established plantings in March. Light pruning can be done anytime. Make major prunings in late winter.

Recommended Varieties
This one is sold generic, but there are dozens of viburnums that should be in the landscape. Hybrids 'Chippewa' and 'Huron' have extra cold hardiness.

Japanese Yew

Podocarpus macrophyllus

This exotic-looking plant is a conifer, which surprises some gardeners. It lends a wonderful leaf texture to the shrub border.

How to Grow
Plant in full sun to partial shade. Choose a protected area or containers if growing in zone 7. Incorporate 3 to 4 inches of organic matter, along with 2 pounds of a 5-10-5 fertilizer per 100 square feet, tilling deeply. Dig the planting hole three to five times as wide as the rootball, but no deeper. Place the plant in the hole and backfill to two-thirds. Tamp the soil and water to settle. Add the remaining backfill, repeat the process, and apply mulch.

Landscape Merit
The Japanese yew is unique in leaf texture and overall shape. It is the best for fitting tall but somewhat narrow spaces. It can be used as a hedge or topiary, but it is ideally a specimen with smaller shrubs grouped around it. It is well suited to "Japanese-style" gardens.

Care and Maintenance
Pay close attention to moisture the first year, and water deeply when required. Feed four weeks after transplanting with a slow-release balanced fertilizer like an 8-8-8, at 1 pound per 100 square feet. Make light annual applications in early spring. Light pruning can be done anytime to shape. Make restorative prunings just before growth resumes in spring.

Recommended Varieties
Mostly sold generic, named varieties are 'Brodie' (3 ft. × 6 ft., compact), 'Nana' (compact), and 'Varigatus' (creamy-white variegation).

Other Name:
Bigleaf Podocarp

Light Needs:

Added Benefit:

Zones: (7), 8, 9

Bloom Time:
Late spring

Bloom Color:
No ornamental value

Height: 10 to 25 ft.

Spacing: 5 to 10 ft.

Water Needs:
Moderate/frequent

Soil:
Moist, well drained

Did You Know?
There are male and female podocarpus, and when you have both you may end up with fruit that is loved by birds.

Color photo on page 137

Mahonia

Other Name:
Holly Grape

Light Needs:

Added Benefit:

Zones: 7, 8, (9)

Bloom Time:
Late winter, early spring

Bloom Color:
Yellow

Height: 4 to 6 ft.

Spacing: 3 to 4 ft.

Water Needs:
Moderate/frequent

Soil:
Moist, well drained

Did You Know?
The mahonia is related to the nandina and Japanese Barberry.

Color photo on page 137

Mahonia species

The Mahonia is a plant that changes throughout the year but is always attractive.

How to Grow
Plant in full sun to partial shade. Incorporate 3 to 4 inches of organic matter, along with 2 pounds of a 5-10-5 fertilizer per 100 square feet, tilling deeply. Dig the planting hole three to five times as wide as the rootball, but no deeper. Place the plant in the hole and backfill to two-thirds. Tamp the soil and water to settle. Add the remaining backfill, repeat the process, and apply mulch.

Landscape Merit
Mahonia deserves a place in the landscape similar to a piece of statuary; use as an accent near the front door or just off the patio. It's in the barberry family and has distinctive evergreen foliage that will be different colors throughout the year. Steel-blue fruit are formed in huge clusters, commanding our attention, and that of the birds who devour them. Late-winter or early-spring yellow blossoms are unique in their growth habit, blooming when not too many other plants are in bloom. Everyone needs at least one of these plants.

Care and Maintenance
Moisture is especially important the first year; water deeply when required. Feed four weeks after transplanting with a slow-release balanced fertilizer like an 8-8-8, at 1 pound per 100 square feet. In beds less than three years old, feed as above in March and August. Feed established plantings in March. Remove old woody canes to encourage new young shoots.

Recommended Varieties
M. aquifolium (Oregon holly grape) 'Golden Abundance', 'Kings Ransom', and *M. beali* 'Leatherleaf Mahonia' all have appeal.

Nandina

Nandina domestica

Nandinas give us bright, bold fruit and foliage colors all winter.

How to Grow

Plant in sun for best color, though all sites are tolerated. Prepare soil, incorporating 3 to 4 inches of organic matter, along with 2 pounds of a 5-10-5 fertilizer per 100 square feet, tilling deeply. Dig the planting hole three to five times as wide as the rootball, but no deeper. Place the plant in the hole and backfill to two-thirds. Tamp the soil and water to settle. Add the remaining backfill, repeat the process, and apply mulch.

Landscape Merit

Also called heavenly bamboo, the old-fashioned nandina gives a lush tropical feel. Winter invites thousands of bright-red berries, giving the plant a new look. The dwarf versions develop a spectacular display of red, orange, yellow, and purple leaf color that persists all winter. Plant as a specimen or in groups.

Care and Maintenance

Moisture is especially important the first year; water deeply when required. Feed four weeks after transplanting with a slow-release balanced fertilizer like an 8-8-8, at 1 pound per 100 square feet. In beds less than three years old, feed as above in March and August. Feed established plantings in March. Remove one-third of the tallest canes each year to keep compact and full.

Recommended Varieties

In addition to grandma's old favorite, there are some dwarf varieties that have captured the market: 'Fire Power', 'Gulf Stream', 'Harbour Dwarf', 'Nana', and about twenty more.

Other Name:
Heavenly Bamboo

Light Needs:

Added Benefits:

Zones: 7 to 9

Bloom Time:
Late spring,
early summer

Bloom Color:
Pink to white

Height:
2 to 8 ft.
(variety dependent)

Spacing: Large,
3 to 4 ft.; dwarf, 2 ft.

Water Needs:
Moderate

Soil:
Moist, well drained

Did You Know?

Nandina berries make good holiday decorations.

Color photo on page 137

Southern Wax Myrtle

Myrica cerifera

Other Names:
Candleberry, Bayberry

Light Needs:

Added Benefits:

Zones: 7 to 9

Bloom Time:
Spring

Bloom Color:
Inconspicuous
(blue berries)

Height: 15 to 20 ft.

Spacing: 10 to 15 ft.

Water Needs:
Moderate/frequent

Soil:
Moist, well drained

Did You Know?

Early Americans boiled the berries, yielding wax for candles.

Color photo on page 138

The wax myrtle is not only one of our best evergreens, but is among the best for feeding birds during the winter.

How to Grow

Plant in full sun to partial shade. Male and female flowers are on separate plants. For berries, and therefore birds, select a female plant. Incorporate 3 to 4 inches of organic matter, along with 2 pounds of a 5-10-5 fertilizer per 100 square feet, tilling deeply. Dig the planting hole three to five times as wide as the rootball, but no deeper. Place the plant in the hole and backfill to two-thirds. Tamp the soil and water to settle. Add the remaining backfill, repeat the process, and apply mulch.

Landscape Merit

The wax myrtle is a tough native evergreen best used as a small tree or large shrub. Plant in groups of three to five for screening around patios. The blue-gray waxy berries, which were once used in making candles, feed forty species of birds. Combine with the yaupon for a winter bird sanctuary.

Care and Maintenance

Moisture is especially important the first year; water deeply when required. Feed four weeks after transplanting with a slow-release balanced fertilizer like an 8-8-8, at 1 pound per 100 square feet. Established plantings need to be fed in April and August. Wax myrtles with heavy berry crops need this last application. Make major prunings in late winter and light prunings anytime.

Recommended Varieties

They are usually sold generic, but 'Emperor' (with serrated leaves) and 'Hiwassee' (with extra cold hardiness) should be more available.

Yaupon and Possumhaw Holly

Ilex vomitoria and *Ilex decidua*

These species represent the best of native hollies, one deciduous and the other evergreen and both loaded with berries.

How to Grow

Choose a female variety for berry production. Full sun is needed for a large berry crop, but other than that, it will grow anywhere. Incorporate 3 to 4 inches of organic matter, along with 2 pounds of a 5-10-5 fertilizer per 100 square feet, tilling deeply. Dig the planting hole three to five times as wide as the rootball, but no deeper. Place the plant in the hole and backfill to two-thirds. Tamp the soil and water to settle. Add the remaining backfill, repeat the process, and apply mulch.

Landscape Merit

The berries provide great winter color and feed many bird species. These hollies are great in clumps, or as a specimen. The weeping forms make great accents, and the dwarf forms are among the most adaptable small evergreen shrubs.

Care and Maintenance

Moisture is especially important the first year; water deeply when required. Feed four weeks after transplanting with a slow-release balanced fertilizer like an 8-8-8, at 1 pound per 100 square feet. Established plantings need to be fed in April and August. Hollies with heavy berry crops benefit from this last application. Light pruning can be done anytime. Make major prunings in late winter.

Recommended Varieties

I. vomitoria, Yaupon, 'Jewel', 'Pride of Houston', and 'Kathy Ann' are champion berry producers. *I. decidua* 'Possomhaw', 'Warrens Red', 'Pocahontas', and 'Sentry' are also noteworthy.

Other Name: Winterberry

Light Needs:

Added Benefits:

Zones: 7 to 9

Bloom Time: Spring

Bloom Color: Inconspicuous, berries ornamental

Height: 15 to 20 ft. (dwarf, 3 to 5 ft.)

Spacing: 5 to 8 ft. (dwarf, 3 to 5 ft.)

Water Needs: Low/moderate

Soil: Slightly moist, well drained

Did You Know?

Stems with berries are well suited to decorating the mantle for the holidays.

Color photo on page 138

FLOWERING SHRUBS

Have you ever shopped for a house and discovered you liked the ones with gorgeous landscapes better? Homes with attractive landscapes generally bring a premium price. While we don't necessarily plant a landscape to help sell our home, we should avoid displaying anything that hurts our investment, including a mundane landscape.

You will find a wonderful mixture of flowering shrubs on the following pages: shrubs that bloom in February, shrubs whose flowers have an intoxicating fragrance, and those that bear flowers that butterflies find irresistible, as if they contained nectar from heaven.

A "mundane landscape" is one that has no flowering shrubs.

There are shrubs whose flower size defies logic and yet can be dried for indoor enjoyment for years to come. There are shrubs whose flowers are fragrant and whose leaves are unparalleled for fall color. There are other shrubs whose bloom is spectacular, yet even if they did not bloom, they would still be considered ideal as evergreens. Flowering shrubs have to be a part of any Southern landscape.

Shrub beds should be well drained to moist, loose, and nutrient- and humus-rich, with a layer of mulch to prevent moisture loss, deter weeds, and moderate summer temperatures. Notice I said "beds," because shrubs need improved soil and deserve it just as flowers do.

This soil will be the home for the life of the plant's roots. A successful start of new shrubs and trees in the landscape depends upon planting techniques and care. You have only one chance to get a new plant off to a good start.

After carefully making plans, people often fail to properly place the individual plants in the landscape. Putting even a 5-dollar plant in a 10-dollar planting hole does have merit! Dig the planting hole three to five times wider than the diameter of the rootball, but no deeper. Gently tease the roots to break the circular root pattern. If the plant is potbound, separate the roots by making three vertical cuts through the root system.

Nurseries and garden centers have a prepared landscape mix perfect for raised beds of azaleas, camellias, or any shrub you like. Purchase these soil mixes by the bag, cubic yard, or truckful. The economical price of a cubic yard of mix will make you wonder why you have been torturing your plants with heavy clay. Metal edging, landscape timbers, brick, and masonry work well to separate turf from beds and allow the soil to be raised with the addition of amendments.

Azaleas are an attractive shrub that also combines well with other spring colors found in such plantings as bulbs, phlox, or pansies. For the rest of the year, we can use them as background for summer pockets of color from impatiens and begonias.

Don't forget that deciduous native azaleas offer wonderful fragrance!

Many gardeners simply stick azaleas in the yard where, during the eleven months they are not in bloom, they give the appearance of giant meatballs. Try them in borders, where they can serve as a background for color.

Many Mississippi gardeners who relish azaleas fail to take advantage of a group called the Satsuki. Satsuki means "fifth month" in Japanese, and that is when they bloom, some even into June. There are over forty varieties of Satsuki azaleas to choose from, enabling gardeners to really extend the growing season.

When the pocketbook is tight, buy larger container-grown shrubs and smaller trees—you will not need as many, and you will be more likely to plant at the correct spacing.

Azalea

Light Needs:

Added Benefits:

Zones: 7 to 9

Bloom Time:
Spring

Bloom Color:
Many colors and blends

Height: 4 to 8 ft.

Spacing: 3 to 6 ft.

Water Needs:
Frequent

Soil:
Moist, well drained

Did You Know?

There are several varieties, like 'Watchet', that also bloom in the fall!

Color photo on page 138

Rhododendron species

Hundreds of bright 2- to 4-inch flowers make azaleas the most revered of all shrubs.

How to Grow

Plant in partial shade with moist, well-drained, acid soil. Incorporate 3 to 4 inches of organic matter, along with 2 pounds of a 5-10-5 fertilizer per 100 square feet, tilling deeply. Dig the planting hole three to five times as wide as the rootball, but no deeper. Azaleas are often potbound; score the roots with a knife. Place the azalea in the hole and backfill with soil. Tamp and water to settle. Apply 3 to 4 inches of mulch.

Landscape Merit

The Southeastern spring landscape is spectacular, thanks to azaleas. They are well suited to shrub beds when combined with hollies, small trees like the dogwood and Japanese maple, and other spring-blooming shrubs.

Care and Maintenance

Watch the moisture the first year. Feed four weeks after transplanting with a slow-release 8-8-8 fertilizer at 1 pound per 100 square feet. Azaleas have shallow root systems; maintain moisture and apply fresh mulch yearly. Feed in later winter and mid-summer with an azalea fertilizer. Prune after spring bloom if needed. Watch leaves for first sign of azalea lacebugs and treat early.

Recommended Varieties

'Southern Indica' hybrids are great, but hardy only to around 10 degrees Fahrenheit. More cold hardy are 'Kurumes', and 'Girard' hybrids. 'Robin Hill' hybrids and 'Satsukis' are known for later bloom, allowing the grower to lengthen the season. Deciduous native azaleas *R. austrinum* and *R. canescens* offer varieties with beauty and fragrance.

Bottlebrush Buckeye

Aesculus parviflora

Bottlebrush flowers are 4 inches wide and 12 inches long and produced in huge quantities.

How to Grow

Plant in full sun to partial shade. Prepare a bed for the bottlebrush buckeye and companion shrubs by incorporating 3 to 4 inches of organic matter, along with 2 pounds of a 5-10-5 fertilizer per 100 square feet, tilling deeply. Dig the planting hole three to five times as wide as the rootball, but no deeper. Place the buckeye in the hole and backfill to two-thirds. Tamp the soil, and water to settle. Add the remaining backfill, repeat the process, and apply mulch.

Landscape Merit

This is the poster child for underused plants. The huge white blossoms, in contrast with the dark green leaves and followed by attractive fall yellow foliage, make this a plant for all shrub beds. It is good combined with evergreens or planted as understory to pines.

Care and Maintenance

Feed in late winter with a light application of slow-release balanced fertilizer. Prune suckers as they develop to keep it confined. It can be cut to the ground in a rejuvenation-type pruning and will return faithfully. Maintain mulch and moisture similar to those used for azalea. Enjoy!

Recommended Varieties

It is sold generic. You will have to search, but it will be worth it.

Light Needs:

Zones: 7 to 9

Bloom Time:
Early summer

Bloom Color:
White

Height: 8 to 12 ft.

Spacing: 4 to 6 ft.

Water Needs:
Frequent

Soil:
Moist, well drained

Did You Know?

The bottlebrush buckeye is native to the southeastern United States as far south as Alabama.

Color photo on page 138

Bridal Wreath Spiraea

Spiraea × vanhouttei

Other Name:
Van Houtte Spiraea

Light Needs:

Added Benefit:

Zones: 7 to 9

Bloom Time:
Spring

Bloom Color:
White

Height: 6 to 8 ft.

Spacing: 5 to 8 ft.

Water Needs:
Frequent

Soil:
Moist, well drained

Did You Know?

The name *spiraea* comes from the Greek, meaning "a plant used for garlands."

Color photo on page 138

Long, arching stems loaded with hundreds of glistening white flowers make this beloved old-timer a permanent fixture in the spring garden.

How to Grow

Plant in full sun to partial shade. Prepare a bed for the spiraea and companion shrubs by incorporating 3 to 4 inches of organic matter, along with 2 pounds of a 5-10-5 fertilizer per 100 square feet, tilling deeply. Dig the planting hole three to five times as wide as the rootball, but no deeper. Place the spiraea in the hole and backfill to two-thirds. Tamp the soil, and water to settle. Add the remaining backfill, repeat the process, and apply mulch.

Landscape Merit

The graceful weeping of the branches adorned with white spring flowers make this plant ideal for shrub beds that have azaleas and evergreens. The bluish green foliage stands out against the dark green of other plants. The fall foliage is also a welcome yellow or orange.

Care and Maintenance

Feed with light applications of a slow-release balanced fertilizer in late winter and midsummer. Keep well watered and mulched. Next year's bloom is produced on this year's growth. Prune after bloom by selectively removing old unproductive branches.

Recommended Varieties

This spiraea is almost totally generic, though 'Renaissance' is a named selection. Try the several selections of *Spiraea bumalda*, such as 'Anthony Waterer', which has pink blooms in summer and fall.

Butterfly Bush

Buddleia davidii

There is a huge revival of this wonderful plant of our ancestors. It yields fragrance, cutflowers, and long bloom, and attracts countless butterflies.

How to Grow

Plant in full sun for best bloom. Prepare the bed for the buddleia and companion plants by incorporating 3 to 4 inches of organic matter, along with 2 pounds of a 5-10-5 fertilizer per 100 square feet, tilling deeply. Dig the planting hole three to five times as wide as the rootball, but no deeper. Place the buddleia in the hole and backfill to two-thirds. Tamp the soil, and water to settle. Add the remaining backfill, repeat the process, and apply mulch.

Landscape Merit

Buddleia is at home in the shrub bed, perennial garden, and butterfly garden. The graceful stems arch over for you to admire. The foliage serves as a nice contrast to the dark green of most shrubs. Use indoors as cutflowers for several days of enjoyment.

Care and Maintenance

Feed in late winter with a light application of slow-release balanced fertilizer. The buddleia blooms in new growth, so hard pruning in late winter yields productive new growth. Should plants freeze to the ground, new growth will emerge in the spring. Keep watered and mulched for active growth.

Recommended Varieties

B. davidii varieties are some of the most popular. 'Black Knight' (dark purple), 'Charming' (pink), 'Empire Blue' (blue), 'Pink Delight' (pink), 'White Delight', and Nanho hybrids 'Nanho blue' and 'Nanho purple' should all be tried. There are many, many more.

Other Name:
Summer Lilac

Light Needs:

Added Benefits:

Zones: 7 to 9

Bloom Time:
Spring, summer, and fall

Bloom Color:
Many colors

Height: 6 to 10 ft.

Spacing: 4 to 6 ft.

Water Needs:
Moderate/frequent

Soil:
Moist, well drained

Did You Know?

Several of the varieties, like 'Empire Blue', have orange eyes.

Color photo on page 138

Camellia

Camellia japonica and *sasanqua*

When you consider the waxy, leathery leaves of these evergreens, coupled with blooms as pretty as a rose, you wonder why anyone would plant anything else.

How to Grow

Plant in partial shade. Prepare the bed for camellias by incorporating 3 to 4 inches of organic matter, along with 2 pounds of a 5-10-5 fertilizer per 100 square feet, tilling deeply. Dig the planting hole three to five times as wide as the rootball, but no deeper. Place the camellia in the hole and backfill with soil. Tamp and water to settle. Apply mulch.

Landscape Merit

By choosing *Camellia sasanqua* and *Camellia japonica* varieties, we can have the best of all worlds: fall and winter bloom (*sasanqua*), winter and spring bloom (*japonica*), and great summer foliage as pretty as a ligustrum. Combine with hollies and azaleas.

Care and Maintenance

Moisture is important the first summer, so keep well watered. Feed a month after transplanting with a light application of slow-release balanced fertilizer. Feed established plantings with a slow-release camellia or balanced (8-8-8) fertilizer in late spring at 1 pound per 100 square feet. Water during dry periods, and keep well mulched. Use a dormant oil to control scale. Prune after bloom to shape.

Recommended Varieties

There are gigantic books just on camellia varieties, so recommendation is almost pointless. A few favorite sasanquas are 'Yuletide' (red with yellow stamens), 'Pink Snow' (light pink, semi-double), 'Cleopatra' (pink, semi-double), and 'Shishigashira' (rose, very compact plant). Japonica favorites are 'Professor Charles S. Sargent' (red, peony) and 'Pink Perfection' (pink, formal).

Other Names:
Japanese Camellia,
Sasanqua

Light Needs:

Added Benefits:

Zones: 7 to 9

Bloom Time:
Fall and winter or winter and spring

Bloom Color:
Many colors and blends

Height:
Sasanqua 2 to 12 ft.,
japonica 6 to 12 ft.

Spacing: 3 to 6 ft.

Water Needs:
Moderate

Soil:
Moist, well drained

Did You Know?

Camellias also work great in large decorative containers.

Color photo on page 138

Flowering Quince

Chaenomeles speciosa

Like a trumpet announcing royalty, flowering quince shouts with its bright red flowers, "You have survived winter, spring is just days away!"

How to Grow

Plant in full sun. Prepare a bed for flowering quince and other spring shrubs by incorporating 3 to 4 inches of organic matter, along with 2 pounds of a 5-10-5 fertilizer per 100 square feet, tilling deeply. Dig the planting hole three to five times as wide as the rootball, but no deeper. Place the flowering quince in the hole and backfill to two-thirds. Tamp the soil, and water to settle. Add the remaining backfill, repeat the process, and apply mulch.

Landscape Merit

The bold scarlet to red color lasts for a long time and brings out the first bees of the year. Some say to plant it away from the house so that its stiff twiggy growth habit won't stand out. I say, plant it in a shrub bed framed by evergreen shrubs. They work in hedges and massed in clumps. Use branches in a vase.

Care and Maintenance

Feed in late winter with a light application of slow-release balanced (8-8-8) fertilizer. Prune to desired shape anytime. Take out old canes, allowing new wood to develop for next year's blooms.

Recommended Varieties

Known for bright-scarlet flowers, varieties like 'Texas Scarlet' and 'Super Red' are the most common. Pink forms are 'Pink Beauty' and 'Enchantress'; white selections are 'Jet Trail' and 'Low-n-White'. There are also unique double forms like 'Phyllis Moore' and 'Cameo'.

Other Name:
Japanese Quince

Light Needs:

Added Benefits:

Zones: 7 to 9

Bloom Time:
Late winter, early spring

Bloom Color:
Red, pink, white, and blends

Height: 3 to 6 ft.

Spacing: 4 to 6 ft.

Water Needs:
Moderate

Soil:
Moist, well drained

Did You Know?

The fruit of the flowering quince can be made into jelly.

Color photo on page 138

Forsythia

Other Name:
Golden Bell

Light Needs:

Added Benefits:

Zones: 7 to 9

Bloom Time:
Late winter, early spring

Bloom Color:
Yellow

Height: 2 to 10 ft.

Spacing: 4 to 8 ft.

Water Needs:
Moderate/frequent

Soil:
Moist, well drained

Did You Know?
The forsythia is really easy to root by tip-layering in adjacent soil.

Color photo on page 138

Forsythia × intermedia

Like quince, the forsythia with its unbelievable bright-yellow flowers is a harbinger of spring.

How to Grow
Plant in full sun, keeping in mind that this plant grows to 8 feet tall and wide. Prepare the bed for the forsythia and other spring shrubs by incorporating 3 to 4 inches of organic matter, along with 2 pounds of a 5-10-5 fertilizer per 100 square feet, tilling deeply. Dig the planting hole three to five times as wide as the rootball, but no deeper. Place the forsythia in the hole and backfill to two-thirds. Tamp the soil, and water to settle. Add the remaining backfill, repeat the process, and apply mulch.

Landscape Merit
The long, arching branches of forsythia are covered with bold, yellow, bell-shaped flowers. The plant develops its graceful habit when left almost natural. It works great in a large shrub border with evergreens and other spring-blooming shrubs when it is allowed at its own pace to be all it can be.

Care and Maintenance
Feed in late winter with a light application of slow-release balanced (8-8-8) fertilizer. Prune after flowering by removing old canes from the base of the plant. Selectively hand-prune to maintain its natural shape.

Recommended Varieties
Many gardeners will be surprised to know that there are varieties—over 30, in fact. Dwarf compact forms are 'Gold Tide' and 'Golden Nugget'. Those of typical height are 'Spring Glory', 'Linwood Gold', and 'Spectabilis'.

Gardenia

Gardenia jasminoides

Go near a gardenia. Like Ulysses lured by the Sirens, you will come under the spell of the smell.

How to Grow

Plant in full sun to partial shade. Choose a protected micro-climate in zone 7. Prepare the gardenia bed by incorporating 3 to 4 inches of organic matter, along with 2 pounds of a 5-10-5 fertilizer per 100 square feet, tilling deeply. Dig the planting hole three to five times as wide as the rootball, but no deeper. Place the gardenia in the hole and backfill to two-thirds. Tamp the soil, and water to settle. Add the remaining backfill, repeat the process, and apply mulch.

Landscape Merit

As a specimen near the porch or patio, it is unsurpassed. Plant smaller evergreen shrubs or liriope as companion plants. They excel in large decorative containers. The 'Radicans' dwarf spreading variety is suitable as a low-growing shrub or ground cover. It is not as cold hardy.

Care and Maintenance

Feed in late winter with a light application of an azalea camellia fertilizer. If leaf yellowing following bloom has occurred in years past, feed with a product containing iron. Use a dormant oil as needed to combat scale in late winter. Control whiteflies and aphids as needed with a recommended insecticide.

Recommended Varieties

'August Beauty' and 'Mystery' have been the leading varieties, 'Chuck Hayes' and 'Daisy' are known for extra cold hardiness, and 'Vetchii' is a compact 3- to 4-ft. plant.

Other Name:
Cape Jasmine

Light Needs:

Added Benefits:

Zones: (7), 8, 9

Bloom Time:
Early summer, few to fall

Bloom Color:
White

Height: 2 to 6 ft.

Spacing: 3 to 6 ft.

Water Needs:
Moderate/frequent

Soil:
Moist, well drained

Did You Know?

Pick a gardenia and set in a dish for hours of fragrance indoors.

Color photo on page 138

Glossy Abelia

Abelia × grandiflora

Other Name:
Abelia

Light Needs:

Added Benefits:

Zones: 7 to 9

Bloom Time:
Summer, fall

Bloom Color:
Lilac, white, pink

Height: 2 to 8 ft.

Spacing: 2 to 6 ft.

Water Needs:
Moderate/frequent

Soil:
Moist, well drained

Did You Know?

The abelia is in the honeysuckle family.

Color photo on page 138

Many think of abelia as the Millard Filmore of plants—boring. They bloom for months, however, with clusters of flowers, and have no pests.

How to Grow

Plant in full sun for best bloom. Prepare the bed for abelias by incorporating 3 to 4 inches of organic matter, along with 2 pounds of a 5-10-5 fertilizer per 100 square feet, tilling deeply. Dig the planting hole three to five times as wide as the rootball, but no deeper. Place the abelia in the hole and backfill to two-thirds. Tamp the soil, and water to settle. Add the remaining backfill, repeat the process, and apply mulch.

Landscape Merit

Abelia has a graceful arching habit suited to the shrub border and mass planting. The glossy reddish foliage is attractive, and the plant is among the most pest-free shrubs for sale. Taller varieties are well suited for use as a privacy screen.

Care and Maintenance

Feed in late winter with a light application of a balanced fertilizer (8-8-8), 1 pound per 100 square feet. Your happiness with the abelia may well depend on your pruning. In late winter, prune out one-third of the old canes at the base of the plant. Maintain an even supply of moisture during prolonged dry spells.

Recommended Varieties

'Edward Goucher', a hybrid with lilac flowers, is the most popular in Mississippi. Others to try are 'Francis Mason', with variegated foliage and pink flowers, and 'Prostrata', a white-flowered 3-foot-tall spreading type.

Hydrangea

Hydrangea macrophylla

Hydrangea has been called (and rightfully so) the queen of the late-blooming shrubs.

How to Grow

Plant in partial shade. Prepare a bed for the hydrangea and companion plants by incorporating 3 to 4 inches of organic matter, along with 2 pounds of a 5-10-5 fertilizer per 100 square feet, tilling deeply. Dig the planting hole three to five times as wide as the rootball, but no deeper. Place the hydrangea in the hole and backfill to two-thirds. Tamp the soil, and water to settle. Add the remaining backfill, repeat the process, and apply mulch.

Landscape Merit

The large mophead-shaped, delicate-looking lacecap hydrangeas brighten partially shady areas of the landscape. The hydrangea is suited to massing, using as a specimen in-between evergreens, and planting in large containers. The flowers are great for cutting and bringing indoors for drying.

Care and Maintenance

Feed in late winter with a light application of a balanced (8-8-8) fertilizer. Use 1 pound per 100 square feet of bed space. Do not prune until after bloom. Next season's buds are formed in late summer. Acidic soil where aluminum is available yields blue flowers, and alkaline soil yields pink flowers. If you want blue, add aluminum sulfate; for pink add dolomitic lime. The process may take two years. Keep them well watered and mulched through the summer.

Recommended Varieties

'Blue Prince', 'Nikko Blue', and 'Westfalen' are three of many to try. 'Bluebird', 'Blue Wave', and 'Variegata' are a sampling of many lacecaps.

Other Name:
Bigleaf Hydrangea

Light Needs:

Added Benefits:

Zones: 7 to 9

Bloom Time:
Early summer

Bloom Color:
Blue, pink

Height: 4 to 8 ft.

Spacing: 3 to 5 ft.

Water Needs:
Moderate/frequent

Soil:
Moist, well drained

Did You Know?

There is a native hydrangea called the oakleaf (see page 189).

Color photo on page 138

Indian Hawthorn

Rhaphiolepis indica

The glossy, leathery leaves, coupled with gorgeous delicate-looking pink or white blooms, make Indian hawthorn one of the best-loved shrubs.

How to Grow
Plant in full sun for best performance. Give protection in zone 7. Prepare a bed for Indian hawthorns and companion plants by incorporating 3 to 4 inches of organic matter, along with 2 pounds of a 5-10-5 fertilizer per 100 square feet, tilling deeply. Dig the planting hole three to five times as wide as the rootball, but no deeper. Place the Indian hawthorn in the hole and backfill to two-thirds. Tamp the soil, and water to settle. Add the remaining backfill, repeat the process, and apply mulch.

Landscape Merit
Indian hawthorn is one of the best low-growing border shrubs. There are also large varieties that make outstanding specimens. They are well utilized as small hedges or massed plantings.

Care and Maintenance
Feed after blooming with a slow-release 8-8-8 fertilizer at 1 pound per 100 square feet. Use hand pruners to selectively shape and size. Indian hawthorns are susceptible to the same disease that attacks photinia. Planting in sun and providing good air circulation aids in prevention. Prolonged cool, wet weather may trigger the disease. Fungicides help, as does watering from underneath with a wand or soaker hose. White varieties appear to be less susceptible to disease.

Recommended Varieties
'Eleanor Taber'™, 'Jack Evans', 'Ballerina', 'Snow White', and 'Indian Princess' are well-known varieties. Try the large, fragrant 'Majestic Beauty'.

Other Name:
Rhaphiolepis

Light Needs:

Added Benefit:

Zones: (7), 8, 9

Bloom Time:
Late fall to late spring

Bloom Color:
Pink, white

Height: 3 to 10 ft.

Spacing: 3 to 6 ft.

Water Needs:
Moderate/frequent

Soil:
Moist, well drained

Did You Know?
The Indian hawthorn is in the rose family.

Color photo on page 139

Lorapetalum

Lorapetalum chinense var. *rubrum*

Red lorapetalums have been among the most exciting new shrubs of the 1990s. Their hot pink flowers are showy in the spring landscape.

How to Grow

Plant in full sun to partial shade. Prepare a bed for the lorapetalum by incorporating 3 to 4 inches of organic matter, along with 2 pounds of a 5-10-5 fertilizer per 100 square feet, tilling deeply. Dig the planting hole three to five times as wide as the rootball, but no deeper. Place the lorapetalum in the hole and backfill to two-thirds. Tamp the soil, and water to settle. Add the remaining backfill, repeat the process, and apply mulch.

Landscape Merit

Lorapetalum is suited to specimen plantings, massing, and use as a screen. The foliage of some varieties holds a deep maroon color, especially attractive as a backdrop to pink-fringed flowers. Eventual size is still unknown. In Japan they have been seen growing to 20 to 30 feet tall.

Care and Maintenance

Feed in late winter with a light application of an 8-8-8 fertilizer. If growing massed in a bed, fertilize at a rate of 1 pound per 100 square feet. Lower limbs can be pruned to develop into a tree, or pruned like a forsythia, removing old canes in the center for a vase shape. Keep slightly moist and well mulched. Choose spring planting over fall planting to give longer adjustment time before winter.

Recommended Varieties

Popular varieties are 'Blush', 'Burgundy', 'Zhuzhou Fuchsia', and 'Plum Delight'™.

Other Name:
Chinese Fringe Flower

Light Needs:

Zones: 7 to 9

Bloom Time:
Spring

Bloom Color:
Pink, red

Height: 6 to 10 ft.

Spacing:
8 to 10 ft.

Water Needs:
Moderate

Soil:
Moist, well drained

Did You Know?

The lorapetalum is in the Witch Hazel family.

Color photo on page 139

Mock Orange

Other Name:
English Dogwood

Light Needs:

Added Benefits:

Zones: 7 to 9

Bloom Time:
Late spring

Bloom Color:
White

Height: 5 to 8 ft.

Spacing: 4 to 6 ft.

Water Needs:
Moderate

Soil:
Moist, well drained

Did You Know?

The name *Philadelphus* is thought to come from Ptolemy II Philadelphus, who ruled Egypt from 285 to 246 BC.

Color photo on page 139

Philadelphus coronarius

The mock orange blooms for weeks with fragrant dogwood-type blossoms literally covering the plant. It is one of the showiest plants of late spring.

How to Grow
Purchase mock orange while in bloom to ensure fragrance. Plant in full sun to partial shade. Prepare a bed by incorporating 3 to 4 inches of organic matter, along with 2 pounds of a 5-10-5 fertilizer per 100 square feet, tilling deeply. Dig the planting hole three to five times as wide as the rootball, but no deeper. Place the mock orange in the hole and backfill to two-thirds. Tamp the soil, and water to settle. Add the remaining backfill, repeat the process, and apply mulch.

Landscape Merit
Some prefer not to grow mock orange due to its stiff, upright habit, but its virtues outweigh this habit by a ton. It is a long-lived shrub suitable for use as a specimen-type planting in the shrub border, corner plantings, and screens. Fragrant and showy flowers are produced by the hundreds.

Care and Maintenance
Feed in late winter with a light application of an 8-8-8 fertilizer. Prune after blooming by removing old wood, which will induce new stems for next year's flowers. Suckers will appear at the base of the plant to form a clumping shrub. Remove any unwanted sprouts in the winter for use in other parts of the landscape.

Recommended Varieties
They are usually sold generic. Varieties to look for are 'Primuliflorus', 'Deutziflorus', and 'Nanus'.

ⓝ Oakleaf Hydrangea

Hydrangea quercifolia

The oakleaf hydrangea is a 2000 Mississippi Medallion winner that has outstanding landscape attributes.

How to Grow
Plant in partial shade. Prepare a bed for the oakleaf hydrangea by incorporating 3 to 4 inches of organic matter, along with 2 pounds of a 5-10-5 fertilizer per 100 square feet, tilling deeply. Dig the planting hole three to five times as wide as the rootball, but no deeper. Place the oakleaf hydrangea in the hole and backfill to two-thirds. Tamp the soil, and water to settle. Add the remaining backfill, repeat the process, and apply mulch.

Landscape Merit
Oakleaf hydrangea was made for the partial-shade shrub border. The 12-inch-long white blossoms adorn this shrub in late spring and early summer, and are well suited to cutting and drying. These plants also work as specimens between larger evergreen shrubs. The foliage turns deep maroon in fall and persists through much of winter.

Care and Maintenance
Feed in late winter with a light application of slow-release 8-8-8 fertilizer. If planted in a mass, apply fertilizer at a rate of 1 pound per 100 square feet of bed space. Prune selectively immediately after blooming to shape the plant and induce new growth. Keep oakleaf hydrangea well watered during the summer and, as always, maintain a good layer of mulch.

Recommended Varieties
'Snowflake', 'Snow Queen', and 'Harmony' are old standards. The relatively new 'Alice', with blossoms that age to pink, is getting the industry's attention.

Light Needs:

Added Benefit:

Zones: 7 to 9

Bloom Time:
Late spring, early summer

Bloom Color:
White

Height: 3 to 8 ft.

Spacing: 4 to 6 ft.

Water Needs:
Moderate/frequent

Soil:
Moist, well drained

Did You Know?
The oakleaf hydrangea is native to Mississippi.

Color photo on page 139

Rose-of-Sharon

Hibiscus syriacus

Someone described the old-fashioned version of this plant as a shrub with hollyhock flowers. New selections look a lot like an exquisite tropical hibiscus.

How to Grow

Plant in full sun. Prepare a bed for rose-of-Sharon by incorporating 3 to 4 inches of organic matter, along with 2 pounds of a 5-10-5 fertilizer per 100 square feet, tilling deeply. Dig the planting hole three to five times as wide as the rootball, but no deeper. Place the plant in the hole and backfill to two-thirds. Tamp the soil, and water to settle. Add the remaining backfill, repeat the process, and apply mulch.

Landscape Merit

Althaea's long blooming season has strong appeal. Tuck it in the shrub border for pockets of head-high color. Use in the back of the perennial border. New varieties like 'Diana' and 'Helen' work well in the tropical garden.

Care and Maintenance

Feed with a light application of an 8-8-8 fertilizer in early spring and again in midsummer. Prune in early spring, removing much of the previous season's growth down to a few buds. This will induce more and larger blooms. Keep well watered and mulched during the summer.

Recommended Varieties

'Bluebird' (blue with a red eye), 'Red Heart' (white with a red eye), and the double 'Ardens' are choice selections to try. The new varieties from the United States National Arboretum, 'Aphrodite' (pink with a red eye), 'Diana' (white), and 'Helene' (white with red), are all worth growing.

Other Name:
Shrub Althaea

Light Needs:

Added Benefit:

Zones: 7 to 9

Bloom Time:
Summer

Bloom Color:
Many colors and blends

Height: 5 to 10 ft.

Spacing: 4 to 8 ft.

Water Needs:
Moderate/frequent

Soil:
Moist, well drained

Did You Know?
The althaea, or rose-of-Sharon, is related to okra and cotton.

Color photo on page 139

Virginia Sweetspire

Itea virginica

The Virginia sweetspire is a much-underused native with fragrant white flowers and wide landscape appeal.

How to Grow

Plant in full sun to partial shade. Prepare a bed for the sweetspire by incorporating 3 to 4 inches of organic matter, along with 2 pounds of a 5-10-5 fertilizer per 100 square feet, tilling deeply. Dig the planting hole three to five times as wide as the rootball, but no deeper. Place the sweetspire in the hole and backfill to two-thirds. Tamp the soil, and water to settle. Add the remaining backfill, repeat the process, and apply mulch.

Landscape Merit

The fragrant white fingerlike flowers in the spring are enough to warrant growing in the landscape, but the deep-green leaves turn purple to bright red in the fall and hold on for a long time, even into winter. It excels in natural landscape settings, but is also well suited to understory situations. The plant has no serious pests.

Care and Maintenance

Feed in late winter with a light application of an 8-8-8 fertilizer at the rate of 1 pound per 100 square feet. No pruning is necessary except to lightly shape or to remove unwanted suckers that develop. The suckers can be easily rooted. Keep watered and mulched throughout the growing season.

Recommended Varieties

'Henry's Garnet' is the leading variety and was a Louisiana Select winner. It has outstanding fall color. Other varieties to try are 'Little Henry'™ (compact with 4-inch-long flowers) and 'Merlot' (also compact).

Other Name:
Virginia Willow

Light Needs:

Added Benefit:

Zones: 7 to 9

Bloom Time:
April, May

Bloom Color:
White

Height: 4 to 8 ft.

Spacing: 3 to 4 ft.

Water Needs:
Moderate/frequent

Soil:
Moist, well drained

Did You Know?

Itea comes from the Greek word meaning "willow."

Color photo on page 139

TREES

The shade that trees provide is one of life's memorable pleasures. Trees act as windbreaks, screen us from undesirable sights and sounds, and provide homes and shelter for native wildlife—benefits often taken for granted.

Selecting the right tree for your landscape, whether for shade or flower, is one of the most important decisions you will make. Yet while many people put time and research into deciding which new car to buy, they may purchase a tree on a whim. When building a new house, they may spend hours going over floor plans and making decisions on wallpaper without attending to the fact that the stately old tree in the backyard-to-be will soon be lost in the construction process. That tree may or may not have been worth as much as the purchase price of the lot, but no amount of money can replace a hundred-year-old plant.

Trees reign in the landscape, dominating all other plants.

While the cost of a tree is small in dollars spent, the investment potential is high. A tree not only adds value to your home, but can also provide enjoyment and memories for generations to come. The wrong decision can result in a loss of the most precious of investments, time, which cannot be replaced. Thus, a careful analysis of the landscape should be made to determine where trees are needed and for what purpose. The same is true when a new home is being built. Which trees are to be saved? Are they worth saving? Will they perform desired functions in the landscape?

An important consideration is the size of the tree in fifteen or fifty years. After becoming familiar with the mature height and width of available trees, the potential tree grower should consider the choice between evergreen and deciduous. Deciduous trees (those that lose their leaves) offer a greater selection, and they will provide shade in the summer while allowing in welcome sun during the winter.

Evergreens make good year-round screens and windbreaks. They give color to the winter landscape in addition to serving as a backdrop for blooming plants.

Finally, one has to understand the cultural requirements of a tree. Trees need different amounts of light, moisture, drainage, and nutrients. Some are more cold tolerant and others more heat tolerant. Some have features that may be undesirable to the owner, such as fruit drop or problems with insects and disease.

Like shrubs, containerized trees need to be planted properly in a hole three to five times as large as the soilball, but no deeper. Spread the roots by gently teasing to break the circular pattern. If the tree is potbound, separate the root system by making three vertical cuts through the root system.

There is a good tree available for any type of landscape.

For a balled-and-burlapped plant, dig the planting hole no deeper than the height of the soilball. Digging the hole deeper would allow the plant to settle and can cause suffocation of the roots. Lift the plant by the rootball, not the trunk. When filling the hole, be careful not to disturb the rootball. Add backfill up to two-thirds of the depth of the rootball, firm the soil, and settle it with water.

Remove the burlap from the top of the soil by rolling it down the side of the soilball. Cut all strings; if the burlap is actually a synthetic material, remove it from the soilball after the plant is in place. It is not necessary to remove regular burlap since it will rot in the soil.

Fortunately, there are plenty of trees from which to choose.

American Holly

Ilex opaca

The American holly is a wonderful pyramidal evergreen native tree that serves the landscape well, casting shade in the summer and giving color in the winter.

How to Grow

Choose a site in full sun to partial shade in well-drained, moist, fertile soil. Consider the mature size (50 ft. × 30 ft.) when choosing the location. Set out nursery-grown plants anytime. Dig the hole three to five times as wide as the rootball, but no deeper. The rootball's top should be even with the soil line. When planting in midsummer, form a 4-inch berm outside the rootball area. This berm should be able to hold 5 gallons of water. After planting, water deeply and apply mulch. Remove the berm after the first year.

Landscape Merit

The American holly is great as a long-lived specimen or accent. A group on the northern side of the home will act as a screen and shield out cold, blustery winds. The fruit produced on female plants is eaten by 18 species of birds.

Care and Maintenance

Feed in late winter with an application of 8-8-8 fertilizer at 1 pound per 100 square feet of planted area (the area from the trunk to just outside the canopy). Keep well watered and mulched during the first year of establishment. These are low-maintenance trees. Should scale become a problem, treat with dormant oil.

Recommended Varieties

'Jersey Princess', 'Dan Fenton', 'Jersey Delight', 'Jersey Knight' (male pollinator), and 'Merry Christmas' are all acclaimed selections.

Other Name:
Yule Holly

Light Needs:

Added Benefit:

Zones: 7 to 9

Bloom Time:
Spring

Bloom Color:
Inconspicuous
(has red berries)

Height: 40 to 50 ft.

Width: 25 to 30 ft

Water Needs:
Moderate

Soil:
Moist, well drained

Did You Know?

The American holly is native over a wide range, from New York to Pennsylvania to Florida to Texas.

Color photo on page 139

Bald Cypress

Taxodium distichum

The bald cypress is native in the South and is our closest relative to the giant sequoias in California. It is stately, majestic, and unsurpassed in its beauty.

How to Grow
Choose a site in full sun to partial shade, considering the mature size (50 to 70 feet × 20 to 30 feet). Set out nursery-grown plants anytime into well-drained, moist, fertile soil. Dig the hole three to five times as wide as the rootball, but no deeper. The rootball's top should be even with the soil line. When planting in midsummer, form a 4-inch berm outside the rootball area. This berm should be able to hold 5 gallons of water. After planting, water deeply and apply mulch. Remove the berm after the first year.

Landscape Merit
They are fast-growing while young, and long-lived—two traits that don't usually appear together. They have the ability to grow in soils that are dry or that hold water. The wood is extremely durable. The fernlike foliage is very attractive, and the gradual buttressing of the trunk has landscape appeal. The seeds are eaten by ducks and other birds.

Care and Maintenance
Feed in late winter with an application of 8-8-8 fertilizer at the rate of 1 pound per 100 square feet of planted area (the area from the trunk to just outside the canopy). Prune only to remove dead wood or unwanted branches.

Recommended Varieties
Though almost always sold generic, selections have been made, such as 'Shawnee Brave' and 'Apache Chief'.

Other Name:
Swamp Cypress

Light Needs:

Added Benefit:

Zones: 7 to 9

Bloom Time:
Spring

Bloom Color:
Inconspicuous

Height: 50 to 70 ft.

Width: 20 to 30 ft.

Water Needs:
Moderate

Soil: Moist

Did You Know?
The bald cypress is native from Delaware to Indiana to Texas.

Color photo on page 139

Chinese Pistache

Pistacia chinensis

The Chinese pistache is a choice tree for the urban landscape. It grows shapely with age and produces some of the most outstanding fall leaf color.

How to Grow

Choose a site in full sun. Set out nursery-grown plants anytime into well-drained, moist, fertile soil. Dig the hole three to five times as wide as the rootball, but no deeper. The rootball's top should be even with the soil line. When planting in midsummer, form a 4-inch berm outside the rootball area. This berm should be able to hold 5 gallons of water. After planting, water deeply and apply mulch. Remove the berm after the first year.

Landscape Merit

The Chinese pistache is gangly in its early years but turns into a beautiful swan with a nice oval shape. It produces deep-green leaves that turn a fiery red-orange in the fall. The wood is tough and durable in the face of storms. It is considered a long-lived tree.

Care and Maintenance

Container-grown trees rarely require staking. In the second year, prune gangly branches to encourage branch development. Feed in late winter with an application of 8-8-8 fertilizer at 1 pound per 100 square feet of planted area (the area from the trunk to just outside the canopy). Male trees grow slightly faster, and female trees produce an inedible cluster of berries that can be used for decoration.

Recommended Varieties

No named selections are sold at this time.

Did You Know?

The Chinese pistache is used as the rootstock for pistachio nut trees.

Color photo on page 139

Eastern Red Cedar

Juniperus virginiana

Eastern red cedar is the original Southern Christmas tree. It is beautiful and durable, and it is native.

How to Grow

Choose a site in full sun to partial shade. Set out nursery-grown plants anytime into well-drained, moist, fertile soil. Dig the hole three to five times as wide as the rootball, but no deeper. The rootball's top should be even with the soil line. When planting in midsummer, form a 4-inch berm outside the rootball area. This berm should be able to hold 5 gallons of water. After planting, water deeply and apply mulch. Remove the berm after the first year.

Landscape Merit

This is one of the toughest trees for the landscape. When pests attack, it survives. The pyramidal shape is welcome, and the foliage has a pleasant aroma. Fruit produced by female plants is eaten by twenty species of birds. Use as accent, specimen, or screen. The eastern red cedar is a good backdrop for summer flowers.

Care and Maintenance

Feed the eastern red cedar in late winter with an application of 8-8-8 fertilizer at a rate of 1 pound per inch of trunk diameter. Broadcast the fertilizer evenly under the foliage canopy. Bagworms can be a problem; treat with an appropriate insecticide.

Recommended Varieties

I prefer Mississippi-grown natives. Well-known selections from other states are 'Brodie' (20 to 25 feet), 'Burkii' (15 to 20 feet), 'Hillspire' (10 to 15 feet), 'Manhattan Blue' (10 to 12 feet), 'Skyrocket' (15 to 20 feet), and 'Idyllwild' (12 to 15 feet).

Other Name:
Red Juniper

Light Needs:

Added Benefit:

Zones: 7 to 9

Bloom Time:
Early spring

Bloom Color:
Inconspicuous
(blue fruit on females)

Height: 12 to 50 ft.

Width: 6 to 20 ft.

Water Needs:
Low/moderate

Soil:
Slightly moist, well drained

Did You Know?

The fruit which is eaten by birds is also eaten by opossum.

Color photo on page 139

Ginkgo

Other Name:
Maidenhair Tree

Light Needs:

Zones: 7 to 9

Bloom Time:
Spring

Bloom Color:
No ornamental value

Height: 50 to 80 ft.

Width: 30 to 40 ft.

Water Needs:
Moderate/frequent

Soil:
Moist, well drained

Did You Know?
Fossils show that the ginkgo at one time was native in North America—it was reintroduced here in 1784.

Color photo on page 139

Ginkgo biloba

People know this plant from herbal extracts and ginkgo leaf gold-plated earrings, but to grow it and see it every day is to really know it. This tree is one for the ages.

How to Grow
Choose a site in full sun. Set out nursery-grown (males only) ginkgoes in the spring into deep, well-drained soil that is moist and fertile. Dig the hole three to five times as wide as the rootball, but no deeper. The rootball's top should be even with the soil line. When planting in midsummer, form a 4-inch berm outside the rootball area. This berm should be able to hold 5 gallons of water. After planting, water deeply and apply mulch. Remove the berm after the first year.

Landscape Merit
The ginkgo commands attention. Its unique form is admired in all seasons. It is an exceptionally long-lived tree; your children's children will thank you for it. The fall color is bright yellow and catches your eye from a great distance. The sight of yellow leaves lying on the ground is a picture in itself.

Care and Maintenance
In late winter, apply an 8-8-8 fertilizer at the rate of 1 pound per inch of trunk diameter. Broadcast fertilizer evenly under the canopy of the tree. Maintain a 3-inch layer of mulch and water regularly during the summer. If any pruning is necessary, do so in spring.

Recommended Varieties
The most recognized variety is 'Autumn Gold'™; others to consider are 'Saratoga' and 'Shangri-La'®.

Japanese Maple

Acer palmatum

No other plant has the graceful elegance of the Japanese maple. Gaze upon an old arching laceleaf Japanese maple, and a sense of awe and admiration fills your spirit.

How to Grow

Choose a site in partial shade, protected from wind. Set out nursery-grown plants in spring or fall. Plant in well-drained and -prepared moist fertile soil. Spread a 4-inch layer of fine pine bark and peat, tilling to a depth of 10 inches. Dig the hole three to five times as wide as the rootball, but no deeper. The rootball's top should be even with the soil line. After planting, water and apply a 3-inch layer of mulch.

Landscape Merit

Japanese maple is the ultimate accent or focal point for a garden. It deserves to be seen and admired. It is at home in a garden that has azaleas and dogwoods. A large laceleaf in an old mossy pot is welcome on any patio or deck.

Care and Maintenance

Feed in late winter with a light application of slow-release 8-8-8, broadcast evenly under the canopy. If grown in a tub, use time-release granules or water-soluble fertilizer in early spring. Maintain moisture and mulch throughout the summer.

Recommended Varieties

'Bloodgood' (15 to 20 feet), is a 2000 Mississippi Medallion winner. The red color lasts well into the summer. 'Oshio Beni' (15 to 20 feet) and 'Sango Kaku' (20 to 25 feet with coral stems) are famous non-dissected types. 'Crimson Queen' (8 to 10 feet), 'Ever Red' (10 feet), and 'Filigree' (6 feet) are chosen dissected types.

Light Needs:

Zones: 7 to 9

Bloom Time: Spring

Bloom Color: No ornamental value

Height: 15 to 25 ft.

Width: 15 to 25 ft.

Water Needs: Moderate/frequent

Soil: Slightly acid, moist, well drained

Did You Know?

The fruit of the maple (called a samara) is winged, giving it the ability to fly helicopter-like in the wind as it falls.

Color photo on page 139

Lacebark Elm

Other Name:
Chinese Elm

Light Needs:

Zones: 7 to 9

Bloom Time:
Late summer

Bloom Color:
No ornamental value

Height: 40 to 50 ft.

Width: 40 to 50 ft.

Water Needs:
Moderate

Soil:
Moist, well drained

Did You Know?

Dutch elm disease, to which the lacebark elm is resistant, can kill a large American elm in one to two months.

Color photo on page 140

Ulmus parvifolia

This tall stately tree is the best elm for the landscape, providing shade, that much-sought-after summer commodity.

How to Grow
Choose a site in full sun. Set out nursery-grown trees in the spring or fall into well-drained, moist, fertile soil. Dig the hole three to five times as wide as the rootball, but no deeper. The rootball's top should be even with the soil line. When planting in midsummer, form a 4-inch berm outside the rootball area. This berm should be able to hold 5 gallons of water. After planting, water deeply and apply mulch. Remove the berm after the first year.

Landscape Merit
This elm is fast growing, long lived, and resistant to Dutch elm disease and the elm leaf beetle. The wood develops into an attractive feature with age as it exfoliates and becomes mottled. It has a graceful habit, giving good shade to the landscape. It is considered semi-evergreen in milder areas of Mississippi. It is good as an accent or specimen.

Care and Maintenance
Feed in late winter with an application of 8-8-8 fertilizer at 1 pound per 100 square feet of planted area (the area from the trunk to just outside the canopy). Keep well watered and mulched during the first year of establishment.

Recommended Varieties
Most gardeners will be surprised to find that there are named varieties. Acclaimed selections from the University of Georgia are 'Allee'® (70 × 59 feet), 'Athena'® (40 × 55 feet), and 'Burgundy' (red fall leaf color).

Red Maple

Acer rubrum

The native forest comes alive with color in fall thanks to the red maple, which grows on both wet and dry sites.

How to Grow

Choose a site in full sun for best fall color. Set out nursery-grown plants during the fall or winter into well-drained, moist, fertile soil. Dig the hole three to five times as wide as the rootball, but no deeper. The rootball's top should be even with the soil line. When planting in midsummer, form a 4-inch berm outside the rootball area. This berm should be able to hold 5 gallons of water. After planting, water deeply and apply mulch. Remove the berm after the first year.

Landscape Merit

The fall color of red maple is among the best of Southeastern trees. The color from the initial growth in spring is bright red. The tree is a fast grower but is not known to be particularly strong. The bark is a unique silver-gray.

Care and Maintenance

Feed in late winter with an application of 8-8-8 fertilizer at a rate of 1 pound per 100 square feet of planted area (the area from the trunk to just outside the canopy). Broadcast the fertilizer evenly under the limb area. The tree has a shallow root system, so maintain a 3- to 4-inch layer of mulch. Pay attention to watering during the year of establishment. Water established trees deeply and infrequently.

Recommended Varieties

'Autumn Flame', 'October Glory', 'Brandywine', and 'Cumberland' are leading varieties.

Other Names:
Swamp Maple, Scarlet Maple

Light Needs:

Added Benefit:

Zones: 7 to 9

Bloom Time:
Spring

Bloom Color:
Red

Height: 40 to 60 ft.

Width: 30 to 35 ft

Water Needs:
Moderate/frequent

Soil:
Moist, well drained

Did You Know?

The seeds are eaten by squirrels and chipmunks.

Color photo on page 140

River Birch N

Betula nigra

The river birch, native to Mississippi, wins the trophy for having the prettiest bark, making it a landscape feature twelve months of the year.

How to Grow

Choose a site in full sun to partial shade in an area where this tree can be seen and enjoyed. Set out nursery-grown plants in early spring into well-drained, moist, fertile soil. Dig the hole three to five times as wide as the rootball, but no deeper. The rootball's top should be even with the soil line. When planting in midsummer, form a 4-inch berm outside the rootball area. This berm should be able to hold 5 gallons of water. After planting, water deeply and apply mulch. Remove the berm after the first year.

Landscape Merit

The bark of the river birch exfoliates into papery sheets and looks great year 'round. The tree easily forms multiple trunks, adding to its beauty. The fall foliage develops into shades of yellow. It is not long lived, but it is worth growing, enjoying, and then replacing if needed.

Care and Maintenance

Feed in late winter with an application of 8-8-8 fertilizer at a rate of 1 pound per 100 sq. feet of planted area (the area from the trunk to just outside the canopy). Prune to remove unwanted basal branches or dead wood, or to shape. Watch for aphids on young trees and treat as needed. Keep well watered and mulched during the summer months.

Recommended Varieties

'Heritage'® is the most outstanding variety, with salmon-colored bark. 'Dura-Heat'™ is a new selection gaining recognition for aphid resistance and a white bark.

Other Name:
Red Birch

Light Needs:

Zones: 7 to 9

Bloom Time:
Early summer

Bloom Color:
No ornamental value

Height: 40 to 70 ft.

Width: 40 to 60 ft.

Water Needs:
Frequent

Soil:
Moist, well drained, slightly acidic

Did You Know?

The seeds of the river birch are small—374,000 seeds per pound.

Color photo on page 140

Shumard Oak

Quercus shumardii

The shumard oak is one of the prettiest oaks for the urban landscape, with attributes that make it an all-time winner.

How to Grow

Choose a site in full sun. Set out nursery-grown plants during the fall or winter, into well-drained, moist, fertile soil. Dig the hole three to five times as wide as the rootball, but no deeper. The rootball's top should be even with the soil line. When planting in midsummer, form a 4-inch berm outside the rootball area. This berm should be able to hold 5 gallons of water. After planting, water deeply and apply mulch. Remove the berm after the first year.

Landscape Merit

The shumard oak is a fast-growing species with strong, durable wood. The leaves are deeply toothed and glossy. They also provide us with dependable red fall color. The trees grow large, providing welcome shade to a heated summer environment. The acorns are large, 1 inch long and almost as wide. They provide food for wildlife.

Care and Maintenance

Feed in late winter with an application of 8-8-8 fertilizer at the rate of 1 pound per 100 sq. feet of planted area (the area from the trunk to just outside the canopy). Broadcast the fertilizer evenly under the canopy of the tree. Water deeply and infrequently during prolonged dry periods. Maintain a good layer of mulch.

Recommended Varieties

The shumard oak is sold generic. The nuttall oak *Q. nuttallii* is another fine oak with good fall color.

Other Name:
Shumard Red Oak

Light Needs:

Added Benefit:

Zones: 7 to 9

Bloom Time:
Spring

Bloom Color:
No ornamental value (has acorns)

Height: 60 to 70 ft

Width: 40 to 50 ft.

Water Needs:
Moderate

Soil:
Moist, well drained

Did You Know?

The National Champion is in Natchez, Mississippi, and is 144 feet tall and 112 feet wide.

Color photo on page 140

Spruce Pine

Light Needs:

☀ ☽

Added Benefit:

Zones: 8, 9

Bloom Time:
Spring

Bloom Color:
No ornamental value

Height: 50 to 90 ft.

Width: 30 to 40 ft.

Water Needs:
Moderate

Soil:
Moist, well drained,
slightly acidic

Did You Know?
Spruce pine was named
by John Bartram,
September 25, 1765,
near Savannah, Georgia.

Color photo on page 140

Pinus glabra

We can grow several pines in the landscape in Mississippi, but for sheer beauty, the spruce pine is at the top of the list.

How to Grow
Choose a site in full sun to partial shade. Set out nursery-grown plants in spring into well-drained, moist, fertile soil. Dig the hole three to five times as wide as the rootball, but no deeper. The rootball's top should be even with the soil line. When planting in midsummer, form a 4-inch berm outside the rootball area. This berm should be able to hold 5 gallons of water. After planting, water deeply and apply mulch. Remove the berm after the first year.

Landscape Merit
With its unique look, it is easy to spot this pine while driving. The needles are short and dark green, twisted in bundles of two. Dense growth gives it an appearance of belonging in the Rocky Mountains. It serves as a screen for privacy and a windbreak. It's an excellent background for beds of azaleas or small trees like the redbud.

Care and Maintenance
Prune dead branches to keep tidy. Even though it is rugged and native, it will appreciate supplemental irrigation. Irrigate deeply, giving 2 inches of water a week during dry periods. Maintain a layer of mulch underneath.

Recommended Varieties
The spruce pine will take a little extra searching. It is only for zones 8 and 9. For north Mississippi, the white pine *P. strobus* offers varieties giving much the same look with needles that are the same length, but in bundles of five.

Southern Live Oak

Quercus virginiana

The southern live oak is the most majestic of all oaks in Mississippi and reigns like royalty today at old antebellum homes.

How to Grow

Choose a site in full sun. Set out nursery-grown plants during fall and winter into well-drained, moist, fertile soil. Dig the hole three to five times as wide as the rootball, but no deeper. The rootball's top should be even with the soil line. When planting in midsummer, form a 4-inch berm outside the rootball area. This berm should be able to hold 5 gallons of water. After planting, water deeply and apply mulch. Remove the berm after the first year.

Landscape Merit

This is a long-lived species. Plant a southern live oak and your progeny will appreciate and remember you. Its spreading form is ideally suited to children and swings. It is an evergreen tree, shedding leaves with new spring growth. This is the tree reminiscent of *Gone With the Wind*—and you can grow it.

Care and Maintenance

Feed in late winter with an application of 8-8-8 fertilizer at the rate of 2 pounds per 100 sq. feet of planted area (the area from the trunk to just outside the canopy). Broadcast the fertilizer evenly under the canopy of the tree. If needed, prune in late winter. Keep well watered and growing during the summer months.

Recommended Varieties

The live oak is sold generically. Some say it is marginally hardy in zone 7, yet it is native to parts of Oklahoma.

Other Name:
Live Oak

Light Needs:
☼

Added Benefit:

Zones: 7 to 9

Bloom Time:
Spring

Bloom Color:
No ornamental value

Height: 40 to 50 ft.

Width: 50 to 75 ft.

Water Needs:
Moderate/frequent

Soil:
Moist, well drained

Did You Know?
The National Champion is only 55 feet tall but 122 feet wide.

Color photo on page 140

Sweetgum

Other Name:
American Sweetgum

Light Needs:

☼

Added Benefit:

Zones: 7 to 9

Bloom Time:
Spring

Bloom Color:
No ornamental value

Height: 60 to 75 ft.

Width: 25 to 60 ft.

Water Needs:
Moderate/frequent

Soil:
Moist, well drained, slightly acidic

Did You Know?
Sweetgum's wood has long been used in furniture making.

Color photo on page 140

Liquidambar stryaciflua

This tree has wonderful palmate leaves, gives fall color that comes in fiery oranges, reds, and purples, and produces balls suitable for holiday decoration.

How to Grow
Choose a site in full sun. Set out nursery-grown plants in fall or winter into well-drained, moist, fertile soil. Dig the hole three to five times as wide as the rootball, but no deeper. The rootball's top should be even with the soil line. When planting in midsummer, form a 4-inch berm outside the rootball area. This berm should be able to hold 5 gallons of water. After planting, water deeply and apply mulch. Remove the berm after the first year.

Landscape Merit
The leaves are as pretty as those of a Japanese maple and turn color almost as well as a sugar maple, yet many scorn the tree because of those sweetgum balls. The horrid sweetgum balls do feed 25 species of birds, squirrels, and chipmunks, though, and provide good shade and a pyramidal form that lasts for years.

Care and Maintenance
Some quickly list problems, but basically the tree requires no maintenance. Keep watered and mulched during the first year of establishment. Rake those balls just as you do pine cones or pecans.

Recommended Varieties
Named varieties are 'Festival', 'Autumn Gold', and 'Burgundy', all of which claim great fall color, and a fruitless variety called 'Rotundiloba' (leaves are round, not pointed).

Willow Oak

Quercus phellos

This is one of the most stately oaks, with leaves resembling those of the willow. It is native and durable.

How to Grow

Choose a site in full sun. Set out nursery-grown plants in fall or winter into well-drained, moist, fertile soil. Dig the hole three to five times as wide as the rootball, but no deeper. The rootball's top should be even with the soil line. When planting in midsummer, form a 4-inch berm outside the rootball area. This berm should be able to hold 5 gallons of water. After planting, water deeply and apply mulch. Remove the berm after the first year.

Landscape Merit

The willow oak is a large species yielding precious summer shade. It is a long-lived tree, yet it has a fast growth rate. Though deciduous, it holds its leaves a long time, making it almost semi-evergreen.

Care and Maintenance

Feed in late winter with an application of 8-8-8 fertilizer at a rate of 1 pound per 100 sq. feet of planted area (the area from the trunk to just outside the canopy). Broadcast the fertilizer evenly under the canopy of the tree. Make any major pruning in late winter; light pruning can be done anytime. Keep well watered during the first year of establishment. Water deeply but infrequently.

Recommended Varieties

Willow oak is sold generically. Another fine oak to grow is the bur oak *Q. macrocarpa*, which has the largest of all acorns.

Other Name:
Swamp Willow Oak

Light Needs:

Added Benefit:

Zones: 7 to 9

Bloom Time:
Spring

Bloom Color:
No ornamental value

Height: 70 to 80 ft.

Width: 40 to 50 ft.

Water Needs:
Moderate

Soil:
Moist, well drained, slightly acidic

Did You Know?

The acorns are eaten by turkey, quail, blue jay, dove, and squirrel.

Color photo on page 140

FLOWERING TREES

Just about the time gardeners think that winter will never end, many Mississippi landscapes erupt into spectacular bloom with trees like the Taiwan cherry, followed by the giant flowers of the Japanese or saucer magnolias. These give way to blooms from natives like the eastern redbud and the dogwood.

In the summer when temperatures and humidity seem stifling, landscapes are ablaze with color from the trees that have the longest bloom of any trees: the crape myrtles. They have been called the lilacs of the South, and certainly they are among the most prized trees in the Southern landscape. The Mississippi Medallion program has identified award-winning crape myrtles like the white flowered 'Natchez', the red 'Tonto', and the pink 'Sioux'.

Crape myrtles are known not just for fall bloom, but also for beautiful fall foliage and an exfoliating bark that has patches of cinnamon brown and other colors, making these trees useful as winter landscape accents.

Hundreds of thousands of visitors come to Mississippi to gaze at the spring bloom of our trees.

Mississippi gardeners look for small trees to fit today's urban landscape and to add color. Almost all of the flowering trees in this chapter are perfect for those niche places in the landscape. You can grow several of them in shrub beds with azaleas and camellias, or grow them as understory trees for the stately pines.

Container-grown trees can be planted during just about any month in Mississippi, though fall and early spring are best. The hot buys on trees are often during the summer months, but with a little care you can take advantage of these great deals.

Establishing landscape trees successfully depends on the use of good gardening practices, proper soil preparation, correct planting techniques, and good follow-up care. Plants require oxygen, nutrients, and water for proper growth. You have one chance to plant it right and get a tree off to a good start.

If you are planting a group of trees or shrubs, it pays to put them in a bed. Prepare the bed by tilling and double-digging the site 15 to 20 inches deep and working in organic matter such as compost, humus, pine bark, or peat.

If you are planting single trees in the land-scape, there is more to the process than just digging a hole. The hole needs to be three to five times larger than the diameter of the rootball. This tree will have to eventually spread its roots to the native soil, so avoid the temptation to dig a hole in tight clay and use peat or compost as the backfill. You can mix one part compost with two parts native soil to backfill around the rootball. All trees need to be planted at the same depth they were growing in their containers—much deeper, and settling can cause a tree to suffocate.

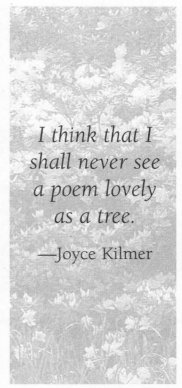

I think that I shall never see a poem lovely as a tree.

—Joyce Kilmer

If you are planting in the summer, use some of the leftover backfill to form a berm or ring around the tree. The berm should be large enough to hold three to five gallons of water, depending on the size of the tree. It will direct water to the tree's root zone, which is especially important if you are planting on a slope where water runs off quickly. The berm can be removed the second year.

Mulch around the trees will conserve moisture, keep soil temperatures moderate, and deter weeds, and it will keep you from damaging your tree with the string trimmer or lawnmower.

Crape Myrtle

Other Name:
Crepe Flower

Light Needs:

Added Benefits:

Zones: 7 to 9

Bloom Time:
Summer, early fall

Bloom Color:
Many colors and blends

Height: 5 to 30 ft.

Spacing: 6 to 15 ft.

Water Needs:
Moderate/frequent

Soil:
Moist, well drained

Did You Know?

The United States National Arboretum has released more than twenty varieties of crape myrtle.

Color photo on page 140

Lagerstroemia indica × *L. fauriei* hybrids

Crape myrtles have been called the "Lilacs of the South." Their long season of richly colored bloom is just one of many outstanding attributes.

How to Grow

Plant in full sun for best flower performance. Container-grown crape myrtles can be planted anytime. The soil must be well drained. Dig the hole three to five times as wide as the rootball, but no deeper. The rootball's top should be even with the soil line. Crape myrtles look good planted in groups as part of a bed. Read about group planting and midsummer planting in the chapter introduction (pages 208–209).

Landscape Merit

Crape myrtles have an exceptionally long bloom cycle. Exfoliating bark makes them useful as accents year 'round. The deep-green leaves of a few varieties turn crimson-orange in the fall. They are well suited for use as small screens.

Care and Maintenance

Feed in late winter and midsummer with an application of 8-8-8 fertilizer equaling 1 pound per 100 square feet of planted area (the area from the trunk to just outside the canopy). In late winter, prune by removing old seedpods and unwanted basal sprouts. Remove any twiggy growth and internal crisscrossing branches. Keep the natural shape, trying not to prune off branches larger than a dime. Deadheading the forming seedpods during the summer will keep growth coming and result in more flowers.

Recommended Varieties

Three have been named Mississippi Medallion winners for long bloom, disease resistance, outstanding bark, and fall foliage: 'Natchez' (white, 21 feet), 'Tonto' (red, 10 feet), and 'Sioux' (pink, 12 feet). There are many other great choices.

Dogwood

Cornus florida

The flowering dogwood is considered by many to be the most beautiful of all native trees.

How to Grow
The dogwood brightens areas of partial shade, but can be grown in full sun with rich, organic, moist soil that is well drained. Choose container-grown plants for best success. Dig the hole three to five times as wide as the rootball, but no deeper. The rootball's top should be even with the soil line. Water deeply and apply mulch. Dogwoods look good when planted as part of a spring shrub and flower border. Read about such planting, and planting in midsummer, in the chapter introduction (pages 208–209).

Landscape Merit
Dogwood blooms, called bracts, reflect light and brighten the partially shady landscape. They serve well as understory trees. The leaves are among the prettiest for fall color. The bright-red fruit is eaten by 28 species of birds, including the turkey.

Care and Maintenance
Feed in late winter with a very light application of 8-8-8 at 1/2 pound per 100 square feet of planted area (the area from the trunk to just outside the canopy). The dogwood is similar to an azalea, with its shallow root system. Maintain moisture and mulch.

Recommended Varieties
Many are sold generic. Some are known for disease resistance: 'Cherokee Princess', 'Cherokee Sunset'™ (red), 'Cloud 9', and 'Fragrant Cloud'. The Stellar® Dogwoods, crosses between *C. florida* and *C. kousa*, are gaining recognition for disease resistance and excellent flowers.

Other Name:
Flowering Dogwood

Light Needs:

Added Benefits:

Zones: 7 to 9

Bloom Time:
Spring

Bloom Color:
White, pink, red

Height: 20 to 30 ft.

Spacing: 17 to 25 ft.

Water Needs:
Moderate/frequent

Soil:
Moist, well drained

Did You Know?
The dogwood fruit is loved by birds, deer, and squirrels.

Color photo on page 140

Golden Raintree

Koelreuteria paniculata

The golden raintree erupts in long 12- to 15-inch sprays of yellow blossoms.

How to Grow

Choose a site in full sun. Set out nursery-grown plants anytime into well-drained soil. Dig the hole three to five times as wide as the rootball, but no deeper. The rootball's top should be even with the soil line. When planting in midsummer, form a 4-inch berm outside the rootball area. This berm should be able to hold 5 gallons of water. After planting, water deeply and apply mulch. Remove the berm after the first year.

Landscape Merit

Today's landscape is in need of small durable trees, and the golden raintree is superb. There are few to no insect or disease threats. The golden flowers are unique, hanging 12 to 15 inches long all over the tree, looking like beautiful tinsel. The fall leaf color is a striking yellow. They are also tough in cold and heat. Use to shade the patio or deck.

Care and Maintenance

Feed in late winter with an application of 8-8-8 fertilizer equaling 1 pound per 100 square feet of planted area (the area from the trunk to just outside the canopy).

Recommended Varieties

Almost always sold generic, two varieties in the trade are 'Fastigiata' and 'September Gold'.

Other Names:
Varnish Tree,
Pride of India

Light Needs:

Zones: 7 to 9

Bloom Time:
Early summer

Bloom Color:
Yellow

Height: 20 to 25 ft.

Spacing: 17 to 25 ft.

Water Needs:
Moderate/frequent

Soil:
Moist, well drained

Did You Know?

The golden raintree is in the soapberry family.

Color photo on page 140

Grancy Graybeard

Chionanthus virginicus

The fluffy white fringe flowers of the Grancy Graybeard have made this flowering tree a favorite since the 1800s.

How to Grow

Choose a site in full sun to partial shade for best flower performance. Plant in an area that is moist, fertile, and well drained. Set out nursery-grown plants in early spring. Dig the hole three to five times as wide as the rootball, but no deeper. The rootball's top should be even with the soil line. When planting in midsummer, form a 4-inch berm outside the rootball area. The berm should be able to hold 5 gallons of water. After planting, water deeply and apply mulch. Remove the berm after the first year.

Landscape Merit

The Grancy Graybeard excels in the urban landscape. The white flowers brighten partially shady areas and lend fragrance. The leaves go from green to bright yellow in the fall. Male trees have larger flowers, but the females produce fruit that is a delicacy for birds.

Care and Maintenance

Feed in late winter with an application of 8-8-8 fertilizer at a rate of 1 pound per 100 square feet of planted area (the area from the trunk to just outside the canopy). No regular pruning is required. There are no serious pests or diseases, but watch for borers.

Recommended Varieties

The Grancy Graybeard is native, and no selections have been made. Shop early in the spring—demand is great and supply is limited.

Other Names:
Fringe Tree,
Old Man's Beard

Light Needs:

Added Benefits:

Zones: 7 to 9

Bloom Time:
Spring

Bloom Color:
White

Height: 12 to 20 ft.

Spacing: 15 to 20 ft.

Water Needs:
Moderate/frequent

Soil:
Moist, well drained

Did You Know?

The word *chionanthus* comes from Greek words meaning "snow flower."

Color photo on page 140

Japanese Magnolia

Magnolia soulangiana

The large tulip-shaped flowers produced in late winter and early spring are a sight long remembered.

How to Grow

Choose a site that is fertile, well drained, and moist, with wind protection. Set out nursery-grown plants in early spring. Dig the hole three to five times as wide as the rootball, but no deeper. The rootball's top should be even with the soil line. When planting in midsummer, form a 4-inch berm outside the rootball area. This berm should be able to hold 5 gallons of water. After planting, water deeply and apply mulch. Remove the berm after the first year.

Landscape Merit

One of these trees can be used as an accent or specimen. The color, shape, size, and fragrance of the flowers all border on the spectacular. Even if they get killed by freezes every other year, those years in bloom are worth it. The large fuzzy buds are unique.

Care and Maintenance

Feed in late winter with an application of 8-8-8 fertilizer at a rate of 1 pound per 100 square feet of planted area (the area from the trunk to just outside the canopy). If any pruning must be done, do so after the bloom cycle. The saucer magnolia has no serious pests or diseases.

Recommended Varieties

'Alexandrina' is one of the most popular, but the color varies—buy in bloom to select your color favorite. 'Burgundy' (deep purple) and 'Rustica Rubra' (reddish purple) are great. Try M. *stellata*, the star magnolia with white star-like flowers

Other Name:
Saucer Magnolia

Light Needs:

Added Benefits:

Zones: 7 to 9

Bloom Time:
Late winter, early spring

Bloom Color:
Purple, pink, rose, white

Height: 15 to 30 ft.

Spacing: 15 to 20 ft.

Water Needs:
Moderate/frequent

Soil:
Moist, well drained

Did You Know?

Magnolia was named after Pierre Magnol (1638-1715), a French botanist.

Color photo on page 141

Ornamental Pear

Pyrus calleryana

One of the most widely planted and beloved trees is the flowering pear.

How to Grow

Choose a site in full sun with moist, well-drained, fertile soil. Set out nursery-grown plants anytime. Dig the hole three to five times as wide as the rootball, but no deeper. The rootball's top should be even with the soil line. When planting in midsummer, form a 4-inch berm outside the rootball area. This berm should be able to hold 5 gallons of water. After planting, water deeply and apply mulch. Remove the berm after the first year.

Landscape Merit

The trees are a mass of white blooms in the spring, followed by glossy green leaves that provide some of the most reliable fall color in shades of orange, yellow, crimson, and burgundy. The small fruit that may be a nuisance if the tree is planted by a sidewalk is food for birds. It's the ideal accent or specimen tree and fits into the urban landscape nicely.

Care and Maintenance

Fireblight is the main enemy. Reducing fertilizer and little to no pruning helps, as well as variety selection. Keep basal sprouts removed. Maintain mulch and water during prolonged dry periods.

Recommended Varieties

'Bradford' gets huge and has the best fall color. It does break in ice and wind storms. 'Chanticleer' is resistant to limb breakage, but fall color is not as showy. 'Aristocrat' resists storm damage but shows signs of being a fireblight target.

Light Needs:

Added Benefit:

Zones: 7 to 9

Bloom Time:
Spring

Bloom Color:
White

Height: 20 to 40 ft.

Spacing: 17 to 25 ft.

Water Needs:
Moderate

Soil:
Moist, well drained

Did You Know?

The 'Bradford' is a USDA release from 1963.

Color photo on page 141

Redbud

Other Name:
Eastern Redbud

Light Needs:

Added Benefits:

Zones: 7 to 9

Bloom Time:
Early spring

Bloom Color:
Pink, purple, white

Height: 25 to 35 ft.

Spacing: 15 to 20 ft

Water Needs:
Moderate/frequent

Soil:
Moist, well drained

Did You Know?
The redbud has been in cultivation since 1641.

Color photo on page 141

Cercis canadensis

Nothing is prettier than a native redbud surrounded by blooming narcissus or towering above a bed of azaleas.

How to Grow
Choose a site in full sun to partial shade that is moist, fertile, and well drained. It is ideal to plant while the tree is dormant, but container-grown trees can be planted anytime. Dig the hole three to five times as wide as the rootball, but no deeper. The rootball's top should be even with the soil line. When planting in midsummer, form a 4-inch berm outside the rootball area. This berm should be able to hold 5 gallons of water. After planting, water deeply and apply mulch. Remove the berm after the first year.

Landscape Merit
They are great as accents, specimen, or understory trees. The purple flowers last for weeks during early spring and deserve to be in well-prepared shrub borders with azaleas, dogwoods, and bulbs. The foliage of the 'Oklahoma' redbud is glossy and attractive.

Care and Maintenance
Feed in late winter and midsummer with an application of 8-8-8 fertilizer at a rate of 1 pound per 100 square feet of planted area (the area from the trunk to just outside the canopy). Maintain moisture during the summer and keep mulched.

Recommended Varieties
It is usually sold generic, but 'Forest Pansy' is a red-leafed variety not known to take full sun; 'Alba' (white) and 'Appalachian Red' (hot pink) are two notable varieties. *C. reniformis* 'Oklahoma' and *C. chinensis* 'Avondale' are also excellent choices.

Southern Magnolia

Magnolia grandifloria

The magnolia, revered and coveted by all gardeners, is both the state flower and state tree for Mississippi.

How to Grow

Choose a site in full sun to partial shade that is well drained, fertile, and moist. The southern magnolia is best planted in late winter or early spring. Dig the hole three to five times as wide as the rootball, but no deeper. The rootball's top should be even with the soil line. When planting in midsummer, form a 4-inch berm outside the rootball area. This berm should be able to hold 5 gallons of water. After planting, water deeply and apply mulch. Remove the berm after the first year.

Landscape Merit

This stately glossy-leafed evergreen gives color and character to the winter landscape. The giant white fragrant blossoms are made for childhood memories and the artist's canvas. They make an excellent screen for privacy and to block the cold north wind. The red seeds are eaten by birds.

Care and Maintenance

Feed in late winter with an application of 8-8-8 fertilizer, 1 pound per 100 square feet of planted area (the area from the trunk to just outside the canopy). If you prune the lower limbs, you have made a commitment to raking leaves. Leave the limbs and let the fallen leaves serve as mulch.

Recommended Varieties

'Little Gem' (21 feet) is a Mississippi Medallion winner and fits all landscapes. 'D.D. Blanchard', 'Bracken's Brown Beauty', and 'Majestic Beauty' are just a few of many good ones.

Other Name:
Large-Flowered Magnolia

Light Needs:

Added Benefits:

Zones: 7 to 9

Bloom Time:
May to June and sporadically

Bloom Color:
White

Height: 25 to 80 ft.

Spacing: 20 to 45 ft.

Water Needs:
Moderate

Soil:
Moist, well drained

Did You Know?

The National Champion magnolia is in Mississippi and has a height of 122 feet and a crown over 63 feet wide.

Color photo on page 141

Taiwan Flowering Cherry

Prunus campanulata

Formosan Cherry,
Bell-Flowered Cherry

Light Needs:

Added Benefits:

Zones: 7 to 9

Bloom Time:
Late winter, early spring

Bloom Color:
Hot pink, pink

Height: 20 to 25 ft.

Spacing: 12 to 15 ft.

Water Needs:
Moderate/frequent

Soil:
Moist, well drained

Did You Know?

The 'Taiwan Flowering Cherry' is ideal for an oriental garden, or placed where its colors reflect off water.

Color photo on page 141

The 'Taiwan Flowering Cherry' explodes with color, its bell-shaped flowers numbering in the tens of thousands.

How to Grow

Plant in full sun in late winter; container-grown trees can be planted anytime. This tree looks good as part of a well-prepared shrub border with evergreens and spring-blooming shrubs. Lawn planting is possible if drainage is good. Both planting techniques can be found in the chapter introduction on pages 208–209. The planting hole must be much wider than the rootball, but no deeper. Use the extra backfill to form a 4-inch berm beyond the edge of the rootball. It should be large enough to hold 5 gallons of water. If drainage is poor, don't form a berm. After the tree is planted and the berm formed, water thoroughly and mulch. Remove the berm at the end of the first year.

Landscape Merit

Taiwan cherries provide the first color of the year. This early bloom may get caught by freezes, but these trees are still a great choice. They are the perfect accent in a landscape planned for four seasons.

Care and Maintenance

Borers can be a problem; treat as needed. Feed with an 8-8-8 fertilizer at 1 pound per 100 square feet in late winter, extending from the trunk to just outside the canopy. Water is especially important the first year. Established trees should be watered deeply and infrequently. No pruning is required other than to remove crossing branches.

Recommended Varieties

The 'Taiwan Flowering Cherry' and the 'Okame', a hybrid, are great for the entire state.

Vitex

Vitex agnus-castus

This is a beautiful heirloom tree that needs to be planted in great numbers again. The blue flowers are a delight to behold.

How to Grow

Choose a site in full sun that is well drained and fertile. Nurseries usually have good quantities that are starting to bloom. Dig the hole three to five times as wide as the rootball, but no deeper. The rootball's top should be even with the soil line. When planting in midsummer, form a 4-inch berm outside the rootball area. This berm should be able to hold 5 gallons of water. After planting, water deeply and apply mulch. Remove the berm after the first year.

Landscape Merit

The vitex has fragrant bright-blue flowers resembling those of a buddleia but held erect. They command attention when in bloom. The vitex is useful as a small urban tree and in shrub form. It is at home in both perennial and herb gardens. Use as an accent or specimen.

Care and Maintenance

Feed in late winter with an application of an 8-8-8, 1 pound per 100 square feet of planted area (the area from the trunk to just outside the canopy). After the bloom cycle, deadhead blossoms and give another application of fertilizer. Maintain moisture and another bloom period will occur, usually toward the end of summer. It can be kept pruned to maintain shrub form.

Recommended Varieties

Almost always sold generic, 'Abbeville Blue', 'Alba' (white), 'Lilac Queen', and 'Rosea' (pink) are named selections.

Other Name:
Lilac Chaste Tree

Light Needs:

Added Benefits:

Zones: 7 to 9

Bloom Time:
Summer

Bloom Color: Blue to purple, white, pink

Height: 15 to 20 ft.

Spacing: 10 to 15 ft.

Water Needs:
Low/moderate

Soil: Slightly moist, well drained

Did You Know?

Also called Monk's Tree, its dried fruit contains a hormone-like substance that reduces libido.

Color photo on page 141

TROPICALS

Thanks to the 250-plus days between freezing temperatures, and more than fifty inches of annual rainfall, Mississippi is a great place to create a mini–Montego Bay in the landscape. Many of the tropical plants grown in the beautiful Caribbean islands and in South America are for sale at your local garden center and nursery. All colors and forms of hibiscus, allamanda, mandevilla, bougainvillea, gingers, bananas, and more are just down the street at your garden center.

The Chinese hibiscus is by far the most popular tropical plant here. Grown largely in containers, selection and price have influenced many to plant them in the landscape much as you would an annual. The hibiscus comes in a wide assortment of colors, blends, and double-flowered selections. While many flowering plants like high-phosphorus fertilizers, the hibiscus does not. Select a complete balanced fertilizer and apply monthly. The optimum soil pH is 5.5 to 7.8. Any container plant that you water daily during the summer needs fertilizer more often. Hibiscus cannot tolerate wet feet, so if you plan to grow them in the landscape, raise your planting area as needed.

Bougainvilleas, with their almost fluorescent, brightly colored bracts, are great for summer color. This native to Brazil comes in a wide variety of colors and is best grown in a container. Home gardeners have long debated how to get them to flower, but professional growers have no problem. Their solution is to water sparingly until they start to bloom. Once bloom begins, they pinch tips to encourage lateral flowering, and give them a little more water.

Another native of Brazil, known there as Brazilian Jasmine, is the mandevilla. Two popular selections are *Mandevilla splendens* and *Mandevilla* × *Alice du Pont*. Both are vines and are prolific summer bloomers. They have dark-green, lustrous leaves and large, pink, funnel-shaped flowers. They are not the least bit

> Try some of these plants and you just might imagine the sounds of steel drums in your yard.

cold tolerant, but are so vigorous and bloom so profusely that they are worth growing in the landscape as annuals, or containerized for enjoying through the winter.

The allamanda is one of the most common flowers of the tropics and has large, yellow, bell-shaped flowers. There are now compact selections and varieties with pink flowers. The flowers last several days and are produced all summer. It is best to grow allamanda as an annual in the landscape, or to grow it in a container, which allows you to protect it during the winter.

Many gingers are available in Mississippi, one of my favorites being the variegated shell ginger (*Alpinia zerumbet variegata*). With its dark-green leaves and yellow stripes, this ginger is absolutely striking. It's worth planting in your landscape even if it never blooms, but the small, crinkled, yellow flowers with red and brown stripes are a conversation piece. Once established in the landscape, propagate this ginger by division. It can be brought indoors for the winter, where it is equally attractive. Even if left outdoors, mulching heavily should allow it to return after most winters.

Many gardeners have realized that even though they are not located in the 'Citrus Belt,' they can grow and harvest delicious fruit by growing in containers. Look for satsumas, 'Improved Meyer lemon', and kumquats. You can grow citrus for years in a container and have the benefit of foliage, flower, and fruit. Move your plant indoors for winter as needed.

With careful thought and planning, you can create your own little garden of paradise.

Allamanda

Other Name:
Golden Trumpet

Light Needs:

Added Benefit:

Zone: 10

Bloom Time:
Almost continuous

Bloom Color:
Golden yellow

Height × Width:
36 to 42 in. × 48 in.

Water Needs:
High in containers,
moderate in soil

Soil:
Moist, well drained

Uses:
Container, vine, shrub

Did You Know?
The allamanda is named
for a Swiss physician
who collected seeds in
the late 1700s.

Color photo on page 141

Allamanda cathartica

Allamanda yields large 3- to 4-inch golden-yellow trumpet-shaped flowers in clusters that last for days throughout the warm growing season.

How to Grow
After the frost-free date, plant in large containers filled with a light, well-drained potting mixture. Consider planting in a well-drained flowerbed and treating it as an annual, or digging it up in the fall and repotting. Give it morning light and protection from the intense midafternoon sun.

Companion Planting
Allamanda combines well with bananas and mandevillas. If you have a white picket fence, try alternating allamandas with mandevillas, tying them to the fence.

Care and Maintenance
When grown in containers, allamanda will probably require watering every day during the summer. Apply a balanced time-release granular fertilizer every four to six weeks, or a diluted water-soluble balanced fertilizer every other week. In the landscape, feed with light monthly applications of slow-release balanced (10-10-10, for example) fertilizer. If grown as a vine, the allamanda will need to be trained (tied) to a trellis or fence, or it can be pruned and trained into a shrub form. Since it is tropical, it will need to be brought indoors before the first frost or treated as an annual. Like many common landscape plants, it is poisonous.

Recommended Varieties
Allamanda is usually sold generic, but occasionally you will see 'Williamsii'. Dwarf varieties include 'Hendersonii Dwarf', 'Hendersonii compacta', 'Dwarf Discovery', and 'Silver Dwarf Discovery'. A pink form ('Cherries Jubilee') is available. A bush species known as *Allamanda schottii* is also available.

Banana

Musa species

The leaves of the banana tree are among the most decorative for lending a touch of the tropics to our backyard. Trees vary from dwarf to giant-sized, and the unique flowers are followed by hands of bananas.

How to Grow

Plant after the last frost of the season in moist, well-drained soil with plenty of sunlight. They are ideal around the pool and other outdoor areas. Dozens of sizes and varieties are available. Some produce gorgeous flowers with inedible fruit (*Musa ornata*), some can be coaxed into producing edible bananas ('Giant Cavendish'), and others, like the 'Bloodleaf', are grown for lush foliage.

Companion Planting

They can be planted at the back of a tropical border combined with Chinese hibiscus or allamandas. Use behind evergreen plants like cleyera so they will not be missed during the winter.

Care and Maintenance

Water and give monthly applications of a slow-release fertilizer with a 3-1-4 ratio (6-2-8, for example). Banana trees will often go from the ground to 20 feet in one season. In zones 8 and 9, bananas return each spring if the soils are well drained and mulch-protected. Even in the coldest regions of the state they may be cut to a manageable size, dug up, and placed in a frost-free environment to be planted again in the spring.

Recommended Varieties

Try *Musa ornata* or ornamental bananas 'Royal Purple' and 'Lavender Beauty', and *Musa acuminata* 'Bloodleaf', 'Giant Cavendish', 'Super Dwarf Cavendish', and 'Raja Puri'. Don't be afraid to experiment!

Other Name:
Plantain

Light Needs:

Added Benefits:

Zones: (7), 8, 9

Bloom Time:
Summer

Bloom Color: Red, lavender, pink, purple

Height × Width:
3 to 20 ft. × 3 to 15 ft.

Water Needs:
Moderate/high

Soil:
Moist, well drained

Uses:
Landscape or containers

Did You Know?

Bananas produce female flowers called "hands," which become the small bananas. After that, the stalk produces only male flowers.

Color photo on page 141

Bougainvillea

Bougainvillea species

Hundreds of brightly colored, almost iridescent, flowers adorn the bougainvillea. Though it climbs walls in tropical or Mediterranean regions, bougainvillea also excels in any region in baskets and containers.

How to Grow

In all regions of our state except the extreme southern coast, bougainvillea has to be grown in a container for winter protection, or treated as an annual. It blooms easily in containers and can be kept potbound for a long time. Grow in full sunlight and keep well watered and fed when in bloom.

Companion Planting

Bougainvilleas that are growing in containers with a supporting trellis can be combined with downward-cascading plants such as 'New Gold' lantana. The real show occurs when different varieties of brightly colored bougainvilleas are planted together.

Care and Maintenance

Getting bougainvilleas to rebloom is a problem often presented to horticulturists. After bloom has ceased, feed with a 1-2-1 ratio fertilizer, watering to encourage new growth. When adequate growth has occurred, water and food must be reduced to induce blooms. Keep the soil barely moist during this time. The plant needs water when in bloom. If growing in the southern Mississippi landscape, plant along a wall for extra winter protection. The older your plant gets, the more cold hardy it will become, so plant immediately after the last frosty weather.

Recommended Varieties

The list is huge. Here are a few: 'Barbara Karst', 'Crimson Jewel', 'Raspberry Ice', 'Texas Dawn', 'San Diego Red'. Many are still offered only by color.

Other Name:
Paper Flower

Light Needs:

Added Benefit:

Zones: 9b, 10

Bloom Time:
Spring, summer

Bloom Color:
Shades of red, purple, orange, pink, white

Height × Width:
Sprawling canes can reach 20 feet or can be kept cut back

Water Needs:
Moderate

Soil:
Moist, well drained

Uses: Containers, hanging baskets

Did You Know?
The bougainvillea is in the same family as the four-o'clock.

Color photo on page 141

Butterfly Ginger

Hedychium coronarium

Butterfly ginger is one of the most cold-hardy gingers we can grow. The butterfly-shaped flowers are enticingly fragrant. It flowers in late summer and fall, which is a welcome time for Southern gardeners who are tired of the heat.

How to Grow

Plant after the last spring frost in moist, well-drained soil, in an area that receives morning sun and afternoon shade, or filtered light. Plant several close to areas of outdoor entertaining—your guests will relish the intoxicating fragrance. In northern Mississippi, consider planting in protected microclimates that will offer extra winter protection.

Companion Planting

The butterfly ginger is tropical in appearance and works well with plants like elephant ears, ferns, hostas, bananas, and, of course, different species of ginger. The butterfly ginger can also be planted to the rear of beds that have impatiens or begonias.

Care and Maintenance

Butterfly ginger needs plenty of moisture and fertilizer to keep it growing vigorously. Fertilize in early spring with a slow-release fertilizer with a 2-1-2 or 3-1-2 ratio (18-6-12, for example) just prior to shoot emergence, and again in midsummer, being careful not to let the fertilizer touch the stalks. Remove frostbitten stalks and be sure to add a good layer of mulch to assist in winter protection. Divide clumps every three to five years or as needed.

Recommended Varieties

Butterfly ginger is usually sold generic or as species. Look also for *Hedychium chrysoleucum*, which is white with yellow in the center.

Other Name: Ginger Lily

Light Needs:

Added Benefits:

Zones: 7 to 9

Bloom Time: Late summer, fall

Bloom Color: White

Height × Width: 4 to 6 ft. × 3 to 6 ft. (clump)

Water Needs: Moderate/high

Soil: Moist, well drained (also at edge of a water garden)

Uses: Beds adjacent to pools, patios, decks

Did You Know?

The name *Hedychium* is Greek for "sweet snow." This is one of the flowers often used to make Hawaiian leis.

Color photo on page 141

Chinese Hibiscus

Other Name:
Rose of China

Light Needs:

Added Benefits:

Zones: (9), 10

Bloom Time:
All season

Bloom Color:
All shades except blue

Height × Width:
4 to 8 ft. × 3 to 6 ft.

Water Needs:
Moderate

Soil:
Moist, well drained

Uses: Tropical beds,
containers

Did You Know?

Hibiscus shrubs in frost-free areas may reach 15 to 20 feet in height. The hibiscus is related to cotton and okra.

Color photo on page 141

Hibiscus rosa-sinensis

Large, beautiful crepe paper–like flowers are produced for months, with little required of the gardener.

How to Grow

Grow in well-drained beds rich in organic material and exposed to plenty of sun. Keep evenly moist. Morning sun and filtered afternoon light is ideal. Hibiscus also excels in containers. Treat as an annual or bring indoors where it can be treated as a protected shrub (not necessary around coastal Mississippi).

Companion Planting

Nothing is more exotic-looking than large banana trees surrounded by colorful hibiscus. Try growing allamandas on a trellis with a red single hibiscus planted in front. Grow upright elephant ears (*Alocasia macrorhiza*) to the rear of the border, behind hibiscus.

Care and Maintenance

Hibiscus flowers bloom on new growth, so it is important to maintain vigorous growth throughout the season. Keep the plants watered during periods of drought, and keep them well fed. Hibiscus prefers a complete fertilizer formula like a slow-release 18-6-12. Light applications made monthly are preferred. If growing in containers, apply a diluted water-soluble fertilizer weekly, or add time-release granules every four to six weeks. Prune old wood in spring to encourage growth.

Recommended Varieties

The list of varieties is staggering. A few are 'American Beauty', 'Brilliant', 'Kona Princess', 'White Wings', and my favorite, 'Norman Lee'.

Citrus

Citrus species

Almost all gardeners have a plant they protect during the winter. Why not try a citrus tree that is evergreen and has wonderfully fragrant flowers and delicious fruit?

How to Grow

Citrus is a handsome addition to the porch, patio, or deck. Plant in a 2-gallon container, working your way up to a 15- to 20-gallon container over the next few years. South of Interstate 10 in the coastal Mississippi area, cold-hardy citrus like satsumas and kumquats (*Fortunella* species) can be planted on the southern side of the home for increased winter protection. Plant after the last freeze of spring.

Companion Planting

Most of us will have to be satisfied with growing citrus in containers, which makes the combination plant choices plentiful. I prefer to use plants that cascade, like the 'Purple Wave' petunia.

Care and Maintenance

Fill your pot with a loose, light potting mix containing sphagnum moss, to 1 to 4 in. below the container rim, allowing for easy watering. Feed every four to six weeks during the growing season with biweekly applications of diluted water-soluble fertilizer or applications of a 2-1-2 ratio time-release granular fertilizer. This should result in deep-green mature foliage. If planting outside in southern Mississippi, choose a site that is well drained, has full sunlight, and offers protection during cold snaps.

Recommended Varieties

'Kimbrough' and 'Owari' satsuma oranges are among the most cold hardy, as are limequats, kumquats, and the calamondin orange. 'Improved Meyer' lemon works great in containers.

Other Names:
Orange, Lemon, Lime, Grapefruit

Light Needs:

Added Benefits:

Zones: (9), 10

Bloom Time: Spring

Bloom Color: White

Height × Width:
4 × 4 ft. (in containers)

Water Needs:
Moderate

Soil:
Moist, well drained

Uses: Containers, landscape in zone 9

Did You Know?

In France, indoor houses for citrus called *orangeries* were popular during the reign of King Louis XIV.

Color photo on page 141

Crepe Ginger

Other Name:
Wild Ginger

Light Needs:

Added Benefits:

Zones: (7), 8, 9

Bloom Time:
Summer, fall

Bloom Color:
Red bract, white flowers

Height × Width:
6 to 8 ft. × 2 to 3 ft.

Water Needs:
Moderate

Soil:
Moist, well drained

Uses: Tropical beds

Did You Know?
Rhizomes of crepe ginger are used for medicinal purposes in India.

Color photo on page 142

Costus speciosus

Native to the East Indies, this ginger is tropical-looking from foliage to bloom. The bloom first appears as a red cone, 4 inches long and 2½ inches wide, which is actually a bract. Crepe-like white flowers open up in a series. The red cone remains attractive weeks after blooms cease.

How to Grow
Plant after spring weather has warmed, in well-drained, moist soil that receives filtered light. Morning sun and afternoon shade are ideal. In northern Mississippi, consider microclimates around the home where extra cold protection may be given. Mulch to conserve moisture, keep soil temperatures moderate, and protect in the winter.

Companion Planting
Crepe ginger works well with other tropical foliage plants like bananas and upright elephant ears. It combines nicely with red or white impatiens, hostas, and ferns.

Care and Maintenance
Crepe ginger needs plenty of moisture and fertilizer to maintain vigorous growth. Fertilize in early spring just prior to shoot emergence, and again in midsummer with a slow-release fertilizer that has a 2-1-2 ratio (10-5-10, for example). Spread fertilizer evenly and carefully, making sure not to let it touch the stalks. Remove foliage after it is frozen back. When clumps get crowded, divide and replant in early spring.

Recommended Varieties
Crepe ginger is not as easy to find as it should be, or (we hope) as it will be. It is usually sold as generic or species. 'Pink Shadow,' a crepe ginger with a pink blush, and 'Tetraploid,' which produces a shorter plant, are both available.

Croton

Codiaeum variegatum

Croton's foliage is like a Caribbean carnival—bright and bold with color. One of the prettiest plants we can grow in containers for the porch, deck, or patio, its color persists year 'round.

How to Grow

Grow in an Old World–style pot as a patio focal point. Plant in a well-drained, loose potting mixture. Prices have dropped—plant in the landscape as an annual. South of Interstate 10 they may survive several years in a protected landscape area. Crotons need sunlight to develop their rich colors, but appreciate shade protection in midafternoon.

Companion Planting

The croton is so bold and bright that green is its companion color. Try growing dwarf bananas with the croton, whether in the landscape or a tub.

Care and Maintenance

Crotons prefer a slightly acidic soil—take caution not to let the plants dry out. Keep well watered and fed every other week during the growing season with a water-soluble fertilizer, or use time-release granules with a 3-1-2 ratio (18-6-12, for example) every four to six weeks. If bringing indoors for the winter, do so gradually, letting the plant get adjusted to lower levels of light. Once indoors, do not overwater. Cut back on fertilizer until you're ready to take the plant back outside. Spider mites may become a problem indoors, so examine regularly. The leaves are attractive in wreaths.

Recommended Varieties

It is usually sold only as 'croton,' but 'Bravo', 'Big Dipper', 'Commotion', 'Imperialis', 'Majesticum', and 'Evening Embers' are a few in the trade.

Light Needs:

Zones: (9), 10

Bloom Time:
Inconspicuous bloom

Bloom Color:
Foliage in variegated shades of orange, red, yellow, green

Height × Width:
3 to 8 ft. × 3 to 5 ft.

Water Needs:
Moderate

Soil: Slightly moist, well drained

Uses: Tubs and landscape in extreme southern Mississippi

Did You Know?

The croton is in the same family as the copper plant and the poinsettia.

Color photo on page 142

Hidden Ginger

Curcuma petiolata

Other Names:
Queen Lily, Surprise Lily

Light Needs:

Added Benefits:

Zones: 7, 8, 9

Bloom Time:
Late summer, early fall

Bloom Color:
Purple, pink, and white
bracts, yellow bloom

Height × Width:
4 × 4 ft.

Water Needs:
Moderate

Soil:
Moist, well drained

Did You Know?

The spice turmeric
comes from the closely
related *Curcuma longa.*
Other *Curcuma* plants
are used for medicinal
purposes in various
parts of the world.

Color photo on page 142

Purple, pink, and white blooms snuggled among canna-like leaves give hidden ginger a look of having just been brought in from Tahiti or Bora Bora. Awesome as a cut flower, it is probably the hardiest of all gingers.

How to Grow

Plant yours after the last spring frost in a moist, loose, well-drained bed. It prefers filtered light and works great as an understory planting for large deciduous trees. In northern Mississippi, plant in a protected area on the southeastern side of the house. Mulch to conserve moisture and add winter protection. Plant in mass for the best effect.

Companion Planting

Plant in bold drifts adjacent to fern drifts. Try behind hostas or next to lavender impatiens. Hidden ginger combines well with white 'Gingerland' caladium, or those with lavender blotches. Do not use tall plants in front of hidden ginger or it will not be seen.

Care and Maintenance

Hidden ginger is undemanding. Keep watered. Feed in spring prior to shoot emergence, and again in summer, with a slow-release 2-1-2 or 3-1-2 ratio fertilizer. When foliage turns yellow in fall, cut to the ground. Clumps can easily be divided in early spring for multiple plants. Plant enough so that you will be able to harvest them as cut flowers. Apply a fresh layer of mulch in the fall.

Recommended Varieties

Hidden ginger is usually sold generic or by species. There are some closely related species in the trade, such as *Curcuma alismatifolia,* or Siam tulip; and *Curcuma alata,* or giant plume ginger.

Mandevilla

Mandevilla species

Large, hot-pink, funnel-shaped flowers are produced on this Brazilian plant throughout the growing season, making it one of the best buys in tropical plants.

How to Grow

Grow in a container filled with light, well-drained potting mixture, using a small trellis for support. Many Mississippi gardeners choose to grow them in well-drained beds, up a mailbox pole, or on an arbor. Provide plenty of sunlight for best flowering.

Companion Planting

Mandevilla looks great planted in a large basket with a long chain, hanging from a tall porch or balcony. Let it climb the chain, and use the 'Pink Frost' ornamental sweet potato to cascade out of the basket. Mandevilla also combines well with blue clematis on a white picket fence.

Care and Maintenance

Mandevilla is a vigorous-growing vine and flower producer. It needs small doses of a balanced water-soluble fertilizer every two to three weeks when grown in containers, or time-release granules every four to six weeks. In the landscape, use light monthly applications of a slow-release balanced (10-10-10, for example) fertilizer. Be sure to maintain moisture during the hot, dry days of summer. A prolonged period without water may prove fatal to the plant. Overwinter by placing them in a brightly lit area of the home. Do not overwater, and reduce fertilizer applications until spring. Watch for mealybugs and spider mites indoors; treat as needed.

Recommended Varieties

Mandevilla × 'Alice du Pont' is still the best of the mandevillas, but 'Red Riding Hood', a different species, is a close second.

Other Name:
Brazilian Jasmine

Light Needs:

Added Benefit:

Zones: (9), 10

Bloom Time:
Spring, summer, fall

Bloom Color:
Pink, red, white, yellow

Height × Width:
Vine over 8 ft. long

Water Needs:
Moderate

Soil:
Moist, well drained

Uses:
Container, climber

Did You Know?

The mandevilla has some distinguished relatives: allamanda, oleander, and periwinkle.

Color photo on page 142

Night Jasmine

Other Name:
Lady of the Night

Light Needs:

Added Benefits:

Zones: (8), 9, 10

Bloom Time:
Spring, summer, fall

Bloom Color:
Creamy yellow

Height × Width:
4 to 6 ft. × 3 to 4 ft.

Water Needs:
Moderate

Soil:
Moist, well drained

Uses: Tender landscape or container

Did You Know?

Night jasmine is in the same family as tomatoes, peppers, and tobacco.

Color photo on page 142

Cestrum nocturnum

It's nothing fancy to look at, but night jasmine is unequaled when it comes to flooding the yard with intoxicatingly wonderful fragrance at night. It's hard to believe that these small, yellow, trumpet-shaped flowers have that kind of power.

How to Grow
When for sale, it is pretty bland-looking. Plant in moist, well-drained soil near a porch, a patio, or windows that you might have open in springtime. It needs plenty of light to bloom its best, but will do fine even in filtered light. Night jasmine will come back from the roots when temperatures hit the middle teens, so add mulch, grow in containers, or treat as an annual.

Companion Planting
Since we are growing this plant for its fragrant nighttime blossoms, we need to grow it where its performance will be enjoyed. Where hostas excel, so will the night jasmine. Try large containers with a night jasmine surrounded by colorful impatiens.

Care and Maintenance
The night jasmine is an easy-to-grow plant as long as the soil is well drained. Prune to shape as desired. Watch the soil moisture in the heat of summer, and feed monthly with a light application of a balanced fertilizer (10-10-10, for example). Feed with a water-soluble fertilizer every two weeks if in a container, or every four to six weeks with time-release granules. The night jasmine is easy to propagate with woody cuttings.

Recommended Varieties
No varieties are known, but there is a day-blooming cousin called *Cestrum diurnum* (its flowers are not as fragrant).

Scarlet Ginger

Hedychium coccineum

Scarlet ginger's foot-long tropical-looking flower spikes in shades of reddish orange are borne on 6- to 7-foot-tall stalks. The plant forms large clumps, sending up numerous flower stalks as the crown ages.

How to Grow

Plant after the last spring frost in a well-prepared bed that is rich in organic matter and well drained. Partial shade, or morning sun and afternoon shade, is ideal. In northern Mississippi, consider microclimates around the home where extra cold protection may be given. Mulch to conserve moisture, keep soil temperatures moderate, and protect in the winter.

Companion Planting

Scarlet ginger is a large plant that works well behind shrubs like azaleas. It is not a tropical combination, but at least the ginger won't be missed in winter. Reddish-orange impatiens work well planted in front of scarlet ginger.

Care and Maintenance

Scarlet ginger needs plenty of moisture and fertilizer to keep it growing vigorously. Fertilize in early spring just prior to shoot emergence, and again in midsummer, with a slow-release 2-1-2 or 3-1-2 ratio (18-6-12, for example) fertilizer. Spread fertilizer evenly and be careful not to let it touch the stalks. In the northern regions of the state, make sure you add a layer of mulch to protect from winter temperatures. Remove foliage after it is frozen back. When clumps get crowded, divide and replant in early spring.

Recommended Varieties

It is usually sold generic, but new varieties like 'Tara' and 'Disney' may change that in the future. 'Tara' is known to have a longer bloom period.

Other Name:
Red Ginger Lily

Light Needs:

Added Benefits:

Zones: (7), 8, 9

Bloom Time:
Summer, early fall

Bloom Color:
Red and orange

Height × Width:
6 to 7 ft. × 1 ft., leaves
(x 4 to 5 ft., clumps)

Water Needs:
Moderate

Soil:
Moist, well drained

Uses:
Tropical-looking beds

Did You Know?

Would you believe there are over 1,400 species of ginger?

Color photo on page 142

Variegated Shell Ginger

Other Name:
Porcelain Lily

Light Needs:

Added Benefits:

Zones: (7), 8, 9

Bloom Time:
Late summer after mild winters

Bloom Color:
Yellow-and-green foliage

Height × Width:
5 to 6 ft. × 5 ft.

Water Needs:
Moderate

Soil:
Moist, well drained

Uses:
Landscape, containers, and sunrooms

Did You Know?

Alpinia is from Alpino, an Italian botanist in the late 1500s who wrote about Egyptian plants.

Color photo on page 142

Alpinia zerumbet variegata

The creamy-yellow-and-green foliage of variegated shell ginger is so pretty that any blooms it may form are inconsequential. This ginger makes an excellent indoor plant for bright sunrooms or atriums.

How to Grow

Plant after the last spring frost in well-prepared beds that drain well and are rich in organic matter. Give it morning sun or filtered light, and it will thrive. It comes back slowly from extreme winters, so in northern Mississippi, plant in a protected area of the landscape and mulch heavily in late fall. This ginger may be easily dug up and enjoyed indoors for the winter. This is definitely the best ginger for beautifying an old European-style decorative container. Blooms are rare in all but coastal areas.

Companion Planting

This ginger is gorgeous when grown on the shady side of large banana trees, or in combination with upright elephant ears. Dark-lavender impatiens work for additional color.

Care and Maintenance

Variegated shell ginger needs plenty of moisture and fertilizer to keep it growing vigorously. Fertilize in early spring just prior to shoot emergence, and again in midsummer, with a slow-release 2-1-2 or 3-1-2 ratio (18-6-12, for example) fertilizer. Spread fertilizer evenly and be careful not to let it touch the stalks. A layer of pine bark mulch is not only effective for conserving moisture and adding winter protection, but is pretty in contrast with the yellow-and-green foliage.

Recommended Varieties

Sold as generic.

Yellow Shrimp Plant

Pachystachys lutea

Handsome dark-green leaves with scores of bright-yellow 5- to 6-inch upright blooming spikes called bracts grace this plant. The bracts support the white flowers, which open in a series and are borne all season long. This is such an outstanding tropical it has been chsen as a Mississippi Medallion winner for the year 2000.

How to Grow
Plant after the last frost in spring in a well-prepared, moist, well-drained bed rich in organic matter. Choose an area that receives morning sun and after-noon shade, or filtered light. It brightens the summer porch, patio, or deck when planted in large containers. Don't stop there—mass-plant a dozen yellow shrimp plants in a bed to stop traffic.

Companion Plantings
Mass-plant in beds with violet-colored impatiens in front. Large plants may be needed in this situation since impatiens grow so fast. Yellow shrimp plant also works well with dwarf bananas.

Care and Maintenance
For vigorous growth, maintain moisture and feed with light monthly applications of a complete and balanced (10-10-10, for example) slow-release fertilizer. Occasional pruning may be needed to keep it bushy. Deadhead for new emerging blossoms. Yellow shrimp plant has to be treated as an annual or grown as a container plant for winter protection. Cuttings root easily.

Recommended Varieties
It is mostly sold generic, but the variety 'Golden Candle' is becoming available. Try the red shrimp plant *Beloperone guttata*, which is a tender perennial in zone 9, southern Mississippi.

Other Name:
Lollipop Plant

Light Needs:

Added Benefits:

Zone: 10

Bloom Time:
Spring, summer, fall

Bloom Color:
Yellow bracts, white flowers

Height × Width:
3 × 3 ft.

Water Needs:
Moderate

Soil:
Moist, well drained

Uses: Containers, landscape, sunrooms

Did You Know?
The white flowers extending from the yellow bracts are much loved by hummingbirds for their sweet nectar.

Color photo on page 142

VINES

There was something about a recent Garden and Patio Show in Jackson, Mississippi, that really surprised me: gardener after gardener was walking out of the show carrying trellises, towers, and even arbors. Climbing plants are back in business.

Of course there are many cottage-style gardens where climbers have always been popular. But there is a new group of gardeners out there, with modern new homes, building flower borders and incorporating vertical growth. I walked out of the Garden and Patio Show with a tower as a present for my wife, Jan. Before I could give her some of my horticultural advice, she had clematis twining around it.

> The clematis is a great choice for climbing.

The clematis is a great choice for climbing, as is the 'Tangerine Beauty' crossvine (*Bignonia capreolata*). We planted it at our Truck Crops Branch Experiment Station three years ago as part of the Mississippi Medallion trials. Every year it borders on the spectacular, with orange trumpet-shaped flowers that number in the thousands. Best of all, it has pretty much done its thing without any close supervision from us.

Another great climber that is always the talk of Fall Flower and Garden Fest at the Experiment Station is the hyacinth bean funnel, formerly known as *Dolichos lablab* and now *Lablab purpureus*. When you see the hyacinth bean vine in October, it is hard to believe that it was planted by seed in midsummer. The flowers are gorgeous, the seedpods are an awesome purple velvet color, and the beans are edible.

Nothing is prettier than a patio with a Southern-style pergola draped with a climbing vine such as wisteria, with its hundreds of delightfully fragrant blooms cascading downward. What could be better than sitting on the patio where a nearby moonvine is blooming with its intoxicating fragrance?

Climbing vines can also play an important role by saving energy and slashing high utility costs. If your home is brick, you can allow vines such as the creeping fig to cover the east or west walls. This will help reduce the amount of heat absorption by your home.

If your home is wood, don't let the vines attach themselves—instead, use a trellis. The trellis system allows you to grow spectacular flowering vines such as the black-eyed Susan vine or queen's-wreath. You can also choose to select one of the vines mentioned in the Tropicals chapter or a climbing rose from the Roses chapter.

An important consideration when using vines is the weight of the plant. Vines like wisteria can reduce a cheap trellis to a pile of rubble in one season. Posts need to be set in concrete and cross supports bolted, or use an iron trellis system.

Some vines climb quickly and naturally; others need a little encouragement by way of tying, weaving, and bending. Many of the blooming vines need to be pruned to generate new growth and flowers, so don't be intimidated. Cut as required by your plant.

A climber gives a sense of depth and dimension to the flower border.

Black-Eyed Susan Vine

Other Name:
Clock Vine

Light Needs:

Added Benefits:

Zones: 7 to 9

Bloom Time:
Summer

Bloom Color:
Yellow, orange, white

Height: 3 to 8 ft.

Spacing: 18 to 24 in.

Water Needs:
Moderate/frequent

Soil:
Moist, well drained

Uses:
Arbor, fence, trellis, tower, basket

Did You Know?
The flower looks as if it has five petals, but in reality it is a funnel form.

Color photo on page 142

Thunbergia alata

Bright orange, yellow, or white flowers resembling black-eyed Susans adorn this vigorous climbing annual, all in one season.

How to Grow
Choose a site in full sun to partial shade, and plant after the last frost of the year. Prepare the soil deeply by adding 3 to 4 inches of composted pine bark and humus, tilling to a depth of 8 to 10 inches. While tilling, incorporate 2 pounds of slow-release 12-6-6 fertilizer per 100 square feet. Set out nursery-grown transplants at the same depth they were growing in the containers. It is also easy to grow from seed. Sow three seed about $1/4$ inch deep, water, and cover with mulch. Germination takes 10 to 21 days. Remove the weakest seedlings.

Companion Planting
Grow black-eyed Susan vine at the entrance to a cottage garden over an arbor or along a fence. Plant perennial blue salvias or angelonias as lower-level plants. Tall perennial summer phlox planted in front also makes an impressive show.

Care and Maintenance
Feed with a light application of the above fertilizer every 4 to 6 weeks. Keep well watered for vigorous growth. The black-eyed Susan vine climbs easily, so provide a sturdy structure. Spider mites are an occasional problem. Watch for and treat early if found.

Recommended Varieties
'Susie' is the most recognized variety and comes in yellow, orange, and white. 'Angel Wings' has white flowers and an ever-so-light fragrance.

Ⓝ Carolina Jessamine

Gelsemium sempervirens

This gorgeous semi-evergreen vine with fragrant yellow flowers is as much a part of the South as fried chicken.

How to Grow

Buy nursery-grown transplants in the fall and you may have spring blooms! Set out plants at the same depth they were growing in the containers. If soil is heavy or tightly compacted, loosen it by tilling in 3 to 4 inches of organic matter like fine pine bark and compost.

Companion Planting

The showy yellow flowers bloom at one of the prettiest times of the year. Grow in combination with redbud and dogwood trees, flowering quince and spiraea. Nearby white narcissus will also add to the beauty.

Care and Maintenance

Carolina jessamine needs a very sturdy support structure. It climbs with ease and can get top-heavy. Annual thinning will probably have to be done in the lower part of the state. Feed with a light application of slow-release 12-6-6 fertilizer in late winter. *All parts of the plant are poisonous if eaten.* The bobwhite quail, however, has been known to eat the seed.

Recommended Varieties

'Pride of Augusta' and 'Plena' are double-flowered forms. 'Margarita', discovered in Georgia, is known for extra cold hardiness. 'Woodlanders Light Yellow' has cream-colored flowers and is recommended only for zones 8 and 9. The *G. rankii*, or swamp jessamine, blooms in fall and is adaptable to wet conditions.

Other Names:
Yellow Jessamine,
Carolina Wild Woodbine

Light Needs:

Added Benefits:

Zones: 7 to 9

Bloom Time:
Late winter, spring

Bloom Color:
Yellow

Height: 10 to 20 ft.

Spacing: 6 to 10 ft.

Water Needs:
Moderate

Soil:
Moist, well drained

Uses:
Posts, lattice, trellis, arbor, pergola

Did You Know?

The Carolina jessamine is the state flower of South Carolina.

Color photo on page 142

Clematis

Other Name:
Virgin's Bower

Light Needs:

Added Benefits:

Zones: 7 to 9

Bloom Time:
Spring, summer, fall

Bloom Color:
Many colors and blends

Height: 10 to 20 ft.

Spacing: 4 to 6 ft.

Water Needs:
Moderate

Soil: Moist, well drained, slightly alkaline

Uses: Fences, towers, trellis, mailbox post

Did You Know?

C. paniculata (sweet autumn clematis) has a wonderful fragrance and is one of the easiest to grow.

Color photo on page 142

Clematis species and hybrids

Flowers up to 10 inches in many colors make this perennial vine a must for the Southern-style cottage garden.

How to Grow

Prepare the bed by incorporating 3 to 4 inches of organic matter and tilling to a depth of 8 to 10 inches. Clematis prefers slightly alkaline soils; add dolomitic lime when tilling, along with a light application of 12-6-6 fertilizer. Plant at the same depth it was growing in the container. Water well and mulch.

Companion Planting

Clematis has often been made to climb a white picket fence in the cottage garden. Try the *C. Jackmanii* (purple) on a fence with mandevilla. 'Piccadilly' (purple-blue) looks good with yellow allamanda. Clematis looks exceptional growing on an old-style Victorian tower in the middle of a cottage garden.

Care and Maintenance

Feed in late winter and midsummer, using a light application of the above fertilizer. Know your varieties before you prune. Members of the *Jackmanii* group, the most popular, bloom on new growth, which means pruning in early spring. 'Henryi' and 'Candida' in the *Lanuginosa* group bloom on old bottom wood and new growth. Prune these by two-thirds in late winter. Clematis like 'The President' and 'Lincoln Star' bloom only on old wood. Prune these after bloom.

Recommended Varieties

'Henryi', 'Candida' and 'Gillian Blades' (white); 'Comtesse de Bouchard' and 'Lincoln Star' (pink); 'Ernest Markham', 'Red Cardinal', and 'Niobi' (red); 'Lady Betty Balfour' and Prince Philip' (blue-violet); and *C. Jackmanii* 'Mrs. M. Thompson' and 'Gypsy Queen' (purple) are all worth trying.

Coral Honeysuckle

Lonicera sempervirens

You may loathe the rampant Japanese honeysuckle, but you will love this evergreen native coral honeysuckle—and the hummingbirds will, too!

How to Grow

Choose a site in full sun for best blooming performance, though partial shade is tolerated. A wide variety of soils is acceptable. Loosen heavy clay by adding organic matter to the planting area. Work in 3 to 4 inches of fine pine bark and compost, tilling to a depth of 8 to 10 inches. Plant nursery-grown transplants in the spring at the same depth they were growing in the containers. Water and apply mulch. The flowers are a favorite of hummingbirds and butterflies. The fruit is eaten by several bird species, such as the cardinal and the purple finch.

Companion Planting

Coral honeysuckle draping over a picket or split-rail fence lends a nostalgic, if not romantic, look to the Southern garden. Plants bloom heaviest in spring and bud all summer. Lower-level plants like gold lantana, shasta daisies, and coreopsis are all good companion plants.

Care and Maintenance

Feed with a light application of a slow-release 12-6-6 fertilizer in late winter. Don't be afraid to prune back lightly to maintain size and form. Occasionally powdery mildew is a problem; treat early and provide good air circulation around the plant.

Recommended Varieties

'Sulphurea' (yellow), 'Alabama Scarlet' (scarlet), 'Magnifica' (red), and 'John Clayton' (yellow) are a few of the varieties in the trade.

Other Name:
Trumpet Honeysuckle

Light Needs:

Added Benefits:

Zones: 7 to 9

Bloom Time:
Spring, summer

Bloom Color:
Coral, yellow, scarlet

Height: 10 to 20 ft.

Spacing: 24 to 36 in.

Water Needs:
Low/moderate

Soil: Slightly moist, well drained

Uses:
Cover for fences, arbors, deck railing, trellis

Did You Know?

The Japanese honeysuckle (usually avoided) has been known to spread 150 feet!

Color photo on page 142

Coral Vine

Other Names:
Rosa de Montana,
Queen's Wreath

Light Needs:

Added Benefit:

Zones: 8, 9

Bloom Time:
Late summer, fall

Bloom Color:
Pink, white, red

Height: 10 to 15 ft.

Spacing: 5 to 10 ft.

Water Needs:
Low/moderate

Soil: Slightly moist,
well drained

Uses: Screen for
privacy, climber for
fence, arbor, pergola

Did You Know?
This vine was used to
camouflage anti-aircraft
guns in World War II.

Color photo on page 143

Antigonon leptopus

Coral vine, with its bows of pink flowers, is more reminiscent of the Old South than just about any plant.

How to Grow
Choose a site with full sun for best bloom. Good drainage is necessary to entice these wonderful vines back from the harsh winter. Amend the planting site with 3 to 4 inches of organic matter like fine pine bark and compost, tilling to a depth of 8 to 10 inches. Northern zone 8 gardeners (and zone 7 gamblers) should plant along the southern exposure of the home or in any other protective microclimate. Set nursery-grown plants out in the spring at the same depth they were growing in the containers. Water and mulch.

Companion Planting
The late-summer and fall blooms are awesome in a cottage garden where tall spiky plants like Mexican bush sage and indigo spires can serve as lower-level plants. They are the best at draping a front porch railing or patio lattice, screening for privacy. Use containers of complementary annuals to go along with queen's-pink flowers in this situation.

Care and Maintenance
This tropical will die down after winter's onslaught and return from underground tubers in spring. Cut back top growth when it has been killed in the fall. Mulch very heavily going into winter. Trim and prune as needed to keep in bounds. Propagation is easy with stem cuttings in late summer.

Recommended Varieties
Though still sold generically, there are a few named varieties. A couple are 'Album' (white) and 'Baja Red' (red).

Crossvine

Bignonia capreolata

This underused semi-evergreen native vine may have more flowers per foot when in bloom than any other plant. The orange trumpet-shaped flowers capture the attention of everyone who sees them.

How to Grow

Choose a site in full sun for the most spectacular flower show. Amend tight soils with the addition of 3 to 4 inches of organic matter, and till to a depth of 8 to 10 inches. Select a sturdy support structure, or let it climb a brick or masonry wall. The vine climbs by tendrils, but has small disks that allow it to attach itself to a wall. Plant superior selections from nursery-grown transplants. Set out at the same depth they were growing in the containers, water, and apply mulch.

Companion Planting

Crossvine blooms for a little over a month during mid-April to May, but will vary slightly from year to year and from zone to zone. Let the crossvine drape a fence or porch railing that borders the flower garden. If blue crown pansies are still looking good, they will contrast nicely with the crossvine. If fresh yellow marigolds or ageratums have been planted, the blooming crossvine will frame the garden nicely.

Care and Maintenance

Feed with a light application of 5-10-5 fertilizer in late winter, and slow-release 12-6-6 in midsummer. Prune to maintain shape and confinement. Do major removing or thinning after spring bloom.

Recommended Varieties

The best-known varieties are 'Tangerine Beauty' (apricot-orange), 'Atrosanguinea' (red-purple), and 'Shalimar Red' (red).

Other Name:
Quartervine

Light Needs:

Added Benefits:

Zones: 7 to 9

Bloom Time: Spring

Bloom Color:
Orange, red

Height: 20 to 30 ft.

Spacing: 10 to 15 ft.

Water Needs:
Moderate

Soil:
Moist, well drained

Uses: Climber for masonry walls, fences, railings, pergolas, arbors

Did You Know?

Bignonia is named after Jean Paul Bignon, King Louis IV's librarian.

Color photo on page 143

Hyacinth Bean

Other Names:
Lubia Bean,
Egyptian Bean

Light Needs:

Added Benefits:

Zones: 7 to 9

Bloom Time:
Late summer, fall

Bloom Color: Lilac

Height: 6 to 10 ft.

Spacing: 24 to 36 in.

Water Needs:
Moderate/frequent

Soil:
Moist, well drained

Uses: Screens,
climbers for arbors,
pergolas, fences, trellises

Did You Know?
Hyacinth bean was a
favorite annual vine of
Thomas Jefferson.

Color photo on page 143

Lablab purpureus

The quick-covering hyacinth bean has lilac flowers followed by velvety purple edible seedpods. What more could ask for?

How to Grow
Choose a site in full sun. Prepare soil by spreading a 3- to 4-inch layer of organic matter, like fine pine bark and compost, and till to a depth of 8 to 10 inches. While tilling, incorporate 2 pounds of a slow-release 5-10-5 fertilizer per 100 square feet of bed space. Plant seed adjacent to a support structure like a fence, trellis, or arbor. Plant seeds 1 inch deep and cover. Water thoroughly and mulch. Seeds should germinate in ten to fourteen days. Group four seedlings at intervals 36 inches apart.

Companion Planting
The hyacinth bean covers an arbor for only one season, but blooms and produces fruit as days get shorter in the early fall. Hyacinth bean looks great on a picket or split-rail fence with lower-level fall-blooming salvias, zinnias, and black-eyed Susans to enhance the cottage look. 'New Gold' lantana makes a nice complement to the purple seedpods.

Care and Maintenance
This is a long season crop, but well worth it. Feed every 4 to 6 weeks with light applications of a slow-release 12-6-6 fertilizer. Keep well watered throughout the long growing season. Watch for spider mites during the summer. The pods are delicious when young and a staple of Oriental, Indian, and Indonesian food markets. Keep mulched throughout the winter, and it may be a perennial in coastal areas.

Recommended Varieties
Sold generically.

Moon Vine

Ipomea alba

Moon vine is one of those plants that you can't explain if you haven't experienced it. Experience it by taking in the exotic fragrance of the huge white flowers *at night!*

How to Grow

Though it is called moon vine, choose a site with full sun where the fragrance will be enjoyed during the evening. Incorporate 3 to 4 inches of organic matter like fine pine bark and compost. Till to a depth of 8 to 10 inches and work in a light application of 5-10-5 fertilizer. The seed has a hard coat, so rub them lightly with sandpaper. Soak the seed overnight and plant ½ inch deep. Water and apply mulch.

Companion Planting

It seems odd to talk about a companion for a night bloomer. Try growing the cousin morning glory *I. tricolor*, which blooms in the morning. With morning and night covered, what about the afternoon? Try the other cousin *I. lobata* (or firecracker vine) with hundreds of tubular flowers that start out lemon yellow, then turn orange, then rusty red.

Care and Maintenance

Keep the moon vine well watered during dry summer periods. Feed with a light application of slow-release 12-6-6 fertilizer every 4 to 6 weeks. Pinch or tip-prune to keep the vine within bounds. Watch for spider mites and treat early.

Recommended Varieties

Moon vine *I. alba* is sold generically. Other great relatives are the morning glory *I. tricolor*, firecracker vine *I. lobata*, and Cypress vine *I. quamoclit*

Other Name:
Moon Flower

Light Needs:

Added Benefit:

Zones: 7 to 9

Bloom Time:
Summer, fall

Bloom Color: White

Height: 20 to 30 ft

Spacing: 5 to 10 ft.

Water Needs:
Moderate

Soil:
Moist, well drained

Uses: Climber for fence, trellis, arbor

Did You Know?

All the moon vines are related to the sweet potato.

Color photo on page 143

Trumpet Vine

Other Name:
Trumpetcreeper

Light Needs:

Added Benefits:

Zones: 7 to 9

Bloom Time:
Summer, fall

Bloom Color:
Orange, red, yellow

Height: 20 to 40 ft.

Spacing: 10 to 15 ft.

Water Needs:
Low/moderate

Soil:
Moist, well drained

Uses:
Fences, pergolas, arbors

Did You Know?
Hummingbirds love the flowers of trumpetcreeper.

Color photo on page 143

Campsis radicans

Trumpet vine is one of the most beautiful and easy-to-grow deciduous vines, yet is maligned because of its vigor—which is easily controlled by pruning.

How to Grow
Select a site in full sun for best blooms. Amend tight clay soils by working in 3 to 4 inches of organic matter like fine pine bark and compost. Till to a depth of 8 to 10 inches. Select a very sturdy structure to support the trumpet vine. In spring set out nursery-grown transplants at the same depth they were growing in the containers. Water and mulch.

Companion Planting
Growing on a fence is the best method. The complementary color for these orange trumpet flowers is blue, and blue anise sage *Salvia guarantica* makes a bold combination. 'Victoria' blue and salvia indigo spires also work as lower-level plants. 'New Gold' lantana works well. These companion plants appeal to butterflies and hummingbirds, making for a nice wildlife garden.

Care and Maintenance
Feed in late winter with a slow-release 10-20-10. The trumpet vine is easy to care for by simply pruning every now and then to keep it in bounds. Remove the long seedpods as they form to keep generating blooms. Hoe or dig suckers as they develop in shrub beds.

Recommended Varieties
Most gardeners don't realize that there are varieties, but 'Madame Galen' (red-orange) is a variety not nearly as invasive. 'Flava' (yellow) and 'Crimson Trumpet' (red) are a couple of better-known selections.

Wisteria

Wisteria sinensis

Many springtime childhood memories have been made at Grandma's house, with the wonderful fragrance of wisteria blossoms permeating the air.

How to Grow

Select a site in full sun for best bloom. Amend tight clay soil by adding 3 to 4 inches of organic matter and tilling to a depth of 8 to 10 inches. Wisteria requires one of the sturdiest supports of all vines. Buy nursery-grown plants blooming in containers; plant at the same depth they were growing in the containers. Avoid planting near trees.

Companion Planting

Wisterias, with their giant grape-cluster-like flowers, bloom at the prettiest time of the year, enabling them to add even more beauty to the show of azaleas, spiraea, forsythia, quince, and spring bulbs. Nothing is prettier than a tree-formed wisteria planted in front of redbuds, or draped over a railing overlooking 'Judge Solomon' azaleas.

Care and Maintenance

Stay focused from the day of planting to maintain the desired shape or space allotment for the wisteria. Remove unwanted growth as it occurs. Many a question arises over failure to bloom, which is usually contributed to by one of the following cultural or environmental factors: too much nitrogen, not enough sunlight, midwinter pruning, or the purchase of a seedling. Do heaviest pruning in late spring after the bloom period.

Recommended Varieties

'Caroline' and 'Cooke's Special' are typical colored varieties that are much underused. The white varieties 'Alba' and 'Jako' are spectacular.

Other Name:
Chinese Wisteria

Light Needs:

Added Benefits:

Zones: 7 to 9

Bloom Time: Spring

Bloom Color:
Blue, white

Height: 30 to 45 ft.

Spacing: 15 to 20 ft.

Water Needs:
Low/moderate

Soil: Slightly moist, well drained

Uses: Climber for railing, fence, arbor, pergola, tree-form specimen

Did You Know?

There are Japanese wisteria, American wisteria, and Kentucky wisteria, too!

Color photo on page 143

1996—'New Gold' *Lantana × hybrida*
1996—'Blue Daze' *Evolvulus pilosus*
1997—'Derby', 'Showstar', 'Medallion' *Melampodium paladosum*
1997—'New Wonder' *Scaevola aemula*
1997—'Little Gem' *Magnolia grandiflora*
1998—'Victoria' *Salvia farinacea*
1998—Narrow-Leaf Zinnia *Zinnia angustifolia*
1998—'Natchez' Crape Myrtle *Lagerstroemia indica × fauriei*
1999—'Biloxi Blue' *Verbena × hybrida*
1999—'Indian Summer' *Rudbeckia hirta*
1999—'Tonto' Crape Myrtle *Lagerstroemia indica × fauriei*
1999—'Sioux' Crape Myrtle *Lagerstroemia indica × fauriei*
2000—'Bloodgood' Japanese Maple *Acer palmatum*
2000—Oakleaf Hydrangea *Hydrangea quercifolia*
2000—Yellow Shrimp Plant *Pachystachus lutea*
2000—'Wave' Petunias, Misty Lilac, Rose, Pink, Purple *Petunia × hybrida*

The Mississippi Medallion Award Program is a cooperative effort of the Mississippi Nurserymen's Association, Mississippi Plant Selections Committee, Mississippi State University Extension Service, and the Mississippi Agricultural and Forestry Experiment Station. Rather than depend on variety recommendations generated thousands of miles away, the Mississippi Medallion award is given based on plants' performance throughout the state. Evaluation sites are located at several locations from north to south to give a broad perspective on a plant's performance in Mississippi.

BIBLIOGRAPHY

Armitage, Allan M. *Herbaceous Perennial Plants*. Champaign, Illinois: Stipes Publishing Co., 1997.

Dirr, Michael A. *Manual of Woody Landscape Plants: Their Identification, Ornamental Characteristics, Culture, Propagation and Uses*. Fifth Edition. Champaign, Illinois: Stipes Publishing Co., revised 1998.

Gill, Dan and Joe White. *Louisiana Gardener's Guide*. Franklin, Tennessee: Cool Springs Press, Inc., 1997.

Hill, Madalene, Gwen Barclay, and Jean Hardy. *Southern Herb Growing*. Fredericksburg, Texas: Shearer Publishing Co., 1987.

Hopkinson, Patricia, Diane Miske, Jerry Parsons, and Holly Shimizu. *Herb Gardening*. New York: Pantheon Books, Knopf Publishing Group, 1994.

Nagel, David, Pat Harris, Mukund Patel, and John Byrd. *Establish and Manage Your Home Lawn*. Mississippi State University Extension Service: Publication 1322, revised 1999.

Odenwald, Neil and James Turner. *Identification, Selection and Use of Southern Plants for Landscape Design*. Third Edition. Baton Rouge, Louisiana: Claitor,s Publishing Division, 1996.

Perry, James, revised by John Davis. *Selecting Landscape Plants*. Mississippi State University Extension Service: Publication 666, 1999.

Royal Horticultural Society Dictionary of Gardening, The New. New York: Stockton Press, 1992.

Southern Living Garden Book, The. Birmingham, Alabama: Oxmoor House, Inc., 1998.

Sperry, Neil. *Texas Gardening*. Second Edition. Dallas, Texas: Taylor Publishing, 1991.

Vines, Robert A. *Trees, Shrubs and Woody Vines of the Southwest*. Austin, Texas: University of Texas Press, 1976.

Welch, William C. *Antique Roses for the South*. Dallas, Texas: Taylor Publishing, 1990.

———. *Perennial Garden Color*. Dallas, Texas: Taylor Publishing, 1989.

PUBLIC GARDENS

Belzoni
Wister Gardens
Hwy. 7 North
Belzoni, Miss
(662) 247-3025

Biloxi
Beauvoir
2244 Beach Boulevard
(228) 388-1313

Jackson
Jackson Zoo
2918 West Capitol St.
(601) 352-2585

Mynelle Gardens
4736 Clinton Boulevard
(601) 960-1894

Lucedale
Palestinian Gardens, Inc.
US Highway 98, 6 miles west of Lucedale
(601) 947-8422

Picayune
The Crosby Arboretum, Mississippi
    State University
1801 Goodyear Road
(601) 799-2311

Starkville
Mississippi State University Arboretum
Mississippi State University Campus
(662) 325-2311

Verona
Magnolia Botanical Gardens
North Mississippi Research and Extension Ctr.
5421 Hwy. 145 South
(662) 566-2201

Mississippi is known nationwide for its historic homes, many including gardens. For more information on pilgrimages and tours, call (800) 927-6378. A few of the homes that may be toured year round are:

Columbus
Amzi Love, 1884
Blewell-Harrison-Lee House and
    Museum, 1847
Liberty Hall, 1832
Rosewood Manor, 1852
Templed Heights, 1837
Waverly Mansion, 1852
White Arches, 1857

Natchez
Auburn, 1812
The Burn, 1832
Dunleith, 1856
The House of Ellicott,s Hall, 1798
Landsdown, 1853
Longwood, 1858
Magnolia Hall, 1858

Monmouth, 1818
Ravenaside, 1870
Rosalie, 1820
Stanton Hall, 1857
Weymouth Hall, 1855

Vicksburg
The Martha Vick House, 1830
The Duff Green Mansion, 1856
Anchuca, 1830
Belle Fleur, 1873
The Corners, 1872
McRaven, 1836
Cedar Grove Mansion-Inn, 1840
Annabelle, 1868
Belle of The Bends, 1876
Tomil Manor, 1910
Grey Oaks, 1834

GLOSSARY

Alkaline soil: soil with a pH greater than 7.0. It lacks acidity, often because it has limestone in it.

All-purpose fertilizer: powdered, liquid, or granular fertilizer with a balanced proportion of the three key nutrients—nitrogen (N), potassium (P), and phosphorus (K). It is suitable for maintenance nutrition for most plants.

Annual: a plant that lives its entire life in one season. It is genetically determined to germinate, grow, flower, set seed, and die the same year.

Balled and burlapped: describes a tree or shrub grown in the field whose soilball was wrapped with protective burlap and twine when the plant was dug up to be sold or transplanted.

Bare root: describes plants that have been packaged without any soil around their roots. (Often young shrubs and trees purchased through the mail arrive with their exposed roots covered with moist peat or sphagnum moss, sawdust, or similar material, and wrapped in plastic.)

Barrier plant: a plant that has intimidating thorns or spines and is sited purposely to block foot traffic or other access to the home or yard.

Beneficial insects: insects or their larvae that prey on pest organisms and their eggs. They may be flying insects, such as ladybugs, parasitic wasps, praying mantids, and soldier bugs, or soil dwellers such as predatory nematodes, spiders, and ants.

Berm: a narrow raised ring of soil around a tree, used to hold water so it will be directed to the root zone.

Bract: a modified leaf structure on a plant stem near its flower that resembles a petal. Often it is more colorful and visible than the actual flower, as in dogwood.

Bud union: the place where the top of a plant was grafted to the rootstock; usually refers to roses.

Canopy: the overhead branching area of a tree, usually referring to its extent including foliage.

Cold hardiness: the ability of a perennial plant to survive the winter cold in a particular area.

Composite: a flower that is actually composed of many tiny flowers. Typically, they are flat clusters of tiny, tight florets, sometimes surrounded by wider-petaled florets. Composite flowers are highly attractive to bees and beneficial insects.

Compost: organic matter that has undergone progressive decomposition by microbial and macrobial activity until it is reduced to a spongy, fluffy texture. Added to soil of any type, it improves the soil's ability to hold air and water and to drain well.

GLOSSARY

Corm: the swollen energy-storing structure, analogous to a bulb, under the soil at the base of the stem of plants such as crocus and gladiolus.

Crown: the base of a plant at, or just beneath, the surface of the soil where the roots meet the stems.

Cultivar: a CULTIvated VARiety. It is a naturally occurring form of a plant that has been identified as special or superior and is purposely selected for propagation and production.

Deadhead: a pruning technique that removes faded flower heads from plants to improve their appearance, abort seed production, and stimulate further flowering.

Deciduous plants: unlike evergreens, these trees and shrubs lose their leaves in the fall.

Desiccation: drying out of foliage tissues, usually due to drought or wind.

Division: the practice of splitting apart perennial plants to create several smaller-rooted segments. The practice is useful for controlling the plant's size and for acquiring more plants; it is also essential to the health and continued flowering of certain ones.

Dormancy: the period, usually the winter, when perennial plants temporarily cease active growth and rest. **Dormant** is the verb form, as used in this sentence: *Some plants, like spring-blooming bulbs, go dormant in the summer.*

Established: the point at which a newly planted tree, shrub, or flower begins to produce new growth, either foliage or stems. This is an indication that the roots have recovered from transplant shock and have begun to grow and spread.

Evergreen: perennial plants that do not lose their foliage annually with the onset of winter. Needled or broadleaf foliage will persist and continues to function on a plant through one or more winters, aging and dropping unobtrusively in cycles of three or four years or more.

Foliar: of or about foliage—usually refers to the practice of spraying foliage, as in fertilizing or treating with insecticide; leaf tissues absorb liquid directly for fast results, and the soil is not affected.

Floret: a tiny flower, usually one of many forming a cluster, that comprises a single blossom.

Germinate: to sprout. Germination is a fertile seed's first stage of development.

Graft (union): the point on the stem of a woody plant with sturdier roots where a stem from a highly ornamental plant is inserted so that it will join with it. Roses are commonly grafted.

Hands: the female flowers on a banana tree; they turn into bananas.

GLOSSARY

Hardscape: the permanent, structural, nonplant part of a landscape, such as walls, sheds, pools, patios, arbors, and walkways.

Herbaceous: plants having fleshy or soft stems that die back with frost; the opposite of **woody.**

Hybrid: a plant that is the result of intentional or natural cross-pollination between two or more plants of the same species or genus.

Low water demand: describes plants that tolerate dry soil for varying periods of time. Typically, they have succulent, hairy, or silvery-gray foliage and tuberous roots or taproots.

Mulch: a layer of material over bare soil to protect it from erosion and compaction by rain, and to discourage weeds. It may be inorganic (gravel, fabric) or organic (wood chips, bark, pine needles, chopped leaves).

Naturalize: (*a*) to plant seeds, bulbs, or plants in a random, informal pattern as they would appear in their natural habitat; (*b*) to adapt to and spread throughout adopted habitats (a tendency of some nonnative plants).

Nectar: the sweet fluid produced by glands on flowers that attract pollinators such as hummingbirds and honeybees, for whom it is a source of energy.

Organic material, organic matter: any material or debris that is derived from plants. It is carbon-based material capable of undergoing decomposition and decay.

Peat moss: organic matter from peat sedges (United States) or sphagnum mosses (Canada), often used to improve soil texture. The acidity of sphagnum peat moss makes it ideal for boosting or maintaining soil acidity while also improving its drainage.

Perennial: a flowering plant that lives over two or more seasons. Many die back with frost, but their roots survive the winter and generate new shoots in the spring.

pH: a measurement of the relative acidity (low pH) or alkalinity (high pH) of soil or water based on a scale of 1 to 14, 7 being neutral. Individual plants require soil to be within a certain range so that nutrients can dissolve in moisture and be available to them.

Pinch: to remove tender stems and/or leaves by pressing them between thumb and forefinger. This pruning technique encourages branching, compactness, and flowering in plants, or it removes aphids clustered at growing tips.

Pollen: the yellow, powdery grains in the center of a flower. A plant's male sex cells, they are transferred to the female plant parts by means of wind or animal pollinators to fertilize them and create seeds.

GLOSSARY

Raceme: an arrangement of single stalked flowers along an elongated, unbranched axis.

Rhizome: a swollen energy-storing stem structure, similar to a bulb, that lies horizontally in the soil, with roots emerging from its lower surface and growth shoots from a growing point at or near its tip, as in bearded iris.

Rootbound (or potbound): the condition of a plant that has been confined in a container too long, its roots having been forced to wrap around themselves and even swell out of the container. Successful transplanting or repotting requires untangling and trimming away of some of the matted roots.

Root flare: the transition at the base of a tree trunk where the bark tissue begins to differentiate and roots begin to form just before entering the soil. This area should not be covered with soil when planting a tree.

Self-seeding: the tendency of some plants to sow their seeds freely around the yard. It creates many seedlings the following season that may or may not be welcome.

Semievergreen: tending to be evergreen in a mild climate but deciduous in a rigorous one.

Shearing: the pruning technique whereby plant stems and branches are cut uniformly with long-bladed pruning shears (hedge shears) or powered hedge trimmers. It is used when creating and maintaining hedges and topiary.

Slow-acting fertilizer: fertilizer that is water insoluble and therefore releases its nutrients gradually as a function of soil temperature, moisture, and related microbial activity. Typically granular, it may be organic or synthetic.

Succulent growth: the sometimes undesirable production of fleshy, water-storing leaves or stems that results from overfertilization.

Sucker: a new growing shoot. Underground plant roots produce suckers to form new stems and spread by means of these suckering roots to form large plantings, or colonies. Some plants produce root suckers or branch suckers as a result of pruning or wounding.

Tuber: a type of underground storage structure in a plant stem, analogous to a bulb. It generates roots below and stems above ground (example: dahlia).

Variegated: having various colors or color patterns. The term usually refers to plant foliage that is streaked, edged, blotched, or mottled with a contrasting color, often green with yellow, cream, or white.

White grubs: fat, off-white, wormlike larvae of Japanese beetles. They reside in the soil and feed on plant (especially grass) roots until summer when they emerge as beetles to feed on plant foliage.

INDEX

INDEX

INDEX

INDEX

INDEX

INDEX

INDEX

ABOUT THE AUTHOR

Norman Winter, who received his bachelor's degree from Hardin-Simmons University and master's degree from Texas A&M University, is no stranger to the world of garden writing. His column, called *Southern Gardening,* is featured weekly in many of Mississippi's leading newspapers.

Norman has managed several organizations in the horticultural field as Executive Director, including The Texas Pecan Growers Association, National Pecan Marketing Council, Texas State Horticultural Society, and American Rose Society. Today, as Extension Horticulturist for Mississippi State University, he serves as coordinator for the Mississippi Medallion Award program, promoting outstanding plants for the state. He received the Outstanding Achievement Award from the Mississippi Nurserymen's Association in 1997.

His award-winning *Southern Gardening* television news segment is seen weekly by an estimated 450,000 viewers, on TV and Cable outlets such as WLOX-TV, Biloxi; WLBT-TV, Jackson; WDAM-TV, Hattiesburg; WXVT-TV, Greenville; WTVA-TV, Tupelo; WTOK-TV, Meridian; WHBQ-TV, Memphis; WABG-TV, Greenville; and Farmweek MS ETV (MSU). His *Southern Gardening* radio program is heard daily on Mississippi Public Radio and several independent stations.

The writing of Norman Winter is regularly found in newspapers such as *The Clarion-Ledger,* Jackson; *Biloxi Sun Herald,* Biloxi; *Brookhaven Leader,* Brookhaven; *Mississippi Press,* Pascagouala; *The Commercial Dispatch,* Columbus; *The Natchez Democrat,* Natchez; *McComb Enterprise-Journal,* McComb; *Starkville Daily News,* Starkville; and *The Daily Sentinel Star,* Grenada.

GARDENING TITLES